MODERN STUDIES IN PHILOSOPHY

ARISTOTLE

D1215369

Modern Studies in Philosophy is a series of anthologies presenting contemporary interpretations and evaluations of the works of major philosophers. The editors have selected articles designed to show the systematic structure of the thought of these philosophers, and to reveal the relevance of their views to the problems of current interest. These volumes are intended to be contributions to contemporary debates as well as to the history of philosophy; they not only trace the origins of many problems important to modern philosophy, but also introduce major philosophers as interlocutors in current discussions.

Modern Studies in Philosophy is prepared under the general editorship of Amelie Rorty, Associate Professor at Douglass College, Rutgers University.

J. M. E. MORAVCSIK, who received his Ph.D. from Harvard University, was born in Budapest, Hungary. Since 1959, he has been a member of the philosophy faculty of the University of Michigan and a regular contributor to journals on ancient Greek philosophy.

MODERN STUDIES IN PHILOSOPHY

ARISTOTLE
A Collection of Critical Essays

EDITED BY J. M. E. MORAVCSIK

UNIVERSITY OF NOTRE DAME PRESS
NOTRE DAME   LONDON

First Hardbound Edition: 1968

University of Notre Dame Press

Notre Dame, Indiana 46556

Printed by special arrangement with Doubleday & Company, Inc.

Anchor Books Edition: 1967
Doubleday & Company, Inc.
Garden City, New York

Copyright © 1967 by J. M. E. Moravcsik
All Rights Reserved

Manufactured in the United States of America

CONTENTS

ARISTOTLE

INTRODUCTION

What is it for us to understand Aristotle?[1] In order to grasp the difficulties involved in answering such a seemingly simple question, it is necessary to consider, briefly, some of the features of the history of philosophy and some of the characteristics of Aristotle's philosophy. Even if this necessarily sketchy introductory discussion fails to yield answers satisfactory to everyone, it should at least help to make clear why this volume is the way it is, and how it is viewed by its editor.

The mere existence of recent and contemporary commentaries on Aristotle might seem to call for an explanation if not an apology. At first glance at least, it might seem that after more than two thousand years Plato and Aristotle should be as well explained as they are ever likely to be, and that historians of philosophy should be turning their attention to the interpretation of less well known figures. And yet the facts are that there is exciting work being done on Aristotle today, that in the view of numerous philosophers and historians of philosophy much of the interpretation done in the past, even when of excellent quality, is not wholly satisfactory for our understanding, and that

[1]The views expressed in this introduction about the nature of the history of philosophy and about Aristotle are those of the editor and are not to be imputed to the contributors to this volume. The editor wishes to express his gratitude to Professor William Dray for a helpful discussion of some of these matters.

future generations are likely to view with dissatisfaction much of the work done today, while doing good and interesting historical work themselves. Under these circumstances the question arises: Why do men feel the need to rewrite the history of philosophy over and over again? One should attempt to answer this question, even if it turns out to be merely a special case of the tantalizing general question: Why must history be rewritten over and over again? In the case of philosophy, this question is sharpened by the fact that the repeated attempts at reconstructing the past are rarely occasioned by the appearance of drastically new empirical evidence. Once an ancient temple or palace is unearthed, it is there for all to see; subsequent excavations seek new targets. The interpreters of ancient philosophy, however, do not behave this way.

Faced with a bewildering variety of materials, one might be tempted to conclude that each school of philosophy feels the need to rewrite the history of the profession in its own image. Perhaps with each so-called "revolution" in philosophy—of which we have recently had such an uncomfortably large number that one is strongly inclined to doubt the genuineness of some—new emphases are given to different aspects of the thinking of the past. Such a line of thought leads to two popular conclusions, which this introduction is intended to combat. One of these is the claim that there is little if any objectivity in histories of philosophy written by philosophers. The other is the view that in order to gain unprejudiced, real insight into the philosophies of classical writers the best thing to do is to turn to the writings of those historians who have little or no systematic interest in current philosophy or at least hold no controversial positions upon this subject.

One way of showing these conclusions to be non sequiturs is to demonstrate that the peculiarly perennial nature of the history of philosophy can be accounted for on the basis of four considerations. First, an illuminating historical account involves comparisons (not necessarily evaluative ones) between the thought of the past and that of the present. (It is, after all, mostly by contrast and comparison that we learn about the thoughts of contemporaries as well.) Such comparisons tend to cast light both ways, and function as a conceptual bridge. Second, much of the explaining of a classical philosopher's thought involves explanations in our own terms, or at least in terms familiar to us. No historical interpretation of an author's works can be complete and adequate if it never breaks out of the circle, no matter how wide, of that author's terminology. These two ingredients of the historian's work, ingredients that link the past to a perpetually changing "present," and a perpetually changing set of terms, "our terms," help to explain the need for rewriting history without abandoning the claim of objectivity.

A third ingredient of the interpreter's task is the tracing of implications and consequences of some of a classical author's key claims. Such logical analysis is aided by the cumulative experience of the centuries, and it is an unending task, since such implications and consequences have no natural boundary. Finally, if we give a wide enough interpretation to the notion of empirical evidence, one can say that the appearance of new evidence fairly frequently plays an important role in new efforts at historical reconstruction. Such evidence may be a large number of quotes embedded in later texts that escaped notice for a long time, or new findings concerning the predominant mode of communication, oral or written, of a certain period. New discoveries in such related fields as the history of science or the history of literature also may lead to revisions

in the history of philosophy. In view of these four factors, one may hold that the history of philosophy is
an empirical enterprise with a corresponding claim of
objectivity,[2] partly cumulative in its progress and partly repetitive for reasons not necessarily linked to lack
of objectivity or the influence on the historian of contemporary philosophic positions.

At the same time these considerations begin to show
the complexity of the task of the historian of philosophy, and they hint at the variety of skills required for
success. Both the complexity and the variety can be
better appreciated if one considers the differences
among the related but distinct questions that a historian can ask about a given text. Examples of these
questions are: (i) What did Aristotle have in mind
when he said that ... ? (ii) What did Aristotle's statement that . . . mean to his contemporaries? (iii) To
what did Aristotle commit himself when he said
that ... ? (iv) How should one take Aristotle's statement that . . . in relation to the problems of our own
times?

What skills are required in order to answer these
questions? In the context of this brief introduction
only one thing needs special emphasis, namely that one
of the requisite skills is that of being a good philosopher. How else, except by being a good philosopher
in his own right, can a historian construct a sufficient
variety of interesting possible interpretations adequate
to the original thought of the subject? Robert Lowell
once said that no translation of a classic in poetry is
adequate unless the translation of a fine poem yields
what is a fine poem in its own right. This point could
easily be extended to the interpretation of classic phi-

---

[2]Some of what Aristotle said is likely to be true or false *a priori*,
but when the historian claims that Aristotle expressed such and
such an *a priori* claim, the historian's claim is empirical.

losophers. Such an extension, however, must meet the possible objection that while poetry is, in a sense, timeless, in an interpretation of a classic philosopher we must distinguish between (a) the treatment of, e.g. Aristotle, as an attempt to rediscover certain thoughts, and (b) the attempt to use this treatment as part of a general inquiry into expressions of timeless verities. With regard to (a) the "Lowell criterion" need not hold, for what is good philosophy in one period might, when viewed from the vantage point of a later period, appear no more than an "adolescent version" of a promising view. Against this objection it can be said that the sharp dichotomy implied by (a) and (b) has already been undermined by our discussion of the interrelatedness of questions (i) to (iv). With regard to the claim that some of the earlier philosophic views may seem "adolescent" to us, the following must be said. Most of the philosophy of our civilization has been organized around a set of loosely connected problems, most of which are not empirical in nature, at least in their original formulation. At times the accumulation of new empirical evidence leads to a reformulation of some of these problems so that they are seen either as not genuine, or as admitting of empirical solutions. In other cases the advances in logic or the availability of other tools of conceptual clarity allow us to arrive at reformulations which have greater clarity in the sense that these reformulations suggest answers that would not have been conceivable under the earlier formulations. There are still other problems, however, which remain with us through the centuries in spite of continuous reformulations. Thus philosophy is cumulative in some ways while in others it is not; some of its problems are perennial while others are not. Much of what Aristotle wrote is centered around issues which are alive today, and thus Robert

Lowell's criterion of adequacy is applicable to most interpretations of Aristotle.

This part of the introduction sheds, one may hope, some light on the nature of the history of philosophy. Our last point also sheds some light on some of the considerations that have guided the construction of this volume. For one of the key considerations in the selection of the material has been that the interpretations should be not only fine pieces of scholarship, but also fine pieces of philosophizing in their own right.

Aristotle's life and its historical context will not be considered here; these matters are discussed adequately in scores of other books. Nor will this introduction summarize Aristotle's views; it may be gathered from what has been said so far, and it will become even clearer from what follows, that according to the editor's view Aristotle's philosophizing does not admit of a summary. Instead, an attempt will be made to elucidate the following questions: (a) Why should one regard Aristotle as a classic philosopher? (b) How does the nature of Aristotle's philosophizing compare with the ways in which more modern philosophers have conducted their inquiries? (c) To what extent and in what ways does Aristotle's philosophy have unity?

With regard to the first question, one should note the variety of ways in which Aristotle's influence has been significant. One of these is manifested in the frequency with which his successors react, positively or negatively, to his writings. Regardless whether the topic is the rules for deductive inferences, or the proper analysis of what it is to explain natural phenomena, or the alleged primacy of material substances, in almost every age philosophers dealing with these topics have conducted a dialogue with Aristotle or with an Aristotelian view. Another manifestation of his influence is that he has been associated, rightly or wrongly, with a coherent view of reality which is supposed to give philosophic foundations to Christian doctrines about God, man, and nature. One may rightly question the extent to which this view can be attributed to Aristotle, but that he inspired it is undeniable. A third, and perhaps most important, way in which Aristotle's influence has been crucial can be seen when we realize the extent to which he set the problems of subsequent philosophy. These problems set for philosophy tasks that have yet to be completed. Such tasks are: *logic* collecting in a systematic fashion all the rules of valid inference, giving a proper analysis of the notion of responsibility, clarifying concepts basic to our understanding, such as the concepts of change, action, thing (or object), mass (or heap), and delineative proper ways of classification. This manifold nature of Aristotle's influence explains why he is a figure to be dealt with by the logician and semantic analyst as well as by the Thomistic theologian, by the student of metaphysics as well as the philosopher of science.

This partial answer to our first question also gives us some conception of the breadth of Aristotle's philosophy, and this—in turn—tells us something about the nature of his philosophizing, the subject of our second question. Aristotle is one of those rare philosophers who wrote about an enormous range of topics within the fields of logic, ethics, philosophy of education, philosophy of science, philosophy of art, philosophy of language, epistemology, and metaphysics. But it is a mistake to think that his philosophizing adds up either to a system or to a world view within which all the answers within all these fields are organized and interrelated. Some of the topics with which Aristotle deals, and his corresponding solutions, are only loosely connected with one another, and he repeatedly emphasizes that different types of topic require different types of approach. Still, neither are we to think of his philosophizing as fragmentary, or as designed only to catch glimpses here and there of the nature of things. In his philosophizing Aristotle seems to have kept in mind the ideal of the self-sufficient man, an ideal that both Plato and he espoused in their ethical writings; a self-sufficient man ought to be able to deal with any problem that he encounters even though he may not organize his answers into an axiomatic pattern, and even though he may come to the conclusion that different types of question require different types of answer. Among his problems epistemological questions did not occupy a central position, and when he came to set for himself questions about knowledge these often cut across the dichotomy of justification and explanation which has dominated most of philosophy since Descartes. But this is only a partial explanation of why he cannot be classified among either the empiricists or the rationalists. Another part of that explanation would be that from his vantage point—as from the vantage point of many philosophers today—these positions seem neither mutually exclusive nor exhaustive of the possibilities. We fare no better if we try another dichotomy, made familiar by Professor I. Berlin,[3] and applicable mainly to the contrast between the dreamers and ideologists of the nineteenth century, and the careful piecemeal thinkers dominating professional philosophy in the twentieth century in England and the United States. Aristotle could be described neither as a hedgehog of the type familiar from the post-Kantian philosophy of the nineteenth century, nor as the intellectual ancestor of that variety of philosophic thought which flourishes in the twentieth and is

[3]*The Hedgehog and the Fox. An Essay on Tolstoy's View of History* (London, 1953).

commonly referred to as "analytic philosophy." Perhaps this elusiveness of Aristotle's philosophy with respect to subsequent classifications helps to account for the fact that both hedgehogs and foxes are often indebted to him. If this brief discussion does not give much of a positive picture of what Aristotle's philosophy was like, at least it should suffice to make the important negative point, that in its nature it was very different from the dominant ways of philosophizing of the last four hundred years.

The foregoing also gives, in outline, the answer to the question about the unity of Aristotle's thought. Today most people tend to think of the great philosophers of the past as system-builders who laid down definitions and basic axioms, and then tried to account for all the salient features of nature, man, and the rules of conduct by means of these basic "truths" and the theorems that can be derived from them. Or, perhaps more loosely, people think that classical philosophers tried to account for all the salient features of the world and man's role in it in terms of an explanation that blends these features into an interrelated organic whole. It is very important to note that neither Aristotle, nor his teacher Plato, was a system-builder of this type. Though some of their concepts ranged over more than one problem, there is no simple truth which either Plato or Aristotle would have regarded as a key to all their answers and suggestions. The only sense of unity that applies to a discussion of Aristotle's views is that of consistency, and even this should be regarded as a desideratum—both Aristotle's and the interpreter's—rather than a fact to be taken for granted. It could be said that Aristotle's metaphysical suggestions were intended to underlie some of what he says about the proper way to explain natural phenomena, but it would be wrong to say that they underlie all his philosophy. (It was reported to me that the late Professor John L. Austin said on one occasion that one of the refreshing features of Aristotle's ethics is its almost total lack of connection with his metaphysics.)

These reflexions suggest that the proper approach to Aristotle's philosophy is a piecemeal, or pluralistic one. What Aristotle says as an answer to one question may not relate to his answers to other questions similar in appearance. Thus acceptance of some of Aristotle's suggestions does not commit one to a wholesale acceptance of his philosophic claims. This remark applies both to content and to methodology. Furthermore, even if it did not have other support, this approach suggests itself as a heuristic principle, for it facilitates the emergence of dialogue between the philosophers of the past and those of the present. The conception of a classic philosopher as a system-builder carries with it the implication that if you reject a part, you must reject all; or conversely that partial acceptance must lead to wholesale acceptance. The approach favored by the editor makes it possible for us to claim with plausibility that one may understand some parts of Aristotle's thought while finding others obscure, that some of his suggestions are acceptable while others do not seem to be, that some of his results seem naïve in the light of subsequent research, while in some other ways (e.g. in his discussion of the variety of types of predication, his analysis of responsibility, and his views on the nature of pleasure and enjoyment) his suggestions are far more profound and far more fruitful than those made by the vast majority of philosophers in the twentieth century.

Right or wrong, these meditations on the nature of the history of philosophy and on the nature of Aristotle's philosophy have influenced the construction of this volume. As we have already seen, one criterion of inclusion was that each contribution should be a good interpretation of Aristotle in the sense that it should also be a good piece of philosophizing. Furthermore, the authors were selected in such a way that there is no common philosophical view or outlook shared by all. An attempt was made to include papers on a variety of topics, but only in this sense does this volume try to convey much of Aristotle's thought; the essays printed here cannot be used as a basis for reconstructing "the philosophy" of Aristotle. Finally, the volume was put together in this manner in the hope that the reader will come to discover the perennial nature of some of the problems with which Aristotle wrestled. But this hope need not be shared by the reader. Perhaps it is only a sign of the editor's Platonistic tendencies.

Thanks and gratitude is due to all those who consented to have their papers reprinted. Special thanks is due to Miss Anscombe who made some corrections in her essay for this volume, and to Mr. Michael Woods and Mr. Urmson for being so kind as to undertake the task of writing new papers. The editor also wishes to thank Mrs. J. L. Austin for having consented to the inclusion of a previously unpublished paper by the late Professor Austin. By far the greatest debt is owed to Mr. Urmson; for in addition to writing his fine paper, he helped to secure permission to publish Professor Austin's manuscript, and without his kind editorial help that manuscript could not have been prepared for publication. Finally, the editor wishes to thank Mrs. Rorty for having asked him to do this volume in her series.

I. LOGIC

ARISTOTLE AND THE SEA BATTLE
De Interpretatione, Chapter IX
G. E. M. ANSCOMBE

1   For what is and for what has come about, then, it is necessary that affirmation, or negation, should be true or false; and for universals universally quantified it is always necessary that one should be true, the other false; and for singulars too, as has been said; while for universals not universally quantified it is not necessary. These have been discussed.

For what is and for what has come about: he has in fact not mentioned these, except to say that a verb or a tense—sc. other than the present, which he regards as the verb *par excellence*—must be part of any proposition.

it is necessary: given an *antiphasis* about the present or past, the affirmative proposition must be true or false; and similarly for the negative. An *antiphasis* is a pair of propositions in which the same predicate is in one affirmed, in the other denied, of the same subject. Note that Aristotle has not the idea of the negation of a proposition, with the negation sign outside the whole proposition; that was (I believe) invented by the Stoics.—What Aristotle says in this sentence is ambiguous; that this is deliberate can be seen by the con-

From *Mind*, LXV (1956), 1–15. Newly revised by the author. Reprinted by permission of the author and the editor of *Mind*.

trast with the next sentence: The ambiguity between necessarily having a truth-value, and having a necessary truth-value—is first sustained, and then resolved at the end of the chapter.

for universals universally quantified: he does not mean, as this place by itself would suggest, that of "All men are white" and "No men are white" one must be true and the other false. But that if you take "All men are white" and "No men are white" and construct the antiphasis of which each is a side, namely, "All men are white—Not all men are white" and "No men are white—Some man is white," then one side of each antiphasis must be true, and the other side must be false.

for singulars too, as has been said: sc. of "Socrates is white—Socrates is not white" one side is necessarily true, the other necessarily false. (This is what a modern reader cannot take in; but see the "Elucidation.")

for universals not universally quantified: his example rendered literally is "man is white—man is not white." From his remarks I infer that these would be correctly rendered "men are...". For, he says, men are beautiful, and they are also not beautiful, for they are ugly too, and if they are ugly they are not beautiful. I believe that we (nowadays) are not interested in these unquantified propositions.

These have been discussed: i.e. in the immediately preceding chapters, by which my explanations can be verified.

2   But for what is singular and future it isn't like this. For if every affirmation and negation is true or false, then it is also necessary for everything to be the case or not be the case. So if one man says something will be, and another says not, clearly it is necessary for one of them to be speaking truly, if every affirmation and negation is true or

3   false. For both will not hold at once on such con-

ditions. For if it is true to say that something is
white or is not white, its being white or not
white is necessary, and if it is white or not white,
it is true to say or deny it. And if it is not the
case, then it is false, and if it is false, it is not the
case; so that it is necessary as regards either the
affirmation or the negation that it is true or false.

singular and future: sc. There will be a relevant discussion tonight; this experiment will result in the mix-
ture's turning green; you will be sent down before the
end of term.

it isn't like this: namely, that these propositions (or
their negations) must be true or false. Throughout this
paragraph the ambiguity is carefully preserved and concealed.

*it is also necessary for everything to be the case
or not be the case:* the Greek "or" is, like the English, ambiguous between being exclusive and being non-
exclusive. Here it is exclusive, as will appear; hence
the "or" in the conditional "if every affirmation and
negation is true or false" is also exclusive, and to point
this he says "every affirmation and negation", not, as
in (1) "every affirmation or negation"; that "or" was
non-exclusive.

For both will not hold on such conditions: namely,
on the conditions that every affirmation is true or false.
This condition is not a universal one; it does not apply
to the unquantified propositions, though if the "or" is
non-exclusive it does. But if the conditions hold, then
just one of the two speakers must be speaking the
truth.

It is true to say or deny it: ἦν is the common philosophical imperfect.

4   So nothing is or comes about by chance or
     'whichever happens'. Nor will it be or not be, but
     everything of necessity and not 'whichever hap-

pens'. For either someone saying something or
someone denying it will be right. For it would
either be happening or not happening accordingly. For whichever happens is not more thus or
not thus than it is going to be.

'whichever happens': the Greek phrase suggests both
"as it may be" and "as it turns out". "As the case
may be" would have been a good translation if it
could have stood as a subject of a sentence. The 'scare-
quotes' are mine; Aristotle is not overtly discussing the
expression "whichever happens".

is not more thus or not thus than it is going to be:
as the Greek for "or" and for "than" are the same, it
is so far as I know a matter of understanding the argument whether you translate as here, or (as is more
usual) e.g.: "isn't or (sc. and) isn't going to be rather
thus than not thus". But this does not make good
sense. Aristotle is arguing: "We say 'whichever happens' or 'as the case may be' about the present as well
as about the future; but you don't think the present
indeterminate, so why say the future is?" Or rather (as
he is not talking about the expression): "Whatever
happens will be just as determinately thus or not thus
as it is."

5   Further, if something is white now, it was true
         earlier to say it was going to be white, so that it
         was always true to say of any of the things that
         have come about: "it is, or will be." But if it was
         always true to say: "it is, or will be", then: im-
         possible for that not to be or be going to be. But if
         it is impossible for something not to come about,
         then it is unable not to come about. But if some-
         thing is unable not to come about it is necessary
6   for it to come about. Therefore it is necessary
         that everything that is going to be should come
         about. So nothing will be 'whichever happens' or
         by chance. For if by chance, then not by necessity.

But if it is impossible for something not to come about, then it is unable not to come about: the reader who works through to the end and understands the solution will examine the dialectic to see where it should be challenged. It will turn out that the point is here, in spite of the equivalence of the two Greek expressions. It is impossible for the thing not to come about, i.e. necessary that it should come about by *necessitas consequentiae*, which does not confer the character of necessity *necessitas consequentis*, on what does come about. A necessary consequence of what is true need not be necessary.

> Still, it is not open to us, either, to say that neither is true, as: that it neither will be nor will
> 7   not be. For firstly, the affirmation being false the negation will not be true, and this being false the affirmation won't be true. —And besides, if it is true to say that something is big and white, both must hold. And if they are going to hold tomorrow, they must hold tomorrow. And if something is neither going to be nor not going to be tomorrow, 'whichever happens' won't be. Take a sea-battle, for example: it would have to be the case that a sea-battle neither came about nor didn't come about tomorrow.

Still, it is not open to us, either, to say that neither is true: And yet Aristotle is often supposed to have adopted this as the solution.

For firstly: this goes against what he has shown at the end of (3): "if it is false, it does not hold." So much, however, is obvious, and so this is not a very strong objection if we are willing to try whether neither is true. What follows is stronger.

And if they are going to hold tomorrow: from here to the end of the paragraph the argument is: if it is the case that something will be, then it will be the case that it is. In more detail: you say, or deny, two things about the future. If what you say is true, then when the time comes you must be able to say those two things in the present or past tenses.

'whichever happens' won't be: i.e. 'whichever happens' won't happen.

8   These are the queer things about it. And there more of the sort, if it is necessary that for every affirmation and negation, whether for universals universally quantified or for singulars, one of the opposites should be true and one false, that there is no 'whichever happens' about what comes about, but that everything is and comes about of necessity. So that there would be no need to deliberate or take trouble, e.g.: "if we do this, this will   happen, if not, not." For there is nothing to prevent its being said by one man and denied by another ten thousand years ahead that this will happen, so that whichever of the two was then true to say will of necessity happen. And indeed it makes no difference either if people have said the opposite things or not; for clearly this is how things are, even if there isn't one man saying something and another denying it; nor is it its having been asserted or denied that makes it going to be or not, nor its having been ten thousand years ahead or at any time you like. So if in the whole of time it held that the one was the truth, then it was necessary that this came about, and for everything that has been it always held, so that it came about by necessity. For if anyone has truly said that something will be, then it can't not happen. And it was always true to say of what comes about: it will be.

9

10

These are the queer things about it. And: I have diverged from the usual punctuation, which leads to the rendering: "These and similar strange things result, if. . . ." This seems illogical.

E.g.: often rendered "since": "since if we do this, this will happen, if not, not." This does not appear to me to make good sense. The Oxford translator sits on the fence here.

So if in the whole of time it held: one must beware of supposing that Aristotle thinks the conclusion stated in the apodosis of this sentence follows from the condition. It only follows if the previous arguments are sound. He is going to reject the conclusion, but there is no reason to think that he rejects the condition: on the contrary.

11   Now if this is impossible! For we see that things that are going to be take their start from deliberating and from acting, and equally that there is in general a possibility of being and not being in things that are not always actual. In them, both are open, both being and not being, and so also both becoming and not becoming. And plenty of
12   things are obviously like this; for example, this coat is capable of getting cut up, and it won't get cut up but will wear out first. And equally it is capable of not getting cut up, for its getting worn out first would not have occurred if it had not been capable of not getting cut up. So this
13   applies too to all other processes that are spoken of in terms of this kind of possibility. So it is clear that not everything is or comes about of necessity, but with some things 'whichever happens', and the affirmation is not true rather than the negation; and with other things one is true rather and for the most part, but still it is open for either to happen, and the other not.

take their start: literally: "there is a starting point of things that are going to be." The word also means "principle". A human being is a prime mover (in the engineer's sense), but one that works by deliberating. As if a calculating machine not merely worked, but was, in part, precisely *qua* calculating, a prime mover. But Aristotle's approach is not that of someone enquiring into human nature, but into causes of events and observing that among them is this one.

acting: he means human action, which is defined in terms of deliberation; see *Nicomachean Ethics* VI 1139: there he repeats the word "ἀρχή": "ἡ τοιαύτη ἀρχὴ ἄνθρωπος": the cause of this sort is man. An animal too or a plant, is a prime mover. Hence his thought is not that there are new starting points constantly coming into existence; that would not matter. It is first of all the nature of deliberation that makes him think that the fact of human action proves the dialectic must be wrong. I cannot pursue this here; though I should like to enter a warning against the idea (which may present itself): "the nature of deliberation presupposes freedom of the will as a condition." That is not an Aristotelian idea.

things that are not always actual: things that are always actual are the sun, moon, planets and stars. Aristotle thought that what these do is necessary. The general possibility that he speaks of is of course a condition required if deliberation and 'action' are to be possible. If what the typewriter is going to do is necessary, I cannot do anything else with the typewriter. Not that this is Aristotle's ground for speaking of the general possibility. That is shown in his consideration about the coat: the assumption that the coat *will be* worn out does not conflict with our knowledge that it *can* be cut up. We know a vast number of possibilities of this sort.

in terms of this kind of possibility: I take it that we have here the starting point for the development of Aristotle's notion of potentiality. The sentence confirms my view of the point where he would say the dialectic went wrong.

with other things one is true rather and for the most part: as we should say: more probable.

14   The existence of what is when it is, and the non-existence of what isn't when it isn't, is necessary. But still, for everything that is to be is not necessary, nor for everything that isn't not to be. For it isn't the same: for everything that is to be of necessity when it' is, and: for it simply to be of necessity. And the same for what isn't. And the same reasoning applies to the antiphasis. For it is necessary that everything should be or not, and should be going to be or not. But it is not the
15   case, separately speaking, that either of the sides is necessary. I mean, e.g. that it is necessary that there will be a sea-battle tomorrow or not, but that it is not necessary that there should be a sea-battle tomorrow, nor that it should not happen. But for it to come about or not is necessary. So that since propositions are true as the facts go, it is clear that where things are such as to allow of 'whichever happens' and of opposites, this must hold for the antiphasis too.

The existence of what is when it is . . . is necessary: i.e. it cannot be otherwise. A modern gloss, which Aristotle could not object to, and without which it is not possible for a modern person to understand his argument, is: and cannot be shown to be otherwise. It will by now have become very clear to a reader that the implications of 'necessary' in this passage are not what he is used to. But see the "Elucidation".

simply to be of necessity: there is a temptation to recognise what we are used to under the title "logical necessity" in this phrase. But I believe that Aristotle thought the heavenly bodies and their movements were necessary in this sense. On the other hand, he seems to have ascribed something like logical necessity to them.

But it is not the case, separately speaking, that either of the sides is necessary: the ambiguity of the opening "it is necessary that an affirmation (or negation) should be true or false" is here resolved. And we learn that when Aristotle said that, he meant that if p is a statement about the present or the past, then either p is necessary or not-p is necessary. But this means that in order to ascribe necessity to certain propositions (the ones, namely, that are not 'simply' necessary) we have to be informed about particular facts. So, one may ask, what has this necessity got to do with logic? —Aristotle, however, states no facts, past, present, or future. (I do in what follows; I hope this will not prove misleading: the purpose is only didactic.) His results could perhaps be summarised as follows: we use indices p and f to the propositional sign to indicate present and past time references on the one hand, and future time reference on the other. Then for all p, p vel not-p is necessary (this covers the unquantified propositions too) and p_p is necessary vel not-p_p is necessary; but it is not the case that for all p, p_f is necessary vel not-p_f is necessary.

> 16   This is how it is for what is not always existent or not always non-existent. For such things it is necessary that a side of the antiphasis should be true or false, but not this one or that one, but whichever happens; and that one should be true rather than the other; but that does not mean that it is true, or false. So it is clear that it is not necessary for every affirmation and negation that this one of the opposites should be true and that one false; for it does not hold for what does not exist but is capable of being or not being; but it is as we have said.

whichever happens: sc.: it is a matter of whichever happens.

that one should be true rather than the other: cf.

"rather and for the most part" above; note that this is governed by "it is necessary"; I infer that Aristotle thought that correct statements of probability were true propositions.

but that does not mean: ἤδη, logical, not temporal;[1] ἤδη works rather like the German "schon" (only here of course it would be "noch nicht"). ἤδη in a non-temporal sense is, like οὐκέτι, frequent in Greek literature. English translators of philosophical texts usually either neglect to translate it or mistranslate it. For examples, see *Theaetetus* 201e4, *Physics* 187a36, *De Interpretatione* 16a8, *Metaphysics* 1006a16. Bonitz gives some more examples.

AN ELUCIDATION OF THE FOREGOING FROM A MODERN POINT OF VIEW

A. The Vice Chancellor will either be run over next week or not. And therefore either he will be run over next week or he will not. Please understand that I was *not* repeating myself!

B. I think I understand what you were trying to do; but I am afraid you were repeating yourself and, what is more, you cannot fail to do so.

A. Can't fail to do so? Well, listen to this: The Vice Chancellor *is* going to be run over next week ...

B. Then I am going to the police as soon as I can.

A. You will only be making a fool of yourself. It's not true.

B. Then why did you say it?

A. I was merely trying to make a point: namely, that I have succeeded in saying something true about the future.

[1] I am indebted to Miss M. Hartley of Somerville College for pointing this out to me.

B.   What have you said about the future that is true?

A.   I don't know: but this I do know, that I have said something true; and I know that it was either when I told you the Vice Chancellor would be run over, or on the other hand when I said he wouldn't.

B.   I am sorry, but that is no more than to say that Either he will or he won't be run over. Have you given me any information about the future? Don't tell me you have, with one of these two remarks, for that is to tell me nothing, just because the two remarks together cover all the possibilities. If what you tell me is an Either/Or and it embraces all possibilities, you tell me nothing.

A.   Can an Either/Or be true except by the truth of one of its components? I seem to remember Quine speaking of Aristotle's "fantasy", that "It is true that either p or q" is not a sufficient condition for "Either it is true that p or it is true that q." Now I will put it like this: Aristotle seems to think that the truth of a truth-functional expression is independent of the truth values of the component propositions.

B.   But that is a howler! The "truth" of Either p or not p is determined, as you know very well, by its truth value's being T for all possible combinations of the truth possibilities of its components; that is why its "truth" gives no information. Having set out the full truth-table and discovered that for all possibilities you get T in the final column, you need make no enquiry to affirm the truth of p∨ ~ p—any enquiry would be comic. If on the other hand you tell me p∨ ~ q (q being different from p) you do give me some information, for certain truth-combinations are excluded. There is therefore the possibility of enquiring whether your information is correct. And that I do by discovering which of the truth-possibilities is fulfilled; and if one of the combinations of truth-possibilities which is a truth-condition for $p \lor \sim q$ is fulfilled, then I discover that your information is correct. But to tell me "It will rain, or it won't", is not to tell me of any truth-possibility that it is—or, if you like, will be, satisfied. Now will you actually tell me something about the future?

A. Very well. Either you are sitting in that chair or it will not rain tomorrow.

B. I agree, that is true, because I am sitting in this chair. But still I have been told nothing about the future, because since I know I am sitting in this chair I know what I have been told is true whether it rains tomorrow or not—i.e. for all truth possibilities of "It will rain tomorrow." But do you mind repeating your information?

A. Either you are sitting in that chair or it will not rain tomorrow.

B. (*Having stood up.*) I am glad to be told it will be fine—but is it certain? Do you get it from the meteorologists? I have heard that they are sometimes wrong.

A. But surely we are talking about truth, not certainty or knowledge.

B. Yes, and I am asking whether your information —which I agree is information this time—is true.

A. I can't tell you till some time tomorrow; perhaps not till midnight. But whatever I tell you then will have been so now—I mean if I tell you then 'True', that means not just that it will be true then but that it was true now.

B. But I thought it was the great point against Aristotle that 'is true' was timeless.

A. Yes—well, what I mean is that if I tell you—as I shall be able to—'True' tomorrow—I mean *if* I am able to, of course—why, then it will have been, I mean is now correct to say it is true.

B. I understand you. If it is going to rain tomorrow it is true that it is going to rain tomorrow. I should be enormously surprised if Aristotle were to deny this.

A. But Aristotle says it isn't true that it is going to rain tomorrow!

B. I did not read a single prediction in what Aristotle said. He only implied that it didn't have to be true that it will rain tomorrow, i.e. it doesn't have to rain tomorrow.

A. What? Even if it is going to rain tomorrow?

B. Oh, of course, if it is going to rain tomorrow, then it necessarily will rain tomorrow: $(p \supset p)$ is necessary. But is it going to?

A. I told you, I can't say, not for certain. But why does that matter?

B. Can't you say anything for certain about tomorrow?

A. I am going to Blackwell's tomorrow.

B. And that is certain?

A. Yes, I am absolutely determined to go. (Partly because of this argument: it is a point of honour with me to go, now.)

B. Good. I fully believe you. At least, I believe you as fully as I can. But do I—or you—know you will go? Can nothing stop you?

A. Of course lots of things can stop me—anything from a change of mind to death or some other catastrophe.

B. Then you aren't necessarily going to Blackwell's?

A. Of course not.

B. Are you necessarily here now?

A. I don't understand you.

B. Could it turn out that this proposition that you, NN., are in All Souls today, May 7, 1954, is untrue? Or is this certain.

A. No, it is quite certain—My reason for saying so is that if you cared to suggest any test, which could turn out one way or the other, I can't see any reason to trust the test if, situated as I am, I have any doubt that I am here. I don't mean I can't imagine doubting it; but I can't imagine anything that would make it doubtful.

B. Then what is true about the present and the past is *necessarily* true?

A. Haven't you passed from certainty to truth?

B. Do you mean to tell me that something can be certain without being true?—And isn't what is true about the present and the past quite necessary?

A. What does 'necessary' mean here, since it obviously doesn't mean that these are what we call necessary propositions?

B. I mean that nothing whatever could make what is certain untrue. Not: if it is true, it is necessary, but: since it is certainly true it is necessary. Now if you can show me that anything about the future is so certain that nothing could falsify it, then (perhaps) I shall agree that it is necessarily true that that thing will happen.

A. Well: the sun will rise tomorrow.

B. That is so certain that nothing could falsify it?

A. Yes.

B. Not even: the sun's not rising tomorrow?

A. But this is absurd! When I say it is certain I am here, am I saying it wouldn't falsify it for me not to be here? But I am here, and the sun will rise tomorrow.

B. Well, let me try again: Could anything that can

happen make it untrue that you are here? If not,
I go on to ask: Could anything that can happen
make it untrue that the sun rises tomorrow?

A.   No.

B.   If we continued in darkness, the appearance of
the night being continued for the rest of our lives,
all the same the sun will have risen; and so on?

A.   But that can't happen.

B.   Is that as certain as that you are here now?

A.   I won't say. —But what does Aristotle mean when
he says that one part of the antiphasis is necessarily true (or false) when it is the present or the
past that was in question? Right at the beginning,
when I said "The Vice Chancellor will either be
run over or not, therefore either he will be run
over or he will not" you said that I was repeating
myself and could not fail to be repeating myself.
And then you referred to the Truth-table-tautolog-
ical account of that proposition. But does not precisely the same point apply to what Aristotle says
about "Either p or not p" when p is a proposition about the present or the past?

B.   You could have avoided repeating yourself if you
had said "The Vice Chancellor will either be run
over or not, therefore either it is necessary that he
should be run over or it is necessary that he should
not be run over." But as you would have been disinclined to say that—seeing no possible meaning
for an ascription of necessity except what we are
used to call 'logical necessity'—you could not
avoid repeating yourself.

Thus Aristotle's point (as we should put it) is that
'Either p or not p' is always necessary, and this necessity is what we are familiar with. But—and this is from
our point of view the right way to put it, for this
is a novelty to us—that when p describes a present or

past situation, then either p is necessarily true, or ~ p is necessarily true; and here 'necessarily true' has a sense which is unfamiliar to us. In this sense I say it is necessarily true that there was not—or necessarily false that there was—a big civil war raging in England from 1850 to 1870; necessarily true that there is a University in Oxford; and so on. But 'necessarily true' is not simply the same as 'true'; for while it may be true that there will be rain tomorrow, it is not necessarily true. As everyone would say: there may be or may not. We also say this about things which we don't know about the past and the present. The question presents itself to us then in this form: does "may" express mere ignorance on our part in both cases?

Suppose I say to someone: "In ten years' time you will have a son; and when he is ten years old he will be killed by a tyrant." Clearly this is something that may be true and may not. But equally clearly there is no way of finding out (unless indeed you say that waiting and seeing is finding out; but it is not finding out that it will happen, only that it does happen.)

Now if I really said this to someone, she would either be awe-struck or think me dotty; and she would be quite right. For such a prediction is a prophecy. Now suppose that what I say comes true. The whole set of circumstances—the prophecy together with its fulfilment—is a miracle; and one's theoretical attitude (if one has one at all) to the supposition of such an occurrence ought to be exactly the same as one's theoretical attitude to the supposition that one knew of someone's rising from the dead and so on.

As Newman remarks, a miracle ought not to be a silly trivial kind of thing—e.g. if my spoon gets up one day and dances a jig on my plate, divides into several pieces and then joins up again, it qualifies ill as a miracle, though it qualifies perfectly well for philosophical

discussion of naturally impossible but imaginable occurrences. Similarly if one were discussing impossible
predictions one would take such an example as the
following: Every day I receive a letter from someone
giving an accurate account of my actions and experiences from the time of posting to the time I received
the letter. And whatever I do (I do random, absurd
actions for example, to see if he will still have written
a true account) the letter records it. Now, since we are
dealing in what can be imagined and therefore can be
supposed to happen, we must settle whether this would
be knowledge of the future: its certainly would surely be a proof that what I did I did necessarily.

It is interesting to note that Wittgenstein agrees
with Aristotle about this problem, in the *Tractatus*.
"The freedom of the will consists in the fact that future actions cannot be known. The connexion of knowing and the known is that of logical necessity. 'A
knows that p' is senseless, if p is a tautology." We are
therefore presented with the logical necessariness of
what is known's being true, together with the logical
non-necessity of the kind of things that are known.
The "logical necessity" of which he speaks in the remark on knowledge is thus not just truth-table necessariness. It is the unfamiliar necessariness of which
Aristotle also speaks. "A knows that p" makes sense
only if p describes a fact about the past or present;
so it comes out in Wittgenstein, and in Aristotle: past
and present facts are necessary. (In more detail, by the
Tractatus account: if A knows p, for some q $(q \supset p)$
is a tautology, and q expresses a fact that A is 'ac-
quainted' with.)

Then this letter about my actions would not have
been knowledge even if what it said was always right.
However often and invariably it was verified, it would
still not be certain, because the facts could go against

it. However Aristotle's considerations are not about knowledge and certainty but about necessity and its correlative possibility. They have probably been made more difficult to understand because they are an instance of his willingness to deny what it does not make sense to assert—for the affirmation of the necessity of p is equivalent to a denial of the possibility of not-p. The possibility in question relates only to the future, hence by some current conceptions the negation of such possibility also relates only to the future.

E.g. 'This plaster can be painted for the next eight hours and not after that since by then it will have set too hard.' Neither the affirmation nor the negation of this sort of possibility can be constructed relative to the past. 'It can be painted yesterday' demands emendation perhaps to 'It may have been painted yesterday,' perhaps to 'It could have been painted yesterday.' (The contingency of the past is that something was possible, not that it is possible. The openness of the future is that something is possible. This is not the same as saying that it *will* be possible, since the possibility may be extinguished. It is a present state of affairs that the plaster can be painted for the next few hours.) Now Aristotle who readily uses 'No men are numbers' as a premise would pass from the denial that possibility of this sort holds in relation to the past (or present) to asserting that the past and present are necessary.

ARISTOTLE'S DIFFERENT POSSIBILITIES

K. JAAKKO J. HINTIKKA

1. *The interrelations of modal notions in Aristotle.*
The results of our examination of the varieties of ambiguity in Aristotle (see *Inquiry*, [1959], 137–51) can be used to analyze his notion of possibility. This notion is closely connected with the other modal notions, notably with those of necessity and impossibility. Since these notions are somewhat more perspicuous than that of possibility, it is advisable to start from them.

Aristotle knew that the contradictory (negation) of 'it is necessary that *p*' is not 'it is necessary that not *p*' but rather 'it is not necessary that *p*' (*De Int.* 12, 22a4 ff.). The last two phrases are not contradictories, either, for they can very well be true together (*De Int.* 13, 22b1 ff.), the latter being wider in application than the former. By parity of form, 'it is not necessary that not *p*' is wider in application than 'it is necessary that *p*'.

These relations are conveniently summed up in the following diagram (which is not used by the Stagirite):

(i)

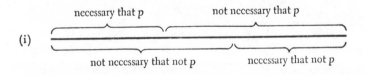

necessary that *p*　　　　not necessary that *p*

not necessary that not *p*　　　necessary that not *p*

From *Inquiry*, III (1960), 18–28. Reprinted by permission of the author and the editors of *Inquiry*.

According to Aristotle, 'impossible' behaves like 'necessary' (*De Int.* 12, 22a7 ff.). We can therefore illustrate it by means of a diagram similar to (i). In fact, the diagram will be virtually the same as the one for 'necessary', for "the proposition 'it is impossible' is equivalent, when used with a contrary subject, to the proposition 'it is necessary'." (See *De Int.* 13, 22b5.) In other words, 'impossible that *p*' is equivalent to 'necessary that not *p*', 'impossible that not *p*' equivalent to 'necessary that *p*', etc. We can therefore complete the diagram (i) as follows:

necessary that *p* =   not necessary that *p* =
impossible that not *p*   not impossible that not *p*

(ii)
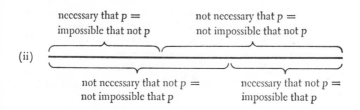

not necessary that not *p* =   necessary that not *p* =
not impossible that *p*   impossible that *p*

2. *The two notions of possibility.* The problem is to fit the notion of possibility into the schema (ii). In this respect, Aristotle was led by two incompatible impulses. On one hand, he was naturally tempted to say that 'possible' and 'impossible' are contradictories; something is possible if and only if it is not impossible (See e.g. *De Int.* 13, 22a16–18, 32–38.) Under this view, we get the following diagram:

not possible that not *p* =   possible that not *p* =
necessary that *p*   not impossible that not *p*

(iii)
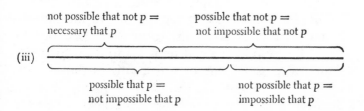

possible that *p* =   not possible that *p* =
not impossible that *p*   impossible that *p*

But this temptation is not the only one. In ordinary discourse, saying that something is possible often serves to indicate that it is *not* necessary. Aristotle catches this implication. For him, "if a thing may be, it may also not be" (*De Int.* 13, 22b20; see also 22a14 ff.). Essentially the same point is elaborated in the *Topica* II 7, 112b1 ff. There Aristotle says that "if a necessary event has been asserted to occur usually, clearly the speaker has denied an attribute to be universal which is universal and so has made a mistake."

Under this view, our diagram will have this look:

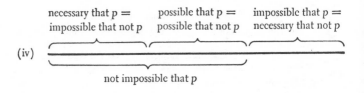

It is seen that (iii) and iv) differ in that in (iii) the range of possibility comprises everything that is necessary, while in (iv) possibility and necessity are incompatible.

It appears from *De Interpretatione* that Aristotle did not immediately see that the assumptions underlying (iii) and (iv) are incompatible. Not surprisingly, he ran into difficulties which he discusses in a not entirely clear way in *De Int.* 13, 22b11–23a7 (although I suspect that the confusion of the usual translations of this passage is not altogether Aristotle's fault). He perceives clearly enough that the gist of the difficulty lies in the relation of possibility to necessity (*De Int.* 13, 22b29 ff.). And at the end he is led to distinguish two senses of 'possible' one of which satisfies (iii) and the other (iv). (*De Int.* 13, 23a7 – 27.) However, Aristotle does not make any terminological distinction between the two. Insofar as the distinction is vital, I shall call the notion of possibility which satisfies (iii) 'possibility proper' and the notion which satisfies (iv) 'contingency'.

3. *Homonymy v. multiplicity of applications.* Now we can see why the distinction between a diversity of applications and homonymy is vital for this essay. We have found a clear-cut case of homonymy: the notions of contingency and of possibility proper have different logical properties. They cannot be covered by a single term 'possibility' except by keeping in mind that this word has different meanings on different occasions. Their relation is therefore one of homonymy (cf. section 10 of the first paper).

But in addition to this duality of 'contingency' and 'possibility proper', there is a different kind of distinction. One of these two logically different notions, viz. possibility proper, covers *two kinds of cases.* When one says that *p* is possible (in the sense of possibility proper), one sometimes could also say that *p* is contingent and sometimes that *p* is necessary. This does not mean, of course, that the term 'possible' is ambiguous; it merely means that its field of application falls into two parts. It was for Aristotle therefore a typical case of multiplicity of applications as distinguished from homonymy (cf. section 10 of the first paper). The following diagram makes the situation clear:

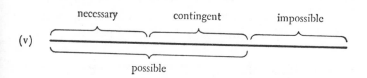

(v)

The distinction between the different applications of 'possibility proper' loomed large for Aristotle because he tended to emphasize the distinction between

necessity and contingency. Thus Aristotle argues in
Met. X 10 that the perishable and the imperishable
are different in kind (εἶδος and γένος). In an earlier
paper ("Necessity, Universality, and Time in Aristotle," Ajatus, XX [1957], 65–90), I have argued that the
distinction between contingency and necessity is for
Aristotle equivalent to that between what is perishable and imperishable. The field of application of 'possibility proper' therefore falls into two parts which are
different in kind. We have already seen in sections 10
and 12 of the first paper that Aristotle viewed situations of this kind with suspicion, although he grudg-
ingly admitted that no logical harm need result. This
is probably one of the reasons why Aristotle in Analytica Priora preferred the notion of contingency to
that of possibility proper.

4. Aristotle's definition of contingency. According to
the results of our examination of the ambiguities of
Aristotelian ambiguity, we may expect that the Stagirite usually refers to the distinction between possibility proper and contingency by means of ὁμωνυμία
and that he always refers to the distinction between
the different cases of possibility proper (i.e. between
necessity and contingency) by means of some other locution, e.g. διχῶς λέγεται, κατὰ δύο τρόπους λέγεται
or πολλαχῶς λέγεται. An examination of the text
will bear out this expectation as far as the first, the
second, and the fourth expressions are concerned. Similarly, the third locution is, we shall find, used by Aristotle in distinguishing two kinds of cases of contingency (see section 6 below).

In Aristotle's discussion of the notion of possibility,
the key passage is in An. Pr. I 13, 32a18–21. It is referred to by Aristotle repeatedly as the definition of
possibility (e.g. An. Pr. I 14, 33b24; 15, 33b28; 15, 34b
28; 17, 37a27). The 'definition' is clear enough (I shall

not discuss here why Aristotle thinks of it as a definition):

> I use the terms 'possibly' and 'the possible' of that which is not necessary but, being assumed, results in nothing impossible.

This is clearly the notion I have called contingency. However, it is not the only variant of possibility, for Aristotle continues:

τὸ γὰρ ἀναγκαῖον ὁμωνύμως ἐνδέχεσθαι λέγομεν

That is, to say of the necessary that it is possible is to use the term 'possible' homonymously. This explanation obviously serves to motivate the qualification "which is not necessary" in Aristotle's definition. The use of the word ὁμωνύμως shows that he knows that he is making a choice between two incompatible meanings of ἐνδέχεσθαι (to be possible). The second meaning, under which even necessary things are called possible, is the notion of possibility which satisfies (iii) and which I have called possibility proper.

We have thus reached two important conclusions: (a) the main notion of possibility employed by Aristotle in *An. Pr.* is what I have called contingency; (b) Aristotle is aware of the existence of the other notion (possibility proper) which is different from contingency to the degree that the same term can be applied to them only homonymously.

These results are confirmed by other passages. A glance at (iv) shows that contingency is symmetrical with respect to negation: *p* is contingent if and only if not-*p* is also contingent. They are therefore convertible to each other. Aristotle makes the same observation and applies it to syllogistic premises in *An. Pr.* I 13, 32a30 ff. This shows that his 'possibility as defined' agrees with my 'contingency'. Essentially the same point is made in *An. Pr.* I 17, 37a22 ff.

Aristotle's awareness of the ambiguity of possibility is also demonstrated by the development of his syllogistic. He frequently points out that the conclusion of a certain syllogism is valid only if one does not understand possibility in the sense defined (i.e. in the sense of contingency) but in a sense in which it is the contradictory of impossibility (e.g. *An. Pr.* I 15, 33b30–33; 15, 34b27–32; 16, 35b33; 17, 36b33; 20, 39a12).

5. *An analysis of An. Pr. I 13, 32a21–28.* The fact that Aristotle was aware of the different logical properties of contingency as distinguished from possibility proper seems to me to be in agreement with what Aristotle writes immediately after the passages I have quoted (*An. Pr.* I 13, 32a21–28). This passage has been censured by the recent commentators in spite of the fact that it occurs in all the MSS and is recognized both by Alexander and by Philoponus (W. D. Ross, *Aristotle's Prior and Posterior Analytics* [Oxford, 1949], p. 327). However, it seems to me that the passage can be understood as it stands by making due allowance for Aristotle's conspicuous conciseness. I shall offer a paraphrase of the passage, enclosing explanatory additions as well as my own comments in brackets. The superscripts refer to further comments.

Aristotle has just explained his sense of ἐνδεχόμενον (possible) and distinguished it from the homonymous notion of possibility proper. He goes on:

> That this [= Aristotle's definition] is the meaning of 'possible' is obvious from the opposing affirmations and denials.[1] For [in the other sense of 'possible'] 'it is not possible to apply', 'it is impossible to apply' and 'it is necessary not to apply' are either the same or imply each other.[2] Consequently their contradictories[3] 'it is possible to apply', 'it is not impossible to apply' and 'it is not necessary not to apply' are the same or imply each other. For either the affirmation or the negation always applies. [This is not correct, however, for we

mean by possibility something more than the absence
of impossibility.[4]] That which is necessary will therefore not be possible, and that which is not necessary
[nor impossible[5]] will be possible.

Further comments: (1) This elliptic sentence poses
two questions:
(a) What are these affirmations and denials affirmations and denials of?
(b) What kind of opposition is Aristotle here referring
to?

As regards (a), the sequel shows that Aristotle is not
dealing with affirmations and denials of possibility in
the sense (of contingency) just defined. It turns out
(cf. (2) below) that the affirmations and denials pertain to the other sense of possibility (possibility proper). Since Aristotle is obviously trying to justify his
own definition, it may be concluded that he is here
starting a *reductio ad absurdum* argument.

As regards (b), a comparison with the occurrences of
ἀντικείμενος later in the passage (cf. (3)) suggests that
this word—which is Aristotle's vaguest and most general term for opposition of any kind—here refers to
contradictory opposition. The alternative would be to
understand the sentence as referring to the opposition
between the two kinds of possibility; this would suit my
interpretation quite as well as the other reading.

(2) This is exactly what we get by accepting the
other sense of ἐνδεχόμενον, i.e. by not excluding necessity from the range of possibility: 'not possible that *p*'
will be equivalent to 'impossible that *p*' which is (cf.
diagram (ii)) tantamount to 'necessarily not *p*'.

(3) The following sentence shows that these contradictories are the ἀντικείμενα referred to here.

(4) It was already pointed out above (in section 2)
that Aristotle took this view. See especially the reference to the *Topica*, loc. cit. It appears from the φανερὸν

in 32a20 that Aristotle thought of this point as being
perfectly obvious; so obvious, indeed, that he neglected
to make it explicit here.

(5) The second part of the last sentence seems
strange. The addition I have indicated is a most tempt-
ing way of making the passage correct. It is very likely,
however, that the passage is Aristotle's as it stands. He
knew that his notion of possibility (i.e. contingency)
is symmetrical with respect to negation in the sense
which best appears from diagram (iv). He may have
thought that this symmetry justifies the transition from
'what is necessary is not possible' to 'what is not necessary is possible'. This leads to a reading of 'not necessary' as an elliptic form of 'not necessary either way',
i.e. 'neither necessary nor impossible'. In the sequel,
we shall find more indications that this was Aristotle's
reading; see section 7 *infra*.

Here I shall only point out that my interpretation is
supported by what we find in *De Interpretatione*. If
it is true that 'not necessary' sometimes does duty for
'neither necessary nor impossible', it may be expected
that 'not necessarily not', i.e. 'not impossible', will
sometimes mean 'neither impossible nor necessary'.
When this is so, 'not impossible' will entail (in fact,
it will be equivalent to) 'not necessary'. And this is
exactly what we find in *De Int.* 13, 22b14–16, where
Aristotle infers 'not necessary' from 'not impossible'.
This inference is very difficult to explain otherwise.
The inference is based on the sequence of implications
(equivalences?) set up by Aristotle in *De Int.* 13,
22a16 ff., where again μὴ ἀδύνατον εἶναι entails μὴ
ἀναγκαῖον εἶναι.

6. *A subdivision of contingency.* Having made these
distinctions, Aristotle goes on to say (in *An. Pr.* I 13,
32b5 ff.) that possibility has two applications (the expression he uses is κατὰ δύο τρόπους λέγεται). On

one hand, it is used to describe what generally happens but falls short of being necessary, on the other hand it is used to describe the indeterminate, that which can be 'thus or not thus' without the prevalence of either alternative. Now the distinction plainly has nothing to do with the difference between possibility proper and contingency. Neither of the two uses distinguished by Aristotle covers what happens necessarily. What we have here is therefore a *subdivision of contingency*. Aristotle's use of the expression κατὰ δύο τρόπους λέγεται suggests that he is not distinguishing two meanings of ἐνδεχόμενον but rather two kinds of cases to which it can be applied. This is verified by his remarks on the conversion of statements of contingency. He says that in both cases the possible premise can be converted into its opposite premise, i.e. '*p* is contingent' into 'not-*p* is contingent'. This is trivial in the case of a *p* which is contingent because it is 'indeterminate'. But Aristotle also holds that the conversion applies to contingency in the sense of that which 'generally happens'. This may seem mistaken; if *p* happens generally but not necessarily, we certainly cannot infer that not-*p* happens generally. What Aristotle means is that even in this case not-*p* is neither necessary nor impossible and hence contingent in the sense of his definition. If 'what happens generally but not necessarily' were one of several *meanings* of 'contingent', Aristotle would not be able to say that 'contingent' always converts with its opposite. What he means is that in each of the different cases that fall under the term 'contingent' we have a conversion to the opposite of some case—not necessarily of the same case— covered by the term.[1] Hence, he is not dealing with

[1]Aristotle's awareness of the fact that a case of a concept may be converted into another case of the same concept is also shown by his remarks on τὸ εἰκός in *Rhet.* II 23, 1402a9 ff.

different meanings of ἐνδεχόμενον, but only with different applications of the term. 'Contingent' is not homonymous although it covers different kinds of cases.

7. *An analysis of An. Pr. I 3, 25a37–25b19.* Some of the passages I have just discussed are referred to by Aristotle earlier in *Analytica Priora* in connection with the conversion of problematic (possible) premises (*An. Pr.* I 3, 25a37–25b19). We are now in a position to understand the context of these references.

In *An. Pr.* I 3, 25b18 Aristotle refers to his later discussions of the conversion of problematic premises. All the remarks on this subject later in *Analytica Priora* pertain to contingent premises. This suggests that the notion Aristotle has in mind in 25b18 is his 'possibility as defined' or contingency. This is confirmed by the way Aristotle explains the notion of possibility which he is here dealing with: "But if anything is said to be possible because it is the general rule and natural..." (*An. Pr.* I 3, 25b14 ff.). This recalls one of the different cases of contingency discussed in *An. Pr.* I 13, 32b5 ff. (*vide supra*). And when Aristotle says that this "is the strict sense we assign to possible" (Ross's translation), he is obviously anticipating his definition of contingency, in 32b18–20.

I conclude, therefore, that in *An. Pr.* I 3, 25b14–18 Aristotle is thinking of contingency rather than possibility proper. Now the passage which was just quoted shows that this variant of possibility is contrasted to the one employed in the immediately preceding passage (*An. Pr.* I 3, 25b8–13). We may therefore expect that this latter notion of possibility is what I have called possibility proper. Aristotle's examples show that this is in fact the case. In one of his examples the term 'man' necessarily does not apply to any horse, while in another the term 'white' does not necessarily apply to any coat. This shows that the meaning of possibility which is used here covers cases of necessity as well as cases of contingency. (The examples are both negative in form because he is discussing the conversion of negative premises.)

Although the testimony of Aristotle's examples thus unambiguously shows that in 25b8–13 he is discussing possibility proper, one may still be puzzled by his own explanation of the variant of possibility he is using: "Whatever is said to be possible because it is necessary or because it is not necessary admits of conversion like other negative statements. . . ." For what one would expect here is 'neither necessary nor impossible' instead of 'not necessary'. Some commentators have tried to emend the passage by inserting the negative particle μὴ so as to make it read 'not necessarily not', although there is no real support for such an insertion in the MSS (see Ross, op. cit.). Moreover, this insertion has the disadvantage of making the clause 'because it is necessary' superfluous. In any case, the emendation is quite unnecessary, for we have already found independent reasons for suspecting that Aristotle sometimes uses 'not necessary' (τὸ μὴ ἀναγκαῖον) and, by analogy, 'not necessarily' (μὴ ἐξ ἀνάγκης) as elliptic expressions for 'neither necessary nor impossible' and 'neither necessarily nor impossibly', respectively (see section 5, comment (5) *supra*). This suspicion is now confirmed by the fact that the same explanation works here: on my reading the quoted passage says just what one is entitled to expect.

Here one may ask whether my reading is contradicted by the fact that in his second example Aristotle says that it is not necessary that 'white' applies to any coat (τὸ δὲ οὐκ ἀνάγκη ὑπάρχειν). If Aristotle were consistently using the elliptic mode of expression, should he not use double negative οὐκ ἀνάγκη μὴ ὑπάρχειν, since he is here dealing with negative premises? To this it may be answered that 'neither necessary nor impossible' is symmetrical with respect to negation, so that no extra μὴ is needed even if the elliptic mode of expression is used. Besides, one of Bekker's MSS as well as Philoponus do have the missing μὴ (see Ross, op. cit.), so that Aristotle may very well have been even pedantically consistent in his usage.

We may conclude that in his treatment of the conversion of negative problematic premises Aristotle first discusses premises in which the notion of 'possibility proper' is used and then those in which the notion of contingency is used. In contrast, both these notions are lumped together in Aristotle's discussion of the conversion of positive problematic premises (25a37 – 25b2). He indicates this as follows: . . . ἐπειδὴ πολλαχῶς λέγεται τὸ ἐνδέχεσθαι (καὶ γὰρ τὸ ἀναγκαῖον καὶ τὸ μὴ ἀναγκαῖον καὶ τὸ δυνατὸν ἐνδέχεσθαι λέγομεν). . . . Here the words πολλαχῶς λέγεται suggest that he is not exclusively concerned with the different meanings of ἐνδεχόμενον. In fact, it has been pointed out by Ross that the three cases listed in the parenthetical clause cannot possibly be as many different meanings of ἐνδεχόμενον. However, it seems to me that it cannot be said, either, that they are just three different cases to which the notion of possibility can be applied. The first two are clear; we have encountered τὸ ἀναγκαῖον and τὸ μὴ ἀναγκαῖον before as the two cases covered by the notion of possibility proper. The recurrence for the fourth time of the elliptic expression τὸ μὴ ἀναγκαῖον (or of one of its variants) where one expects 'neither necessary nor impossible' gives further support to my interpretation of this phrase. But τὸ δυνατὸν cannot very well be a third case to which the notion of possibility is applied, for there is no third case comparable with the two already listed. Rather, we must understand τὸ ἀναγκαῖον καὶ τὸ μὴ ἀναγκαῖον as referring to the notion of possibility proper, and understand τὸ δυνατὸν as referring to the other notion of possibility, viz. contingency. This, in fact, seems to be the way Ross understands the passage. Its meaning may hence be expressed somewhat as follows: "...seeing that possibility has many applications (for we call possible both that which is necessary or is not necessary either way and that which is capable of being)...."

This interpretation is supported by the fact that the context shows that Aristotle is here treating both the variants of possibility at the same time. If they are here mentioned in the same order in which they are subsequently treated (in the connection of the conversion of negative problematic premises) we can scarcely separate Aristotle's references to the two variants in any way different from the one just suggested.

Our interpretation also agrees with the way δυνατόν is used elsewhere in *Analytica Priora*. The most important passage in which this term occurs is *An. Pr.* I 15, 34a6 ff. And it is indicated by Aristotle (in 34a14) that the arguments he there gives pertain to possibility with respect to generation. Now this variant of possibility is very likely just our contingency. For something which is generated will sometimes be (viz. after having been generated) and sometimes not be (viz. before it is generated). It is therefore possible in the very sense (in that of contingency) which we wanted to give δυνατόν in *An. Pr.* I 3, 25a39.

8. Remarks on *An. Pr.* I *13, 32b25–32*. What we have found in this paper and its predecessor confirms my earlier analysis of *An. Pr.* I 13, 32b25–32 (in "Necessity, Universality, and Time in Aristotle," pp. 86–88). Here I shall only briefly outline the argument, adding such new evidence as was not mentioned in the earlier paper.

In the passage under discussion Aristotle seems to be saying that

(P)   it is possible for A to apply to all B

is ambiguous in that it may mean either

(P_1)   it is possible for A to apply to everything
       to which B in fact applies

or

(P_2)   it is possible for A to apply to everything
       to which B possibly applies.

This cannot be his meaning, however. For one thing, he never seems to use (P_1) but only (P_2) in his subsequent discussion of syllogisms from possible premises. He seems even to say that (P_2) is what (P) was defined to mean (*An. Pr.* I 14, 33a24–25). For another, the term Aristotle uses is διχῶς, which strongly suggests that he is not at all distinguishing two different meanings of (P). Rather, he is saying that (P) covers two kinds of cases, i.e. that (P) is tantamount to the conjunction of (P_1) and (P_2). This suffices to explain everything that Aristotle says and does. It may be expected that the variant of possibility Aristotle is using in (P_2) is the one he usually employs, viz. contingency. Expressed as explicitly as possible, Aristotle's point therefore is that (P) is equivalent to the conjunction of (P_1) and (P_{21}), where the latter is

(P_{21})   it is possible for A to apply to everything
        to which B applies contingently.

Now this conjunction is clearly equivalent to what we get by assuming that the variant of possibility used in (P_2) is my 'possibility proper':

(P_{22})   it is possible for A to apply to everything
        to which B possibly applies (in the sense of

'possibility proper'), i.e. to everything to which
B applies necessarily or contingently.

This explains why Aristotle seems to deal exclusively
with (P_2) in his syllogistic theory; for what he is really
dealing with is (P_{22}) which is equivalent to the conjunction of (P_1) and (P_{21}) and therefore also to (P).

Further evidence is perhaps found in *An. Pr.* I 29,
45b31–32. Having just explained how the different
kinds of assertoric syllogisms are established, Aristotle
goes on to say that apodeictic (necessary) and problematic (possible) syllogisms are established in the same
way. But he adds a warning:

> In the case of problematic propositions, however, we
> must include those terms which, although they do not
> apply, might possibly do so; for it has been shown that
> the problematic syllogism is effected by means of
> these. . . . (H. Tredennick's translation in the Loeb
> Library edition)

Prima facie this is completely tautologous. For problematic syllogisms contain by definition terms which
do not apply but may apply. What can Aristotle mean
here? It is clear that the *predicate term* A of a premise like (P) may apply possibly but not actually. But
it is not equally obvious whether the *subject term* B
is to be taken to apply possibly or actually; whether,
in other words, (P) is to be understood as being equivalent to (P_1) or to (P_{22}). Unless we assume that Aristotle's statement is pointless, we can scarcely interpret
it except as a repetition of the point which we found
him making in *An. Pr.* I 13, 32b25–32, viz. as identifying (P) and (P_{22}). Notice in particular that there is
no semblance here of a distinction between two meanings.

9. *Concluding remarks.* We have discussed the most
important passages of *An. Pr.* I which turn on the dis-

tinction between the various notions of possibility used by Aristotle. Insofar as we have been successful in applying the results of my earlier analysis of the ambiguities of ambiguity in Aristotle, our success conversely serves as a further confirmation of the earlier analysis. In particular, it supports what was said in section 10 of the first paper. Aristotle's own definition of contingency (see *supra*, section 4) establishes a connection between contingency and possibility proper: contingent is that which is (properly) possible but not necessary. If homonymy were tantamount to the absence of any common element in definition, contingency and possibility proper would not be homonyms. The fact that Aristotle calls them homonyms shows that there is more to his notion of homonymy than that.

ON ARISTOTLE'S SQUARE
OF OPPOSITION

M. THOMPSON

Arguments have recently been offered that purportedly save Aristotle's square of opposition from the charges which modern logicians have brought against it.[1] The main argument in this defense, as I understood it, is the contention that the principle of excluded middle, or the principle that "every meaningful statement is either true or false," is subject to certain qualifications. These qualifications have nothing to do with multivalued logics or the adoption of some new formal principle, but concern an alleged "feature of ordinary speech." In brief, this feature is that in order for an empirical descriptive sentence to be meaningful it is not necessary for it to yield a true or false statement on *every* occasion of its utterance. Thus, the sentence "All Smith's children are girls" is meaningful because it would yield a true and not also a false statement if uttered on an occasion when Smith had

From *The Philosophical Review*, LXII (1953), 251–65. Reprinted by permission of the author and the editor of *The Philosophical Review*.

[1] The most lengthy statement of this defense of Aristotle is given by H. L. A. Hart, "A Logician's Fairy Tale," *The Philosophical Review*, LX (1951), 198–212. Hart says he owes the "substance" of his criticism of "modern logical doctrine" to P. F. Strawson, and refers to the latter's article, "On Referring," *Mind*, LIX (1950), especially pp. 343–44. For a shorter statement of a similar defense of Aristotle, see P. T. Geach, "Subject and Predicate," *Mind*, LIX (1950), esp. 480.

children all of whom were girls. It would likewise yield a false and not also a true statement if uttered on an occasion when Smith had at least one child who was a boy. But if uttered on an occasion when Smith had no children at all it would yield neither a true nor a false statement—"the question of its truth or falsity simply would not arise."

Bearing in mind this feature of ordinary speech, we are to interpret Aristotle's square of opposition as applicable to empirical descriptive sentences only on those occasions when their utterance would yield a statement that it is either true or false but not both. Thus, when an Aristotelian logician affirms that the logical relation of "All ogres are wicked" to "Some ogres are wicked" is one of super-implication, he is not also affirming that some ogres exist. He is merely affirming that the two sentences are so related that on any occasion when an utterance of the first yields a true statement, an utterance of the second must also yield a true statement. The fact that we believe there could be no such occasion is beside the point. The sentences are meaningful because we can imagine what would have to obtain on such an occasion. An Aristotelian logician is then no more guilty of affirming ogres into existence than is the teller of a fairy tale who makes statements about ogres. For the logician like the story teller speaks only of what would be the case *if there were* ogres.

The modern interpretation which permits us to say that "All ogres are wicked" is true though "Some ogres are wicked" is false is thus not only unnecessary in order to avoid the paradoxes of existential import, but it also leads to a misunderstanding of ordinary speech. For it assumes that every meaningful empirical descriptive sentence yields a true or false statement on every occasion of its utterance, and overlooks those occasions when common sense would say that the question of its truth or falsity simply does not arise. If we interrupted the story teller with the question, "But is it true that all ogres are wicked?" this would be a clear indication that we had misunderstood his use of language. Similarly, if we argued about the truth or falsity of "All Smith's children are girls" when we knew that Smith had no children, we could hardly be said to have understood the conditions under which this statement would ordinarily be taken as true or false.

Now I want first of all to argue that these proposed qualifications of the principle of excluded middle are of dubious value since they make any application of the supposedly simple and elementary logical relations in the square of opposition extremely complex.

I

Classical logicians from Aristotle on have taken the relations in the square of opposition as connecting entities which must be either true or false, even though these entities have been variously identified as linguistic expressions, as propositions, and as judgments. While the relations themselves may on occasion have been defined without reference to truth or falsity, such a mode of definition does not mean that sometimes the relations may hold when neither truth nor falsity is applicable. The prerogative of the logician extends only to the point of not having to specify in a given case which one obtains, truth or falsity; it does not extend to the point of casting aside the question of truth and falsity altogether. Yet the latter appears to be what the new defenders of Aristotle are proposing. For according to the new defense, we are to say that "All ogres are wicked" and "Some ogres are not wicked" are related as contradictories, even though neither truth nor falsity is applicable to either of them.

Any assertion here of the commonplace that one of a pair of contradictories must be true and the other false will take the form of a contrary-to-fact conditional. If there were ogres, i.e. if the question of the truth or falsity of these statements were to arise, then one would have to be true and the other false.

Thus, what has traditionally been a simple and straight-forward specification of relations of truth conditions has now been made to involve the complicated logical distinctions required to cope with contrary-to-fact conditionals. Even if we succeed in defining the relations in the square without reference to truth or falsity, we must resort to contrary-to-fact conditionals in order to specify how any of the relations are applicable to all ordinary statements in a way that logical relations have traditionally been supposed applicable. The decision of modern logicians to regard the truth conditions of a universal affirmative statement as satisfied when nothing of the kind named exists enables us to preserve the traditional simplicity in the application of the relation of contradictoriness. Even though this decision does away with the applicability of contrariety, sub-contrariety, and super- and sub-implication, it seems preferable to a decision which makes the application of any of the relations exceedingly complex. The traditional square can be retained as a valid schema relating by contradictoriness four of the most frequent types of quantified statements. The remaining relations indicated by the square can be defined by other schemata in accordance with which they are always applicable, and the traditional simplicity of application for any of the relations can be retained.

Even if we agree with the new defenders of Aristotle that the decision which leads to the modern analysis is repugnant to ordinary speech, we can still argue that this is more desirable than a decision repugnant to logical analysis itself. For surely a decision which makes any specification of the conditions under which a simple logical relation is universally applicable take the form of a contrary-to-fact conditional sins against our conception of what logical analysis should achieve. It seems to me fairly easy to show that the sin is against Aristotle's as well as against our modern conception.

I propose in the remainder of this paper to argue (a) that the account of the square of opposition given in Aristotle's *On Interpretation* is fundamentally different from what is usually taken as the traditional analysis of the square,[2] and (b) that Aristotle's account is free from the contradictions and absurdities which arise from the latter, this freedom being achieved, not by qualifying the principle of excluded middle, but by Aristotle's own peculiar restrictions on the existential import of statements. For reasons that should soon become apparent, I shall begin with some remarks about singular statements.

II

The applicability of truth or falsity to statements when the subject named does not exist is explicitly declared by Aristotle to hold for singular statements.[3]

---

[2]By "traditional analysis" I mean simply the sort that is presented today in most logic texts as the Aristotelian one. As will be made clear in the sequel, the essential features of this analysis are (1) the usual doctrine of immediate inferences, including obversion, contraposition, and inversion; (2) all the logical relations purportedly expressed in Aristotle's square of opposition. When I speak of contradictions and absurdities in this analysis, I do not mean to deny that some classical logicians may have intended some special assumptions not in Aristotle (such as the proposed qualifications of the excluded middle) which keep the analysis consistent. I am concerned only with the analysis as it stands without such assumptions.

[3]*Cat.* 13b26–35. All quotations from Aristotle, unless otherwise specified, are from the Oxford translation.

> But in the case of affirmation and negation, whether the subject exists or not, one is always false and the other true. For manifestly, if Socrates exists, one of the two propositions 'Socrates is ill,' 'Socrates is not ill,' is true, and the other false. This is likewise the case if he does not exist; for if he does not exist, to say that he is ill is false, to say that he is not ill is true.

This clearly suggests that any affirmation about a singular subject implies that the subject exists, while a negative statement about such a subject cannot have this implication. Yet in another passage Aristotle seems to contradict what he says here by arguing that "Homer is a poet" does not imply "Homer is." "Take the proposition 'Homer is so-and-so,' say 'a poet'; does it follow that Homer is, or does it not? The verb 'is' is here used of Homer only incidentally, the proposition being that Homer is a poet, not that he is, in the independent sense of the word."[4]

The crucial point in understanding this second passage is the meaning of "is, in the independent sense of the word," i.e. of "is per se." Clearly this is "is" in the substantive sense of the word and means the same as "is a substance." What Aristotle is denying in this passage, then, is that "Homer is a substance" follows from "Homer is a poet." Now in the first passage quoted above the word "exists" is used to translate *ontos*, which of course literally means just *being* and not necessarily *being a substance*. Hence we should take "exists" as meaning the same as "being" without the specification of the sense of being, as being a substance or being an accident, and then there is no contradiction. "Homer exists" does follow from "Homer is a poet," since if Homer did not exist, i.e. if he were simply nonbeing, it would not be true to say that he is anything. This point is suggested by Aristotle's re-

[4]*On Interpretation* 21a26–28.

marks almost immediately following the second passage quoted above. "But in the case of that which is not, it is not true to say that because it is the object of opinion, it is; for the opinion held about it is that it is not, not that it is." In other words, the fact that a non-existent Homer may be the object of opinion, as he would be if we were to construct a myth about him, does not mean that it is true to say Homer is something.[5] The assertions "Homer is merely the object of opinion" and "Homer is a mythical being" are about Homer only in the sense of denying that he is in fact anything. While we might say that "Homer is a poet" is true in fiction, what is true in this case is true of the myth and not of Homer. And the myth does exist, even though not *per se* as a substance does.[6]

An affirmation about a singular subject, then, is false and its contradictory is true when either of the following conditions obtains.

C-1   The subject exists, either *per se* as a substance or as something dependent on a substance (as an accident of a substance), but does not possess the predicate affirmed of it (e.g. when Socrates exists and is healthy, "Socrates is ill" is false, and when the color of this table exists but is not dull, "The color of this table is dull" is false).

[5]The Oxford translation of the passage just quoted above (21a32–33) obscures the fact that the question is whether non-being is *something* because it is the object of opinion. The Greek just before the semicolon in this translation reads *on ti*. The Loeb translation gives "it is not true to say that it 'is' somewhat, because it is matter of opinion."

[6]The myth may be said to exist as an artificial substance, dependent on its maker. With this interpretation of the text, we must of course deny that Aristotle would allow a realm of fictitious things as a realm of being. This point admittedly calls for further consideration, but it will be passed over here as simply one of the assumptions required in order to make sense out of Aristotle's remarks that are relevant to his account of the square of opposition.

C-2   This subject does not exist, i.e. is neither a sub-
       stance nor something dependent on a substance.

There is thus no need to qualify the principle that
every meaningful statement is either true or false, as
this principle applies to statements about singulars.

There is one further point to be considered before
we turn to the square of opposition. What about the
relation of "Socrates is not-ill" to "Socrates is not ill"?
As Aristotle analyzed this relation it is an implication
with the first statement as antecedent; it is not an
equivalence. "Socrates is not-ill" counts as an affirmation, although one of a very peculiar sort. For the predicate "is not-ill" is not strictly what Aristotle calls a
verb, and after complaining that there is no specified
name for such a predicate, he proposes to call it an
indefinite (or infinite) verb, since it applies "equally
well to that which exists and to that which does not."[7]
Thus, we might say "Socrates is not-ill" when we wish
to affirm that Socrates is a not-ill man, though we
might also use this same affirmation when we want
merely to deny that Socrates is ill. When C-2 obtains,
our assertion is false in the first case but not in the
second.[8] We, of course, could overcome this indefiniteness by adopting the convention that in logic a singular statement with an indefinite verb as predicate
will always be taken in one sense and not the other.
But this would be to retreat from the problem rather
than solve it. Statements of the sort in question are

[7]16b12–16.
[8]Aristotle remarks in 20a25–27 that if the negative answer to
"Is Socrates wise?" is true, then an inference affirming that Socrates is unwise (or not-wise) is correct. In the light of 13b26–35
(quoted above) we must interpret this remark as assuming that
the question would not be asked if Socrates were nonexistent.
The purpose of such an assumption at this point is to show a
difference between universal and singular statements. Even though
men exist, a negative answer to "Is every man wise?" does not
allow the inference that every man is unwise.

logically indefinite and the logician must accept them as such and make what he can of them. Aristotle pointed out that if "Socrates is not-ill" is true, then, whether this is equivalent to affirming that Socrates is a not-ill man or merely to the denial that he is ill, "Socrates is not ill" must be true. However, because of the indefiniteness of the antecedent in this implication the relation does not hold the other way around. When C-2 obtains, the antecedent is false in its strictly affirmative sense while the consequent remains true, and the relation thus cannot be an equivalence.[9]

The recognition of statements with indefinite terms as peculiar entities for the logician to cope with rather than to obliterate by convention is essential to Aristotle's account of the square of opposition.

Aristotle does not say explicitly that a universal affirmative or A statement is false when nothing of the kind named exists, but what he does say about the logical relations of quantified statements seems to me to make the best sense when we take this interpretation of the universal affirmative. Let us see, then, how far we can go toward making sense out of Aristotle's account when we begin with the seemingly rash assumption that an A statement is false when either of the following conditions obtains.

C'-1   At least one thing of the kind named exists, i.e. is either a substance or something dependent on a substance, but does not possess the predicate affirmed of it.

C'-2   Nothing of the kind named exists, i.e. is either a substance or something dependent on a substance.

We must first make sense out of saying that the corresponding O statement, the contradictory of A, is

---

[9]This point is made in the *An. Pr.* 51b36–52a17.

true when C'-2 obtains. Now it is clear that Aristotle regarded O as denying precisely what A affirmed, and that he took these statements as forms of simple affirmation and denial, respectively. Yet the usual rendering of O as "Some S exists and is not P" certainly does not express what Aristotle meant by a simple denial. We have instead a compound statement in which one thing is affirmed and another denied. A literal translation of his examples of O gives "Not every S is P," which is to be taken as simply the denial that P is truly affirmed universally of S. In this simple denial we do not affirm anything, and hence if C'-2 obtains, our denial is true because if there are no S's, it is not true to affirm P universally of them, any more than it is true to affirm illness of Socrates when Socrates does not exist. We must next explain how the corresponding E statement, the contrary of A, is likewise true when C'-2 is the case. For if E is false its contradictory I must be true and we would have the absurdity that "Some S is P" is true when there are no S's. But E and O do not differ in being more or less simple, or more or less a denial. They are both simple denials, though E denies that P can be particularly affirmed (affirmed in at least one instance) of S while O denies that P can be universally affirmed. But clearly, then, if C'-2 obtains E is true since P cannot be particularly affirmed.

With this interpretation of the square, the existential import of a statement is determined by its quality rather than its quantity.[10] While this means that

---

[10]C. S. Peirce remarks, "It is probable that Kant also understood the affirmative proposition to assert the existence of its subject, while the negative did not do so: so that 'some phoenixes do not rise from their ashes' would be true, and 'All phoenixes do rise from their ashes' would be false" (*Collected Papers*, Vol. II, par. 381). Peirce refers, Vol. III, par. 178, to the view that ex-

in any case at least one of the two particular statements in the square must be true, it does not result in the absurdity of forcing us to affirm the existence of whatever may be the subject of a statement. In all cases where C'-2 obtains, both affirmative statements are false and we do not affirm the existence of anything.

This interpretation of the square, however, is impossible if we accept the usual treatment of what Aristotle called indefinite (or infinite) nouns and verbs. As they are normally used in logic books these indefinite terms permit us to assert equivalences between affirmative and negative statements, so that the quality of a statement remains relative to a particular mode of expression and clearly cannot serve as the determination of its existential import. But Aristotle seems to deny these equivalences in his discussion of indefinite terms as they occur in universal and particular statements.

We noted above that, according to Aristotle, the logical relation between a singular affirmation with an

istential import is determined by the quality of the statement as a view "usually understood" in the traditional account.

Peirce does not cite evidence in support of this interpretation of Kant, but it is not difficult to find passages in the *Critique of Pure Reason* that suggest it. For example, "As far as *logical* form is concerned, we can make negative any proposition we like; but in respect to the content of our knowledge in general, which is either extended or limited by a judgment, the task peculiar to negative judgments is that of *rejecting error*" (A 709, B 737; tr. N. Kemp Smith; italics in original). Viewed in this way, then, negative judgments simply reject affirmative judgments as erroneous and affirm nothing about objects in the world. The remark that, as regards logical form, we can make negative any proposition we like, is relevant to the consideration; in the remainder of the present paper. We should note in passing that in accordance with this remark the quality of a statement as determining its existential import is not, for Kant, to be identified with its quality as determined by its logical form.

Evidence that Kant assumed affirmative statements to have existential import may be found in his well-known denial that "existence" is a predicate, plus his insistence on the distinction between categorical and hypothetical judgments.

indefinite verb as predicate and the corresponding denial with respect to the same subject was not equivalence but implication with the first statement as antecedent. Although Aristotle's account of universal and
particular statements with indefinite terms is difficult
in its details and the text seems corrupt at a few places,
I believe there is little room for doubt about the following two points. (1) Whenever a statement containing no indefinite terms and representing one of the
four categorical forms is logically related to another
statement containing indefinite terms, the relation
seems to be implication rather than equivalence.[11]
(2) In every case the affirmative statement is the antecedent of the implication.

The following four implications are clearly indicated
by Aristotle's remarks in Chapter X of his *On Interpretation* (the implications run horizontally and the antecedent is always first).

(1) Every man is just.   Not every man is not-just.
(2) Every man is not-just.   Not every man is just.
(3) Every man is not-just.   No man is just.
(4) Some men are just.   Not every man is not-just.

The first two pairs in this list occur in a context where
Aristotle is concerned primarily with the contradictory
oppositions indicated by the diagonals rather than the
implications and the latter emerge from the schema of

[11]The verb used to express this relation is *akolouthein*, which
means literally "to follow," "to go after," or "with." The most
obvious translation when the verb occurs in a logical treatise is
"to follow from," "to be implied by," and this is the practice
followed by the Oxford and Loeb translators. However, many
commentators have read Aristotle as often using the verb with
the force of "to be equivalent to." This reading is ruled out by
the present interpretation of Aristotle, but the exclusion rests on
an attempt to make sense out of his logical doctrine rather than
on the claim that it is necessitated by the Greek alone. When,
on the other hand, the text gives *tauton semainein* the logical
relation must of course be equivalence rather than implication.

oppositions. The last two pairs are stated separately as implications and are not presented as part of a schema of oppositions. Since an A statement with an indefinite verb as predicate implies both an O and E statement, a definite A statement would also seem to have two corresponding implications. Further, since the list of antecedents includes both the definite and indefinite forms of A it would seem that this list should also include both forms of the I statement. It might thus appear that we can add the following two implications which are not explicitly stated in the text.

(5) Every man is just.   No man is not-just.
(6) Some men are not-just.   Not every man is just.

However, I believe we can argue plausibly that, with Aristotle's analysis, these two additional implications are fundamentally different from the preceding ones, and that his failure to include them here is probably not an oversight. We should note first of all that in none of the four implications listed by Aristotle is there a statement with an indefinite term as subject. All the indefinite terms are predicates. Secondly, the two categorical statements that convert *simpliciter*, viz. E and I do not occur in the list with an indefinite term. Yet our proposed additions to the list involve such occurrences. By simple conversion, we get the following equivalent forms of our new implications.[12]

(5.1) Every man is just.   No not-just is a man.
(6.1) Some not-just is a man.   Not every man is just.

The difficulty here is in explaining how indefinite nouns function as subjects. We should note next that

[12]It is assumed here that for Aristotle simple conversion (as distinct from obversion) yields an equivalent statement. Justification for this assumption can be found in Aristotle's use of conversion in the reduction of syllogisms. He of course did not use obversion in the reductions.

after (1) and (2) are presented as pairs of opposites Aristotle lists two more such pairs that occur
when "not-man" is taken as "a kind of subject." He
cautions that this new set of opposites "should remain distinct from those which preceded it, since it
employs as its subject the expression 'not-man'." The
two further pairs of opposites (with oppositions indicated by the diagonals) are:

(7) Not-man is just.   ✕   Not-man is not not-just.
(8) Not-man is not-just. ✕   Not-man is not just.

Aristotle does not comment on the quantification of
these statements, nor does he give any explicit indication that implications hold here as in (1) and (2), but
a little later in the same chapter he gives the following
pair as equivalents.[13]

(9) Every not-man is not just.   No not-man is just.

Yet if treated as an ordinary categorical statement, the
first member of this equivalence is ambiguous and
might mean "Not every not-man is just" instead of
"No not-man is just." In order for the equivalence to
hold, "every" and "no" must be taken with the force
of "everything" and "nothing." We should thus understand the equivalence as between

(9.1)   Everything that is   Nothing that is not man
        not man is not just. is just.

The necessity for this interpretation of "every" and
"no" arises from the indefiniteness of the subject "not-
man." With this term as subject the only things about
which we can make assertions are those which are not
some definite kind of thing. We can thus never make
an assertion about every member of a collection, but

---

[13]The Greek here is *tauton semainein* as opposed to *akolouthein*. Cf. note 11. The translation in (9) is literal. The Oxford
translation is that given in (9.1).

only about every member that is not such and such. Our assertions will be like the statement a teacher might make after collecting examination papers. "Every paper in this group that does not receive a score of 50 or above is not passing," or in other words, "Every not-50-or-above-paper is not passing." But when we use an indefinite noun as subject without reference to some particular collection, such as a group of examination papers, we make a reference to the collection that comprises the totality of real things. Thus, the statements in (9) and (9.1) are equivalent to "Everything in the totality of real things that is not a man is not just." This reference to the totality of real things results from the peculiar way that an indefinite term signifies things.

These considerations should make it apparent that the statements in question do not have existential import in so far as they are assertions about those members of a collection that are not such and such. The teacher's statement does not imply that there is at least one not-50-or-above-paper in the group nor do (9) and (9.1) imply that there is at least one not-man. From this point of view, the statements are compound denials rather than affirmations—they deny that there is at least one member of the collection which is both not-50-or-above and passing, both not-man and just. This equivalence to a compound denial is again a result of the peculiar signification of indefinite terms, and is no less the case when the statement appears to be a universal affirmative. "Every not-man is just" is equivalent to the denial that there is at least one thing which is both not-man and not just. Particular statements with indefinite terms as subjects, on the other hand, are always equivalent to compound affirmations of existence, even though they appear to be particular negatives. "Not every not-man is just" is equivalent to "Something in the totality of real things is both not-man and not just." The statement must be construed in this way if it is to contradict the compound denial expressed by "Every not-man is just."

The above remarks may suffice to explain why Aristotle regarded indefinite terms as providing only "a kind of subject," and cautioned that the resulting statements should remain distinct from the ones previously considered. His failure to comment on the quantification of the statements in (7) and (8) is perhaps due to the fact that the contradictory oppositions, which seem to have been his primary interest here, are not altered when the statements are quantified as in (1) and (2). A list of the quantified forms would have been superfluous unless he intended also to add a specific account of the peculiarities which resulted from the indefinite subject.

A similar explanation may be given for the failure to mention the implications stated in (5) and (6). Unlike any of the preceding, each of these implications related a simple affirmation or denial to one whose subject is an indefinite term. Had Aristotle mentioned these two implications, it certainly would have been an oversight on his part if he had then omitted the other implications of this sort. But since he did not give the two in question, it seems fair to conclude that he did not intend here to consider any of them.

In light of the above considerations, we now have the following account of the immediate inferences that arise from the introduction of indefinite terms, i.e. of the processes usually called obversion and contraposition.

An A statement implies, but is not equivalent to, its obverse, its partial contrapositive, and its full contrapositive. Thus, "If every S is P, then no S is not-P, no not-P is S, and every not-P is not-S." Each of these three statements in the consequent is equivalent to the other two. "No not-P is S" is equivalent to its obverse, because unlike the original A or a simple E, it has an indefinite term as subject so that neither it nor its obverse has existential import. The inference from "Every not-P is not-S" to "Some not-P is not-S," the so-called full inverse of "Every S is P," is illegitimate because the antecedent in this case does not have existential import while the consequent does.

An E statement is implied by, but is not equivalent to, its obverse, just as the definite denial "Socrates is not ill" is implied by the indefinite affirmation "Socrates is not-ill." Hence the inference from an original E to its contrapositive or its inverse (whether these are full or partial) is never permissible. We cannot infer from "No mathematicians are circle-squarers" that some nonmathematicians are circle-squarers. In order to obtain this conclusion we need independently the premise, "Every circle-squarer is a nonmathematician." This premise is the obverted converse of the original E, and while with the present analysis it implies the E, it is logically independent of the obverse of E, since "Every mathematician is a noncircle-squarer" does not affirm anything about circle-squarers.

An I statement implies its obverse but is not equivalent to it (see (4), while an O statement is implied by its obverse but is not equivalent to it (see (6)). An O is also implied by its partial and full contrapositives, which are both equivalent to its obverse. These equivalences obtain because particular statements with indefinite terms as subjects always have existential import, in contrast to the original O, which asserted a simple denial.

The fundamental difference between this account of immediate inferences and the one which is usually accepted as characteristic of traditional logic is the treatment given the distinction between statements with

definite and indefinite subjects. Before we consider
how this account avoids the contradictions and absurdities in the traditional analysis, there is one further
point to be noted about Aristotle's analysis.

Aristotle seems to have begun construction of his
square with an A statement taken as a simple affirmation about every member of a collection rather than
about every member that is not such and such. In
other words, with a statement like "Every man is
just" as opposed to "Everything that is not a man is
just." As we have already indicated, with Aristotle's
analysis we should take the first but not the second of
these statements as having existential import. Yet
granting this point, we still have the problem of deciding which of the following two statements we shall
take as the contrary of our A statement.

(10)   No man is just.
(10.1)   Every man is not-just.

Either of these statements is so related to our original A that it cannot be true when the A is true,
though it can be true or false when the A is false. If
this reference to truth conditions is our only criterion
for determining the contrary, we should have to admit both statements, even though they are not equivalent, as contraries of our original. Yet clearly, (10) is
the only one that will satisfy the present interpretation of Aristotle's square of opposition. If this interpretation is correct, we would expect Aristotle to offer
arguments for selecting (10) rather than (10.1), and
this is precisely what he does in the last chapter of
On Interpretation. He devotes this chapter to the problem he poses in the opening sentence: "The question
arises whether an affirmation finds its contrary in a denial or in another affirmation; whether the proposition
'every man is just' finds its contrary in the proposition

'no man is just', or in the proposition 'every man is unjust'."[14]

It is unnecessary for our purposes here to analyze separately each of the various arguments Aristotle offers for selecting the denial rather than the affirmation as the contrary. His main point may be summed up by saying that since (10) is implied by but does not imply (10.1), (10) is more opposed to the original A because when the latter is false (10) may be true even though (10.1) is also false. I do not propose to debate the logical merits of this decision, as the relevant point here is simply that with Aristotle's analysis, (10) and (10.1) are not equivalent and that (10) alone represents an E statement in the square of opposition. This determination of E does not prevent it from implying O, since the latter is likewise a simple denial without existential import. Thus, the logical relations which Aristotle claimed for his square of opposition hold if we grant that the statements related in the square are of the peculiar sort that he seems to have intended them to be.

We may now turn to the contradictions and absurdities in what is usually taken as the traditional analysis of the square. When an A statement is taken as equivalent to its obverse, Aristotle's distinction between statements with definite and indefinite terms as subjects is ignored. A statement which has existential import with his analysis is made equivalent to one that cannot have this import as he construed it. The traditional analysis then becomes inconsistent by ac-

[14] 23a28–31. The logical relations in question here remain the same if the privative "unjust" is replaced by the indefinite "not-just." Cf. *An. Pr.* 52a15–17. While one might intend by this replacement to make the statement equivalent to (10), he does not succeed in doing so because the result, (10.1), remains an affirmation and thus, like the original "every man is unjust," implies but is not implied by (10).

cepting *in toto* Aristotle's account of the square of opposition along with this equivalence which Aristotle rejected. It must then be affirmed that "Every S is P" implies "Some S is P," and denied that "Every S is P" can be false while "No S is not-P," "No not-P is S," and "Every not-P is not-S" are all true. This procedure becomes inconsistent when one admits, as Aristotle does, that any of these last three statements is compatible with the falsity of "Some S is P." Inconsistency is avoided in Aristotle's account, not by qualifying the principle of excluded middle, but by restricting existential import in accordance with the quality of the statement and the definite or indefinite character of the subject term.

The traditional procedure also leads to the absurdity that any object of opinion (anything thinkable) must be said to exist. We have characterized statements with indefinite terms as subjects as like statements about every member that is not such and such in a certain collection, but clearly as far as existential import is concerned, they are also like statements about every member that is such and such. "Every paper in this group that scores 50 or above is passing" is just as free of existential import as our former example. There is obviously something absurd about a logic that allows us to infer from this that some paper in the group scores 50 or above and is passing. Yet this is analogous to what the traditional account allows us to do. For a statement like

(11)   Every ogre is wicked.

is construed as equivalent to "Every not-wicked is not-ogre," which clearly means the same as "Everything in the totality of real things that is not wicked is not an ogre." But then with this equivalence (11) must mean the same as

(11.1)   Everything in the totality of real things that
        is an ogre is wicked.

We thus end with the absurdity that we cannot assert (11.1) without implying that ogres exist. And even
worse, we cannot deny (11.1) without making the same
implication. For

(12)   Not every ogre is wicked.

is also assumed to have existential import.

Aristotle's account avoids such absurdity by denying
the equivalence between (11) and (11.1) and holding
that (12) has existential import only when taken as
the contradictory of the latter. In this way there is no
need to qualify the application of the principles of excluded middle. In order to preserve Aristotle's square
in toto we must of course deny the equivalence between (10) and (10.1), and accept only the former as
properly an E statement. The contradictory of such a
statement has existential import and is implied by the
corresponding A. In contrast, modern analysis accepts
the traditional position that (10) is equivalent to
(10.1), and (11) to (11.1), but remains consistent and
avoids absurdity by refusing to accept Aristotle's square
without qualification.

I do not propose here to examine the adequacy of
the Aristotelian account or to subject it to criticism
in the light of modern analysis. But it should be noted
in conclusion that if the present interpretation of Aristotle is correct, his analysis cannot, as the traditional
one can, be taken simply as an inconsistent account
which modern analysis has rectified. In accepting the
equivalences mentioned above, the traditional doctrine
of immediate inferences has already taken an essential step toward the modern position. Consistency can
be restored (without special assumptions, such as that
restricting the applicability of the principle of excluded

middle) only by completing the break with Aristotle
or by returning to his analysis. There is thus a fundamental difference between the Aristotelian and modern analyses which I believe it would be profitable to
examine. This difference is concerned in part at least
with the role of indefinite terms in procedures of quantification and with the existential import of affirmations as distinct from denials. When we say that
"-(x)fx" is equivalent to "($\exists$x)-fx," or that "-($\exists$x)
fx" is equivalent to "(x)-fx," we have replaced what
seems to be a denial by an affirmation with an indefinite predicate, and we are not talking about the categorical statements Aristotle intended when he constructed his square of opposition.

II. CATEGORIES

CATEGORIES IN ARISTOTLE
AND IN KANT

JOHN COOK WILSON

§ 438. If our reasoning is correct, the universalities of the various species of a genus are not particulars of the universality of the genus but kinds (or parts) of it. Suppose now an abstraction beginning from individual things till we come to so-called *summa genera*, or, as they would be more correctly termed, *summae species*. The universalities of all other universals would be comprised in 'the universalities of these, not as their particulars but as kinds, forms, parts, or aspects of them. If, then, we considered these *summae species* as kinds which Being or Reality must take, where Being is more accurately the Being of Things (that is, the universal of which Things are the particulars), the Being of Things is in the position of *genus* to these *summae species* and their several universalities are all comprised in the universality of this genus. In regard to this we must avoid the fallacy of creating a universal of universalities, with an infinite regress. That fallacy has been already sufficiently exposed. There is no universal of universalityness of which the universalities of universals would be particulars, for the universality of one genus universal as distinguished from that of another lies not in its being a unity which is

From *Statement and Inference* (Oxford, 1926), Vol. II, pp. 696–706. Reprinted by permission of the Clarendon Press, Oxford.

particularized but in being particularized in these precise individuals, in being the particularization of its
own peculiar quality or characteristic; but this is precisely itself, and its universality is indistinguishable
from itself in the fullness of its being. Thus the classification of universalities can only be, if possible at
all, the classification of universals; there is no universal
of universalityness of which the universalities of universals would be particulars.

§ 439. This genus, then, of the *summae species* is
not mere Being but the universal of the being of
Things or Substances, and is therefore the generalization of Substance, Substanceness, or Substance-in-gen-
eral. Now in this system every universal has things for
its particulars, and thus the universals of attribute and
relation will not appear in the system. Nevertheless,
every variety of being, attribute, and relation as well
as substance, must be comprised in the system, because all these are comprised in the existence of things.
The nature of substance involves in itself attributes
and relations; its universal therefore involves the universal of possession of attributes and the universal of
relatedness. We have now to consider the relation of
such a universal as attributeness in general or the universal of a particular attribute such as colour(edness)
to the universal of substance in general and to the universals of substances. We may note in passing that we
can understand why Aristotle said that Being was not
a genus if we remember that the genera *par excellence*
(in the *Categories*, for example) are in fact universals
whose particulars are substances.[1]

Attributeness means being an attribute of a substance, hence the universal of substance involves in its
own being the being of attributeness. Nevertheless,
the latter is not an element in the universal substance-

[1]*Cat.* 2a11 ff.

ness, the corresponding element is 'having-attributes'-ness. Moreover, the latter is not a differentiation of substanceness. The question, then, is whether these universals are capable of being unified by any unity beside the unity that one involves the existence of the other. They cannot be differentiations of one and the same universal because differentiations of the same universal must have identical particulars with that universal. Nor can they be particulars of the same universal, for if two universals are particulars of the same universal, they must be differentiations of a common universal though not of that universal. Thus, though we can state of attributeness and substanceness that they are, Being is not a universal of which they are differentiations, nor is Being a universal of which they are particulars.

§ 440. Thus the form 'S is', which as opposed to 'S is P' does not occur in ordinary linguistic usage whether in ancient Greek or in modern languages, does not represent in its subject particulars of a universal which is Being or Beingness. If, then, Aristotle had carried out fully the thought which appears to be implicit in chapter 5 of the *Categories*, with the distinction there made between 'said of a particular subject' and 'existing in a particular subject', the result would have been a system of universals classified as in the section above and based on his view that the only true independent reality is the individual thing (or person). The *summum genus* would be Thingness, and for this the only word in his terminology that appears to be suitable is Being (οὐσία), a word which both in the *Categories* and in *Metaphysics*, Book Z, is sometimes the name for Thing as such, or First (Primary) Being. This, however, is nowhere unmistakably stated; he appears indeed to have virtually stopped in his classification at certain highest genera and his own expression, 'the highest of the genera',[2] favours this interpretation.

§ 441. For his view that Being is not a genus, the important passages are three in the *Metaphysics* with which one in the *Topics* agrees, a passage in the *De Interpretatione*, and one in the *Posterior Analytics*.[3]

The first of the passages from the *Metaphysics* does not turn on his view that the genera *par excellence* are secondary essences and is a little difficult to interpret. It runs as follows: 'But it is not possible for One or Being to be a genus. For each difference of a genus must have one and being said of it (sc. when we speak of it), whereas it is impossible that either the species of the genus or the genus without the species should be said of the differences. Thus, if One or Being were a genus, none of their differences could have one or being stated of it'. By difference he here means not the differentiated universal (e.g. rectilinearity) but the *differentia* (straight, etc.).[4] This suggests that he had not realized that, according to his own theory, Being would be the proper name for the highest genus. The passage from the *Posterior Analytics*, 'to exist is not the being (essence) of anything, since the being existent (that which exists) is not a genus', does seem to be connected with his doctrine that the individual is the only real existent and that the true genera have 'beings' for their particulars. Finally, the passage in the *De Interpretatione* runs as follows: 'for not even "to be" or "not to be" is a sign of a thing, not even if you mention "being" by itself merely. In itself it is nothing, but it signifies in addition a kind of compounding which cannot be understood without the

---

[2]*Met.* 998b18.

[3]*Met.* 998b22, 1053b23, 1059b30; *Top.* 121a16; *De Int.* 16b22; *An. Po.* 92b13.

[4]Cf. his language in the *Topics* 144a37 ff.

things so compounded'. This is most important for the linguistic point involved in our problem.

It is singular that Aristotle, who in the *Metaphysics* is attacking those who made Being and Unity the essence of things, does not adopt the seemingly clear and decisive argument based upon his own theory of true being as the individual and the true genus as that of which the individuals are the particulars. His argument, however, and this is important, is directed to showing that Being as a universal cannot be differentiated, though he has not realized what seems to be the direct proof required (he gives instead a single *reductio ad absurdum*), viz. that if being were the genus or class universal of the universals which we say 'are', those universals, as we have shown, would necessarily have the same kind of particulars as it and consequently the same kind as one another. But, obviously, the universals of a substance, an attribute, a relation, cannot have the same particulars. To reach this positive point of view Aristotle would have required to have had before him the point of view from which a universal could be represented as a particularization, not a differentiation, of another universal.

§ 442. We miss, then, two things in Aristotle's discussion. The line of thought which led him to say 'being is not a genus', at least when it took the shape it seems to have in the *Posterior Analytics*, might have made him recognize that though the universal 'being' was not a highest genus, yet in his own terminology such a genus was exactly 'essence' as the being of things or, more accurately, 'the being a thing'. How far he was from this may be seen when he says,[5] 'Unity cannot be a genus for the same reasons that neither being (existent) nor essence can be'. Secondly, he might have been led to see that though Being is not a clas-

[5]*Met.* 1053b23.

sifying genus which unified everything in that way, yet there is a unifying principle in all reality. Instead he rested content with the negative statement that Being is not such a principle, where being is that 'is' which is universally predicable. He may have been prejudiced by his justifiable criticism of Plato who had sought this unifying principle in the Idea of goodness. Had he followed up his thought he might have reflected that just as a genus demands its own differentiation into species and individuals, so by the same inward necessity the unity of reality demands the kinds and things into which reality actually is differentiated.

§ 443. Taking his own categories, they are obviously unified in the reality of (primary) Being or Substance, and he does elsewhere recognize that the other categories depend on the first. But he never put this as the unity and the real unity which corresponds to what is common to the statement of 'being'. In fact he never cleared up his mind about it, or he could not, so to speak, have so degraded 'being', as he does in the passage translated from the *De Interpretatione*, and have merely left it at that. What he has said there is true and important, but it is misleading, as it stands.

Moreover, the formula 'Being is not a genus', although it shows from one point of view an accurate insight into the nature of classification, is extraordinary and misleading when considered in relation to his own terminology. He must speak of the categories as categories of being; this being cannot be merely the common predicate of everything, if we are to take categories literally as predicates. For we cannot state of this 'being-in-general' that it is a substance. On the other hand, if it does mean 'being-in-general', categories would surely have to mean species or kinds, so that being would indeed be a genus and the formula be contradicted. It is most natural to leave category its proper meaning and then 'being' will stand for 'that which is', not for being in general. This again, if all the categories are asserted of it, as the formula 'categories of that which is' naturally implies, could only be complete being, that which is in the fullest sense. Now that with Aristotle is the individual thing. This agrees with the fact that the categories are given not as abstract universals in the noun form (whiteness, as an example of quality) but in the adjectival form (white, double, etc.). If so, what is meant by the categories of being (that which is) is that each of them is an attribute of the true and real being of the individual thing, the primary being of this treatise. It is the thing in fact of which we can properly state that it is a substance, two cubits long, in the market-place, etc. The only word form which causes any difficulty in this interpretation is that of the adverb of time (e.g. yesterday). This, however, is again not put as an abstract universal but as it would occur in a statement, and it is true (and the truth) that as every happening belongs to a substance, so the temporal qualification ultimately also belongs to a substance (e.g. this substance was in the market-place yesterday). This appears, then, to be the meaning, for it is difficult to see how anything else could be meant.

§ 444. But now, if this is so, in the categories of being, of 'that which is', the latter expression is used in the general sense, and 'that which is' represents the universal of all particular 'beings' and so is the universal of substanceness. It is just in relation to the distinction of the categories that the meaning of 'being is not a genus' becomes of great importance. On the above view 'that which is' is equivalent to substance (being) when the categories are termed categories of that which is. Thus 'that which is' is not only a genus of which real complete things are the particulars (com-

plete, that is, in the Aristotelian sense as equivalent
to things) but the highest and most comprehensive
genus, though *not* the genus of the categories, including all reality whatever. This discussion seems to con-
firm the hypothesis that Aristotle did not pursue the
train of thought which his view that 'being' taken in
one sense is not a genus might have suggested to him.

§ 445. What, then, is the fallacy in Aristotle's proof
that being is not a genus? He contemplates two ways
of stating the genus X in regard to a given subject S.
Either a species AX is stated in S is an AX and therefore mediately the genus S is an X, or the genus is
stated 'without its species', and we say immediately S
is an X. In neither way, he says, can we state the genus
of the difference A. He seems to mean that odd being
the differentia of odd number, we can't say that odd
is an odd number and so a number, nor directly that
odd is a number.

But is the argument free from verbal fallacy? When
we state that S is a species, we mean that S is an AX,
and when we say that the genus belongs to the species, we state X, the genus universal of a member of
the species AX, we mean an AX is an X. If, then,
we state the species of the differentia we ought to
mean that we state that an A is an AX. Now if the
differentia necessarily presupposes X the genus, the
statement must be true. We do not say that odd numberness is numberness, but that an odd number is a
number. So if we state odd number of odd, we mean
that an odd thing is an odd number, which is necessarily true. It looks as though Aristotle meant that
linearity cannot be predicated of straightness because
straightness is not a line; but neither is rectilinearity
a line, and thus he would appear to have fallen into a
verbal fallacy.

§ 446. There is a danger that in appreciating the

insight shown by Aristotle in his dictum 'being is not a genus', we may ourselves fall into the same one-sidedness. There are certain characteristics of Being which, if not identical with those of a true genus, are parallel to them in a remarkable way and must therefore not be neglected. These characteristics are not destroyed by the discovery that being is not a true genus; only a certain way of regarding them, i.e. as particularizations or differentiations of a universal, is destroyed. An attribute or a relation may rightly be said to have being as well as a substance, and this being is not identical with that of substance. We can study the attribute in abstraction from the subject, as we do in the mathematical sciences, and this proves that it is distinguishable in being. So of relation, it is essential to relation that it should be 'between' things which have some other nature than that of standing in a given relation. Hence it is natural at first sight to say that Being is a genus with its species 'being of attribute', etc. Again we think that Being in its own nature necessitates these forms of itself, and this is parallel to the self-determination of a universal in its differentiations. If, then, the forms of Being are not species nor kinds as ordinarily understood, nor of course particulars of a universal, how should they be described accurately? We have to revise one of our usual conceptions and either to refuse to call these universals or to admit universals which have no particulars and no differentiation, the universality of one quality (attribute) being identical in kind with the universality of every other. In this difficulty we may provisionally term them common principles. They are live universals because they are a unity in a manifold; universality in each universal, particularity in each particular, and so on, but different from true universals because the manifold is not a particularization or differentiation of the common principle. This will meet the difficulty we found in regard to classes. We say of every class that it is a class, yet we saw that classness is not a true universal of which classes are particulars. Class has no differentiation and no particulars. We have a unity in a manifold, but the manifold is not a particularization of the unity. Instead, then, of our ordinary view we have to recognize that there are some universals which admit of differentiation and particularization but not of individualization, and that some (which we have called common principles) do not admit of either particularization or differentiation.

§ 447. In Being, then, called provisionally a common principle, we recognize a unity in a manifold which is *sui generis*, just as much as the unity of a true universal in its particulars and its species is *sui generis*. Being, like a true universal, also determines its own manifoldness but in a different manner. If we are to seek an illustration or analogy we may refer to the self, which is an absolute unity in its different thoughts, or a body, which is identical in its different positions and aspects, but neither the self nor the body is the universal of those differences nor they its particulars.

§ 448. If we now consider the forms of Being, the manifold which it must assume and which simulates the differentiation of a universal, we may perhaps find the true significance of the philosophical classifications called systems of categories. These categories are obviously of a very special kind and are philosophical and not scientific. They are, that is, though comprehensive, not a classification and could not be reached by abstracting successively from the whole field of individual substances. In this way we should attain to the classifications of the natural sciences but not to categories. Now Kant's criticism of Aristotle's categories has shown that while there may be agreement about some of the main categories, there may be the greatest disagreement about the real meaning and object of them as a whole. Kant believes that Aristotle was led to his grouping of the categories without realizing its true character, and that in consequence he did not carry it out consistently. Whether, then, Kant's own view of the categories was right or wrong (and surely it was not right) this suggests that there may be a certain instinctive impulse to search for categories, without full consciousness of its nature. The impulse will lead to an arrangement of a quite peculiar kind, and reflection must then supervene in order to understand the impulse and to correct its imperfect work. Kant naturally makes the categories forms of the unifying understanding, because of his dominant confusion of the apprehension and the apprehended. Aristotle's tendency is far sounder, for necessity of apprehension can, after all, only mean apprehension of a necessity in the object.

The explanation, then, of systems of categories may well be that we come in time, by reflection on the use of the verb 'to be', to recognize a corresponding unity of being, that the totality of particulars in all their variety is a unity. Long before we have recognized this unity in particular sets or varieties of being. Then comes the philosophic impulse to determine the forms which *being in general* must take, suggested by the analogous determination of such a unity as the section of a cone, and so to cover exhaustively the differentiations of being in general in the whole of existence. This impulse need not be fully aware of itself. Aristotle, for example, doesn't consciously go to work in this way or, if he did so begin, he probably gave it up when through his clear idea of differentiation and classification he realized that Being is not a genus. Still it may have been the fact that we state of everything that it *is*, which suggested the idea of an absolutely unified system of being.

§ 449. Thus the characteristic of Aristotle's system is that it is a sort of exhaustive attempt to cover the whole variety of reality. 'Everything is either substance or an affection of substance' is its implicit meaning. These are in fact his two main categories. But he gets into difficulties about substance, so that his thought in the end is that everything is either substance, or quality of substance, or quantity of substance (or of what belongs to substance), or relation of substance (or of what belongs to it), and so on. Now it is clear from our analysis above that the impulse to determine a sort of differentiation of Being must produce an altogether unique system. For the general forms of Being are not true differentiations of it, nor are the individuals, which 'are' particulars of Being but of other universals. This explains the fact that the classification (as it first seems to be) of all being could not be attained by any abstraction from individuals or any classification of them; because this, the natural form which classification first takes, proceeds to universals of which the original particulars are those very individuals, and the successive universals are differentiations of one another in succession. This systematization is by means of differentiation and particularization, the other (the system of the categories) is achieved by neither. Hence the latter acquires its uniqueness; for the ordinary scientific method, even when carried to the utmost unity, will not bring to light one single category except substance itself. If continued ideally upwards, it cannot even bring to light the universal 'mere being' of which the categories are the unfolding. The same is of course true of any classification proper which starts from the individual, whether thing or individual attribute. Attributeness, for instance, if regarded as the universal of individual attributes, is neither a differentiation nor a particularization of being; the most general universal which could have individual attributes for its particulars is just attributeness. Now substanceness, attributeness, relationness, etc., cannot be treated as *summa genera* because they would then be members of the same classification; this they can never be, for such genera must have the same sort of particulars, and here the particulars of the one would be substances, the particulars of the other attributes.

§ 450. If, then, this is the true account of the philosophic impulse under discussion, we see that it is a most serious and fatal mistake to regard it as a classification, when once we understand what a classification truly is. (That leads to the further error of vainly attempting to adapt the system of categories to the ordinary classifications and to make them departments of it.) Properly understood, it is simply the just endeavour to determine the manifoldness in which Being in general must unfold itself, and Aristotle proceeded correctly when he exhibited as categories such general forms as those of Substance, Attribute, Relation, etc. Contenting himself, however, with pointing out that Being is not a genus and therefore could not constitute the essence of things, he seems by his merely negative attitude to have missed the true significance of his own list of categories.

§§ 438–50. Translation of principal passages referred to in the above investigation.

[Arist. *Cat.* 2a11. 'Substance most properly and primarily and especially so called is that which is neither said of a particular subject nor is in a particular subject, for instance, a particular human being or a particular horse. Secondary substances are what the species are called, in which the substances primarily so

called exist, and besides them the genera of these species; for instance, while a particular human being exists
in the species human being, the genus of the species
is animal. These, then, are called secondary substances,
for example, both human being and animal'.

De Int. 16b22. 'For not even "to be" or "not to be"
is a sign of a thing, and not even if you mention "being" by itself merely. In itself it is nothing but it signifies, in addition, a kind of compounding which cannot be understood without the things compounded'.

An. Po. 92b13. 'Again we say that it is necessary
that everything be proved to exist by demonstration,
unless it be essence. But to exist is not the essence of
anything, since the being existent (that which exists)
is not a genus. That a thing exists therefore will be
(subject of) demonstration. This is what the sciences
in fact do. The geometrician assumes what triangle
means, but proves that it exists'.

Met. 998b22. 'But it is not possible for either being one or being existent to be a genus of existents.
For while it is necessary that the differentiae of each
genus should each both exist and be one, it is impossible either for the species of a genus to be said of the
appropriate differentiae or the genus <to be said of
them> without its species. Therefore if we assume being one or being existent to be a genus, no differentia
will either be or be one'.[6]

The same argument is used in *Met.* 1059b30, and
Top. 121a16. In *Met.* 1053b23 he says, 'being one
cannot be a genus for the same reasons that neither
being existent nor essence can be'.

---

[6]J. C. W. translated: 'It is not possible for One or Being to be
a genus. For each differentia of a genus must have one and being
said of it (in statements), whereas it is impossible that either the
species of the genus should be said of its differentiae or the genus
without the species. So if One or Being were a genus, none of
their differentiae could have one, or being, stated of it.'

Met. 1017a22. 'Whatever the forms of predication signify are said to be essentially. For to be has as many significations as there are forms. Inasmuch, then, as the predicates signify what the subject is, others its quality, etc., . . . to be has a signification equivalent to each of these (for there is no difference between "the man is walking" and "the man walks)".]

ARISTOTLE'S *CATEGORIES*

TRANSLATED BY J. L. ACKRILL

CHAPTER 1

1a1. When things have only a name in common and the definition of being which corresponds to the name is different, they are called *homonymous*. Thus, for example, both a man and a picture are animals. These have only a name in common and the definition of being which corresponds to the name is different; for if one is to say what being an animal is for each of them, one will give two distinct definitions.

1a6. When things have the name in common and the definition of being which corresponds to the name is the same, they are called *synonymous*. Thus, for example, both a man and an ox are animals. Each of these is called by a common name, 'animal', and the definition of being is also the same; for if one is to give the definition of each—what being an animal is for each of them—one will give the same definition.

1a12. When things get their name from something, with a difference of ending, they are called *paronymous*. Thus, for example, the grammarian gets his name from grammar, the brave get theirs from bravery.

From *Aristotle's Categories and De Interpretatione*, tr. with notes by J. L. Ackrill (Oxford, 1963), pp. 3–12 and 71–91. Reprinted by permission of the Clarendon Press, Oxford.

CHAPTER 2

1a16. Of things that are said, some involve combination while others are said without combination. Examples of those involving combination are 'man runs', 'man wins'; and of those without combination 'man', 'ox', 'runs', 'wins'.

1a20. Of things there are: (a) some are *said of* a subject but are not *in* any subject. For example, man is said of a subject, the individual man, but is not in any subject. (b) Some are in a subject but are not said of any subject. (By 'in a subject' I mean what is in something, not as a part, and cannot exist separately from what it is in.) For example, the individual knowledge-of-grammar is in a subject, the soul, but is not said of any subject; and the individual white is in a subject, the body (for all colour is in a body), but is not said of any subject. (c) Some are both said of a subject and in a subject. For example, knowledge is in a subject, the soul, and is also said of a subject, knowledge-of-grammar. (d) Some are neither in a subject nor said of a subject, for example, the individual man or individual horse—for nothing of this sort is either in a subject or said of a subject. Things that are individual and numerically one are, without exception, not said of any subject, but there is nothing to prevent some of them from being in a subject—the individual knowledge-of-grammar is one of the things in a subject.

CHAPTER 3

1b10. Whenever one thing is predicated of another as of a subject, all things said of what is predicated will be said of the subject also. For example, man is predicated of the individual man, and animal of man; so animal will be predicated of the individual man also—for the individual man is both a man and an animal.

1b16. The differentiae of genera which are different[1] and not subordinate one to the other are themselves different in kind. For example, animal and knowledge: footed, winged, aquatic, two-footed, are differentiae of animal, but none of these is a differentia of knowledge; one sort of knowledge does not differ from another by being two-footed. However, there is nothing to prevent genera subordinate one to the other from having the same differentiae. For the higher are predicated of the genera below them, so that all differentiae of the predicated genus will be differentiae of the subject also.

CHAPTER 4

1b25. Of things said without any combination, each signifies either substance or quantity or qualification or a relative or where or when or being-in-a-position or having or doing or being-affected. To give a rough idea, examples of substance are man, horse; of quantity: four-foot, five-foot; of qualification: white, grammatical; of a relative: double, half, larger; of where: in the Lyceum, in the market-place; of when: yesterday, last-year; of being-in-a-position: is-lying, is-sitting; of having: has-shoes-on, has-armour-on; of doing: cutting, burning; of being-affected: being-cut, being-burned.

2a4. None of the above is said just by itself in any affirmation, but by the combination of these with one another an affirmation is produced. For every affirmation, it seems, is either true or false; but of things said without any combination none is either true or false (e.g. 'man', 'white', 'runs', 'wins').

CHAPTER 5

2a11. A *substance*—that which is called a substance most strictly, primarily, and most of all—is that which

[1]Read τῶν ἑτέρων γενῶν.

is neither said of a subject nor in a subject, e.g. the individual man or the individual horse. The species in which the things primarily called substances are, are called *secondary substances*, as also are the genera of these species. For example, the individual man belongs in a species, man, and animal is a genus of the species; so these—both man and animal—are called secondary substances.

2a19. It is clear from what has been said that if something is said of a subject both its name and its definition are necessarily predicated of the subject. For example, man is said of a subject, the individual man, and the name is of course predicated (since you will be predicating man of the individual man), and also the definition of man will be predicated of the individual man (since the individual man is also a man). Thus both the name and the definition will be predicated of the subject. But as for things which are in a subject, in most cases neither the name nor the definition is predicated of the subject. In some cases there is nothing to prevent the name from being predicated of the subject, but it is impossible for the definition to be predicated. For example, white, which is in a subject (the body), is predicated of the subject; for a body is called white. But the definition of white will never be predicated of the body.

2a34. All the other things are either said of the primary substances as subjects or in them as subjects. This is clear from an examination of cases. For example, animal is predicated of man and therefore also of the individual man; for were it predicated of none of the individual men it would not be predicated of man at all. Again, colour is in body and therefore also in an individual body; for were it not in some individual body it would not be in body at all. Thus all the other things are either said of the primary substances as subjects or in them as subjects. So if the primary substances did not exist it would be impossible for any of the other things to exist.

2b7. Of the secondary substances the species is more a substance than the genus, since it is nearer to the primary substance. For if one is to say of the primary substance what it is, it will be more informative and apt to give the species than the genus. For example, it would be more informative to say of the individual man that he is a man than that he is an animal (since the one is more distinctive of the individual man while the other is more general); and more informative to say of the individual tree that it is a tree than that it is a plant. Further, it is because the primary substances are subjects for all the other things and all the other things are predicated of them or are in them, that they are called substances most of all. But as the primary substances stand to the other things, so the species stands to the genus: the species is a subject for the genus (for the genera are predicated of the species but the species are not predicated reciprocally of the genera). Hence for this reason too the species is more a substance than the genus.

2b22. But of the species themselves—those which are not genera—one is no more a substance than another: it is no more apt to say of the individual man that he is a man than to say of the individual horse that it is a horse. And similarly of the primary substances one is no more a substance than another: the individual man is no more a substance than the individual ox.

2b29. It is reasonable that, after the primary substances, their species and genera should be the only other things called (secondary) substances. For only they, of things predicated, reveal the primary substance. For if one is to say of the individual man what he is, it will be in place to give the species or the genus (though more informative to give man than animal); but to give any of the other things would be out of place—for example, to say 'white' or 'runs' or anything like that. So it is reasonable that these should be the only other things called substances. Further, it is because the primary substances are subjects for everything else that they are called substances most strictly. But as the primary substances stand to everything else, so the species and genera of the primary substances stand to all the rest: all the rest are predicated of these. For if you will call the individual man grammatical it follows that you will call both a man and an animal grammatical; and similarly in other cases.

3a7. It is a characteristic common to every substance not to be in a subject. For a primary substance is neither said of a subject nor in a subject. And as for secondary substances, it is obvious at once that they are not in a subject. For man is said of the individual man as subject but is not in a subject: man is not *in* the individual man. Similarly, animal also is said of the individual man as subject but animal is not *in* the individual man. Further, while there is nothing to prevent the name of what is in a subject from being sometimes predicated of the subject, it is impossible for the definition to be predicated. But the definition of the secondary substances, as well as the name, is predicated of the subject: you will predicate the definition of man of the individual man, and also that of animal. No substance, therefore, is in a subject.

3a21. This is not, however, peculiar to substance; the differentia also is not in a subject. For footed and two-footed are said of man as subject but are not in a subject; neither two-footed nor footed is *in* man. Moreover, the definition of the differentia is predicated of that of which the differentia is said. For example, if footed is said of man the definition of footed will also be predicated of man; for man is footed.

3a29. We need not be disturbed by any fear that we may be forced to say that the parts of a substance, being in a subject (the whole substance), are not substances. For when we spoke of things *in a subject* we did not mean things belonging in something as *parts*.

3a33. It is a characteristic of substances and differentiae that all things called from them are so called synonymously. For all the predicates from them are predicated either of the individuals or of the species. (For from a primary substance there is no predicate, since it is said of no subject; and as for secondary substances, the species is predicated of the individual, the genus both of the species and of the individual. Similarly, differentiae too are predicated both of the species and of the individuals.) And the primary substances admit the definition of the species and of the genera, and the species admits that of the genus; for everything said of what is predicated will be said of the subject also. Similarly, both the species and the individuals admit the definition of the differentiae. But synonymous things were precisely those with both the name in common and the same definition. Hence all the things called from substances and differentiae are so called synonymously.

3b10. Every substance seems to signify a certain 'this'. As regards the primary substances, it is indisputably true that each of them signifies a certain 'this'; for the thing revealed is individual and numerically one. But as regards the secondary substances, though it appears from the form of the name—when one speaks of man or animal—that a secondary substance likewise signifies a certain 'this', this is not really true; rather, it signifies a certain qualification, for the subject is not, as the primary substance is, one, but man and animal are said of many things. However, it does not signify simply a certain qualification, as white does. White signifies nothing but a qualification, whereas the species and the genus mark off the qualification of substance—they signify substance of a certain qualification. (One draws a wider boundary with the genus than with the species, for in speaking of animal one takes in more than in speaking of man.)

3b24. Another characteristic of substances is that there is nothing contrary to them. For what would be contrary to a primary substance? For example, there is nothing contrary to an individual man, nor yet is there anything contrary to man or to animal. This, however, is not peculiar to substance but holds of many other things also, for example, of quantity. For there is nothing contrary to four-foot or to ten or to anything of this kind—unless someone were to say that many is contrary to few or large to small; but still there is nothing contrary to any *definite* quantity.

3b33. Substance, it seems, does not admit of a more and a less. I do not mean that one substance is not more a substance than another (we have said that it is), but that any given substance is not called more, or less, that which it is. For example, if this substance is a man, it will not be more a man or less a man either than itself or than another man. For one man is not more a man than another, as one pale thing is more pale than another and one beautiful thing more beautiful than another. Again, a thing is called more, or less, such-and-such than itself; for example, the body that is pale is called more pale now than before, and the one that is hot is called more, or less, hot. Substance, however, is not spoken of thus. For a man is not called more a man now than before, nor is anything else that is a substance. Thus substance does not admit of a more and a less.

4a10. It seems most distinctive of substance that what is numerically one and the same is able to receive contraries. In no other case could one bring forward anything, numerically one, which is able to receive contraries. For example, a colour which is numerically one and the same will not be black and white, nor will numerically one and the same action be bad and good; and similarly with everything else that is not substance. A substance, however, numerically one and the same, is able to receive contraries. For example, an individual man—one and the same—becomes pale at one time and dark at another, and hot and cold, and bad and good. Nothing like this is to be seen in any other case.

4a22. But perhaps someone might object and say that statements and beliefs are like this. For the same statement seems to be both true and false. Suppose, for example, that the statement that somebody is sitting is true; after he has got up this same statement will be false. Similarly with beliefs. Suppose you believe truly that somebody is sitting; after he has got up you will believe falsely if you hold the same belief about him. However, even if we were to grant this, there is still a difference in the way contraries are received. For in the case of substances it is by themselves changing that they are able to receive contraries. For what has become cold instead of hot, or dark instead of pale, or good instead of bad, has changed (has altered); similarly in other cases too it is by itself undergoing change that each thing is able to receive contraries. Statements and beliefs, on the other hand, themselves remain completely unchangeable in every way; it is because the *actual thing* changes that the contrary comes to belong to them. For the statement that somebody is sitting remains the same; it is because of a change in the actual thing that it comes to be true at one time and false at another. Similarly with beliefs. Hence at least the way in which it is able to receive contraries—through a change in itself—would be distinctive of substance, even if we were to grant that beliefs and statements are able to receive contraries. However, this is not true. For it is not because they themselves receive anything that statements and beliefs are said to be able to receive contraries, but because of what has happened to something else. For it is because the actual thing exists or does not exist that the statement is said to be true or false, not because it is able itself to receive contraries. No statement, in fact, or belief is changed at all by anything. So, since nothing happens in them, they are not able to receive contraries. A substance, on the other hand, is said to be able to receive contraries because it itself receives contraries. For it receives sickness and health, and paleness and darkness; and because it itself receives the various things of this kind it is said to be able to receive contraries. It is, therefore, distinctive of substance that what is numerically one and the same is able to receive contraries. This brings to an end our discussion of substance.

NOTES ON THE *CATEGORIES*

CHAPTER 1

1a1. The word translated 'animal' originally meant just that; but it had come to be used also of pictures or other artistic representations (whether representations of animals or not).

The terms 'homonymous' and 'synonymous', as defined by Aristotle in this chapter, apply not to words but to things. Roughly, two things are homonymous if the same name applies to both but not in the same sense, synonymous if the same name applies to both in the same sense. Thus two things may be both homonymous and synony-

mous—if there is one name that applies to both but not
in the same sense and another name that applies to both
in the same sense. From Aristotle's distinction between
'homonymous' and 'synonymous' one could evidently derive a distinction between equivocal and unequivocal
names; but it is important to recognize from the start that
the *Categories* is not primarily or explicitly about names,
but about the things that names signify. (It will be necessary in the translation and notes to use the word 'things' as
a blanket-term for items in any category. It often represents the neuter plural of a Greek article, pronoun, etc.)
Aristotle relies greatly on linguistic facts and tests, but his
aim is to discover truths about non-linguistic items. It is
incumbent on the translator not to conceal this, and, in
particular, not to give a misleadingly linguistic appearance
to Aristotle's statements by gratuitously supplying inverted
commas in all the places where *we* might feel that it is
linguistic expressions that are under discussion.

The contrast between synonyms and homonyms, between same definition and different definition, is obviously very crude. Elsewhere Aristotle recognizes that the different meanings of a word may be closely related. Thus
at the beginning of *Metaphysics* Γ 2 as he points out that
though the force of 'healthy' varies it always has a reference to health: a healthy person is one who enjoys
health, a healthy diet one which promotes health, a
healthy complexion one which indicates health. Similarly, he says, with 'being': it is used in different ways when
used of things in different categories, but there is a primary sense (the sense in which *substances* have being) to
which all the others are related. Though the *Categories*
gives emphatic priority to the category of substance it
does not develop any such theory about the systematic
ambiguity of 'being' or 'exists'. Chapter 1 makes it seem
unlikely that Aristotle had yet seen the importance of
distinguishing between words that are straightforwardly
ambiguous and words whose various senses form a family
or have a common nucleus. (See Aristotle's suggestions
about 'good' at *Nicomachean Ethics* 1096b26–28.)

1a12. 'Paronymous' is obviously not a term co-ordinate

with 'homonymous' and 'synonymous', though like them it is applied by Aristotle to things, not names. A thing is paronymous if its name is in a certain way derivative. The derivativeness in question is not etymological. Aristotle is not claiming that the word 'brave' was invented after the word 'bravery'. He is claiming rather that 'brave' *means* 'having bravery'; the brave is so called because of ('from') the bravery he has. For an X to be paronymous requires both that an X is called X because of something (feature, property, etc.) which it has (or which somehow belongs to it), and that 'X' is identical with the name of that something except in ending. To say that an X gets its name from something (or is called X from something) does not necessarily imply that there is a name for the something (10a32–b2), or that, if there is, 'X' has any similarity to that name (10b5–9). But only if these conditions are fulfilled does an X get its name from something *paronymously*.

Paronymy is commonly involved when items in categories other than substance are ascribed to substances. If we say that generosity is a virtue or that giving one's time is a (kind of) generosity, we use the name 'generosity'; but if we wish to ascribe generosity to Callias we do not say that he is generosity, but that he is generous —using a word identical except in ending with the name of the quality we are ascribing. Sometimes, indeed, the name of an item in a category is itself used to indicate the inherence of that item in a substance. In 'white is a colour' 'white' names a quality; in 'Callias is white' 'white' indicates the inherence of the quality in Callias. Here we get homonymy or something like it, since the definition of 'white' in the former sentence cannot be substituted for 'white' in the latter: Callias is not a colour of a certain kind (2a29–34, 3a15–17). There are also the possibilities mentioned above: an adjective indicating the inherence of something in a substance may have no similarity (or not the right kind of similarity) to the name of the something, or there may be no name for the something. So the ascription of qualities, etc., to substances does not always involve paronymy; but it very often does.

The whole idea of an X's being called X *from some-thing* (whether paronymously or not) is of importance in the *Categories*. The categories classify things, not words. The category of quality does not include the words 'generosity' and 'generous'; nor does it include two things corresponding to the two words. It includes generosity. 'Generosity' and 'generous' introduce the very same thing, generosity, though in different ways, 'generosity' simply naming it and 'generous' serving to predicate it. Aristotle will frequently be found using or discussing distinctly predicative expressions like 'generous', because though they are not themselves names of items in categories they serve to introduce such items (e.g. the item whose name is 'generosity'). The person called generous is so called *from* generosity.

CHAPTER 2

1a16. What does Aristotle mean here by 'combination' (literally, 'inter-weaving')? The word is used by Plato in the *Sophist* 262, where he makes the point that a sentence is not just a list of names or a list of verbs, but results from the combination of a name with a verb; this line of thought is taken up in the *De Interpretatione* (16a9–18, 17a17–20). In the present passage Aristotle's examples of expressions involving combination are both indicative sentences, and his examples of expressions without combination are all single words. Yet he ought not to intend only indicative sentences (or only sentences) to count as expressions involving combination. For in Chapter 4 he says that every expression without combination signifies an item in some one category; this implies that an expresion like 'white man' which introduces two items from two categories is an expression involving combination. Nor should he mean that all and only single words are expressions lacking combination. For he treats 'in the Lyceum' and 'in the market-place' as lacking combination (2a1), while, on the other hand, a single word which meant the same as 'white man' ought to count, in view of Chapter 4, as an expression involving combination. There seem to be two possible solutions. (*a*) The necessary and sufficient condition for an expression's being 'without combination' is that it should signify just one item in some category. The statement at the beginning of Chapter 4 is then analytic, but the examples in Chapter 2 are misleadingly selective, since on this criterion a single word could be an expression involving combination and a group of words could be an expression without combination. (*b*) The distinction in Chapter 2 is, as it looks, a purely linguistic one between single words and groups of words (or perhaps sentences). In Chapter 4 Aristotle neglects the possibility of single words with compound meaning and is indifferent to the linguistic complexity of expressions like 'in the Lyceum'. Certainly he does neglect single words with compound meaning in the rest of the *Categories*, though he has something to say about them in *De Interpretatione* 5, 8, and 11.

1a20. The fourfold classification of 'things there are' relies on two phrases, 'being in something as subject' and 'being said of something as subject', which hardly occur as technical terms except in the *Categories*. But the ideas they express play a leading role in nearly all Aristotle's writings. The first phrase serves to distinguish qualities, quantities, and items in other dependent categories from substances, which exist independently and in their own right; the second phrase distinguishes species and genera from individuals. Thus Aristotle's four classes are: (*a*) species and genera in the category of substance; (*b*) individuals in categories other than substance; (*c*) species and genera in categories other than substance; (*d*) individuals in the category of substance.

Aristotle's explanation of 'in a subject' at 1a24–25 is slight indeed. One point deserves emphasis. Aristotle does not define 'in X' as meaning 'incapable of existing separately from X', but as a meaning 'in X, not as part of X, and incapable of existing separately from what it is in'. Clearly the 'in' which occurs twice in this definition cannot be the technical 'in' of the definiendum. It must be a non-technical 'in' which one who is not yet familiar with the technical sense can be expected to understand.

Presumably Aristotle has in mind the occurrence in ordinary Greek of locutions like 'heat in the water', 'courage in Socrates'. Not all non-substances are naturally described in ordinary language as *in* substances, but we can perhaps help Aristotle out by exploiting further ordinary locutions: A is 'in' B (in the technical sense) if and only if (*a*) one could naturally say in ordinaryy language either that A is in B or that A is of B or that A belongs to B or that B has A (or that . . .), and (*b*) A is not a part of B, and (*c*) A is inseparable from B.

The inseparability requirement has the consequence that only *individuals* in non-substance categories can be 'in' individual substances. Aristotle could not say that generosity is in Callias as subject, since there could be generosity without any Callias. Only this individual generosity—Callias's generosity—is *in* Callias. Equally, white is not in chalk as subject, since there could be white even if there were no chalk. White is in body, because every individual white is the white of some individual body. For a property to be in a kind of substance it is not enough that some or every substance of that kind should have that property, nor necessary that every substance of that kind should have it; what is requisite is that every instance of that property should belong to some individual substance of that kind. Thus the inherence of a property in a kind of substance is to be analysed in terms of the inherence of individual instances of the property in individual substances of that kind.

Aristotle does not offer an explanation of 'said of something as subject', but it is clear that he has in mind the distinction between individuals in any category and their species and genera. (Aristotle is willing to speak of species and genera in any category, though, like us, he most often uses the terms in speaking of substances.) He assumes that each thing there is has a unique place in a fixed family-tree. What is 'said of' an individual, X, is what could be mentioned in answer to the question 'What is X?', that is, the things in direct line above X in the family-tree, the species (e.g. man or generosity), the genus (animal or virtue), and so on. Aristotle does not explicitly argue for the view that there are natural kinds or that a certain classificatory scheme is the one and only right one.

It is often held that 'said of' and 'in' introduce notions of radically different types, the former being linguistic or grammatical, the latter metaphysical or ontological; and that, correspondingly, the word translated 'subject' (literally, 'what underlies') means 'grammatical subject' in the phrase 'said of a subject' and 'substrate' in 'in a subject'. In fact, however, it is perfectly clear that Aristotle's fourfold classification is a classification of things and not names, and that what is 'said of' something as subject is itself a thing (a species or genus) and not a name. Sometimes, indeed, Aristotle will speak of 'saying' or 'predicating' a *name* of a subject; but it is not linguistic items but the things they signify which are 'said of a subject' in the sense in which this expression is used in Chapter 2. Thus at 2a19 ff. Aristotle sharply distinguishes things said of subjects from the names of those things: if A is said of B it follows that the name of A, 'A', can be predicated of B, though from the fact that 'A' is predicable of something it does not follow that A is said of that thing. At 2a31–34 Aristotle is careless. He says that white is in a subject and is predicated of the subject; he should have said that white is in a subject and its name is predicated of the subject. But this is a mere slip; the preceding lines maintain a quite clear distinction between the things that are said of or in subjects and the names of those things. Being said of a subject is no more a linguistic property than is being in a subject—though Aristotle's adoption of the phrase 'said of' to express the relation of genus to species and of species to individual may have been due to the fact that if A is the genus or species of B it follows that 'A' can be predicated of B.

As regards 'subject', it is true that if virtue is said of generosity as subject it follows that the sentence 'generosity is (a) virtue'—in which the name 'generosity' is the grammatical subject—expresses a truth. But 'virtue is said of generosity as subject' is not about, and does not mention, the names 'virtue' and 'generosity'. It would be absurd to call generosity a *grammatical* subject: it is not generosity but 'generosity' that can be a grammatical subject. Again, if *A* is in *B* as subject then *B* is a substance. But this does not require or entitle us to take 'subject' in the phrase 'in a subject' as *meaning* 'substance' or 'substrate'. It is the expressions 'said of' and 'in' (in their admittedly technical senses) which bear the weight of the distinctions Aristotle is drawing; 'subject' means neither 'grammatical subject' nor 'substance', but is a mere label for whatever has anything 'said of' it or 'in' it. Thus at 2b15 Aristotle explains his statement that primary substances are subjects for all the other things by adding that 'all the other things are predicated of them or are in them'.

The distinctions drawn in this chapter are made use of mainly in Chapter 5 (on substance). In particular, it is only in his discussion of substance that Aristotle exploits the distinction between individuals and species or genera. He seems to refer to individuals in non-substance categories at 4a10 ff., but they are not mentioned in his chapters on these categories. Why does Aristotle not speak of primary and secondary qualities, etc., as he does of primary and secondary substances?

CHAPTER 3

1b10. Aristotle affirms here the transitivity of the 'said of' relation. He does not distinguish between the relation of an individual to its species and that of a species to its genus. It does not occur to him that 'man' functions differently in 'Socrates is (a) man' and '(a) man is (an) animal' (there is no indefinite article in Greek).

1b16. In the *Topics* (107b19 ff.) Aristotle gives this principle about differentiae as a way of discovering ambiguity. If sharpness is a differentia both of musical notes and of solid bodies, 'sharp' must be ambiguous, since notes and bodies constitute different genera neither of which is subordinate to the other. At 144b12 ff. he argues for the principle, saying that if the same differentia could occur in different genera the same species could be in different genera, since every differentia 'brings in' its proper genus. He goes on to water down the principle, allowing that the same differentia may be found in two genera neither of which is subordinate to the other, provided that both are in a common higher genus. In later works Aristotle preserves it as an ideal of classification and definition that the last differentia should entail all preceding differentiae and genera, although he recognizes that in practice we may fail to find such definitions and classifications (*Metaphysics* Z 12). In the *Metaphysics* Aristotle is motivated by a desire to solve the problem of the 'unity of definition' (*De Interpretatione* 17a13), but no such interest is apparent in the *Topics* and *Categories*. Here he is probably influenced by the obvious cases of ambiguity like 'sharp', and also by the evident economy of a system of classification in which mention of a thing's last differentia makes superfluous any mention of its genus. Certainly the *Categories* gives no argument for the principle here enunciated. The principle may help to explain what Aristotle says about differentiae at 3a21–28, b1–9.

The last sentence probably requires emendation. As it stands it is a howler, unless we take 'differentiae of the predicated genus' to refer to differentiae that divide it into sub-genera (*differentiae divisivae*) and 'differentiae of the subject genus' to refer to differentiae that serve to define it (*differentiae constitutivae*). But there is nothing in the context to justify such an interpretation. Only *differentiae divisivae* are in question. A correct point, following naturally from what goes before, is obtained if the words 'predicated' and 'subject' are transposed. That Aristotle is willing to describe the differentiae of a genus X as differentiae of the genus of X is clear; for he mentions two-footed as well as footed as a differentia of animal at 1b19, though the genus of which two-footed is an immediate differentia is not animal but a sub-genus of the genus animal.

CHAPTER 4

First, some remarks about the translation. 'Substance':
the Greek word is the noun from the verb 'to be', and
'being' or 'entity' would be a literal equivalent. But in
connexion with categories 'substance' is the conventional
rendering and is used in the present translation every-
where (except in Chapter 1: 'definition of *being*'). 'Quantity': the Greek is a word that serves both as an interrogative and as an indefinite adjective (Latin *quantum*).
If Aristotle made use also of an abstract noun it would
be desirable to reserve 'quantity' for that; since he does
not do so in the *Categories* (and only once anywhere else)
it is convenient to allow 'quantity' to render the Greek
interrogative-adjective. 'Qualification': Aristotle does use
an abstract noun for 'quality' and carefully distinguishes
in Chapter 8 (e.g. 10a27) between qualities and things
qualified (Latin *qualia*). So in this translation 'quality'
renders Aristotle's abstract noun, while his corresponding
interrogative-adjective is rendered by 'qualified' or 'qualification'. 'A relative': Aristotle has no noun meaning 'relation'. 'A relative' translates a phrase consisting of a preposition followed by a word which can function as the
interrogative 'what?' or the indefinite 'something'. In some
contexts the preposition will be rendered by 'in relation
to' or 'related to'. 'Where', 'when': the Greek words serve
either as interrogatives or as indefinite adverbs ('some-
where', 'at some time'). 'Place' and 'time' are best kept
to translate the appropriate Greek nouns, as at 4b24. 'Being-in-a-position', 'having', 'doing', 'being-affected': each
translates an infinitive (which can be used in Greek as
a verbal noun). The examples of the first two suggest that
Aristotle construes them narrowly (posture and apparel),
but the labels used are quite general. 'Being-affected' is
preferred to alternative renderings because of the need to
use 'affected' and 'affection' later (e.g. 9a28 ff.) as translations of the same verb and of the corresponding noun.

The labels Aristotle uses for his ten categories are,
then, grammatically heterogeneous. The examples he proceeds to give are also heterogeneous. Man is a substance

and cutting is a (kind of) doing; but grammatical is not a quality and has-shoes-on is not a kind of having. 'Grammatical' and 'has-shoes-on' are predicative expressions which serve to introduce but do not name items in the categories of quality and having.

How did Aristotle arrive at his list of categories? Though the items in categories are not expressions but 'things', the identification and classification of these things could, of course, be achieved only by attention to what we say. One way of classifying things is to distinguish different questions which may be asked about something and to notice that only a limited range of answers can be appropriately given to any particular question. An answer to 'where?' could not serve as an answer to 'when?'. Greek has, as we have not, single-word interrogatives meaning 'of what quality?' and 'of what quantity?' (the abstract nouns 'quality' and 'quantity' were, indeed, invented by philosophers as abstractions from the familiar old interrogatives); and these, too, would normally collect answers from different ranges. Now Aristotle does not have a category corresponding to every one-word Greek interrogative, nor do all of his categories correspond to such interrogatives. Nevertheless, it seems certain that one way in which he reached categorial classification was by observing that different types of answer are appropriate to different questions. This explains some of his labels for categories and the predicative form of some of his examples. The actual examples strongly suggest that he thinks about answers to questions about a *man*. Certainly he will have thought of the questions as being asked of a *substance*. This is why he often (though not in the *Categories*) uses the label 'what is it' as an alternative to the noun 'substance'. For what this question, when asked of a substance, gets for answer is itself the name of a substance (cp. *Categories* 2b31). One must not, of course, suppose that in so far as Aristotle is concerned to distinguish groups of possible answers to different questions he is after all engaged in a study of expressions and not things. That 'generous' but not 'runs' will answer the question 'of-what-quality?' is of interest to him as showing that generosity is a different kind of thing from running.

Alternatively, one may address oneself not to the various answers appropriate to various questions about a substance, but to the various answers to one particular question which can be asked about any thing whatsoever—the question 'what is it?'. We may ask 'what is Callias?', 'what is generosity?', 'what is cutting?'; that is, we may ask in what species, genus, or higher genus an individual, species, or genus is. Repeating the same question with reference to the species, genus, or higher genus mentioned in answer to the first question, and continuing thus, we shall reach some extremely high genera. Aristotle thinks that substance, quality, etc., are supreme and irreducibly different genera under one of which falls each thing that there is. This approach may be said to classify subject-expressions (capable of filling the gap in 'what is . . . ?') whereas the previous one classified predicate expressions (capable of filling the gap in 'Callias is . . .'), though, as before, the point for Aristotle is the classification of the things signified by these expressions.

The only other place where Aristotle lists ten categories is in another early work, the *Topics* (I 9). Here he starts by using 'what is it' as a label for the category of substance. This implies the first approach, a classification derived from grouping the answers appropriate to different questions about some individual substance. But later in the chapter the other approach is clearly indicated. It is plain, Aristotle says, that 'someone who signifies what a thing is sometimes signifies substance, sometimes quantity, sometimes qualification, sometimes one of the other predicates. For when a man is under discussion and one says that what is being discussed is a man or is an animal, one is saying what it is and signifying substance; whereas when the colour white is under discussion and one says that what is being discussed is white or is a colour, one is saying what it is and signifying qualification; similarly, if a foot length is being discussed and one says that what is being discussed is a foot length, one will be saying what it is and signifying quantity'. In *this* passage, where the question 'what is it?' is thought of as addressed to items in *any* category, Aristotle can no longer use 'what is it' as a label for the first category but employs the noun for 'substance'. The whole chapter of the *Topics* deserves study.

It is not surprising that these two ways of grouping things should produce the same results: a thing aptly introduced in answer to the question 'of-what-quality?' will naturally be found, when classified in a generic tree, to fall under the genus of quality. The two approaches involve equivalent assumptions. The assumption that a given question determines a range of answers that does not overlap with any range determined by a different question corresponds to the assumption that no item when defined *per genus et differentiam* will be found to fall under more than one highest genus. The assumption that a certain list of questions contains all the radically different questions that may be asked corresponds to the assumption that a certain list of supreme genera contains all the supreme genera. It should be noticed, however, that only the second method gets *individuals* into categories. For one may ask 'what is it?' of an individual in any category; but items introduced by answers to different questions about Callias are not themselves individuals, and a classification of such items will have no place for Callias himself or for Callias's generosity. It has, indeed, been suggested that individuals have no right to a place in Aristotle's categories because the Greek word transliterated 'category' actually means 'predication' or 'predicate' (it is in fact so rendered in this translation, e.g. 10b21). However, it is substance, quality, quantity themselves which are the 'categories', that is, the ultimate predicates; items belonging to some category need not be items which can themselves be predicated, they are items of which that category can be predicated. Thus the meaning of 'category' provides no reason why Callias should not be given a place in a category, nor why non-substance individuals should be left out.

Some general points: (1) Aristotle does not give argument to justify his selection of key questions or to show that all and only the genera in his list are irreducibly different supreme genera. When speaking of categories in other works he commonly mentions only three or four or five (which nearly always include substance, quantity, and quality), but often adds 'and the rest'. In one place he does seek to *show* that 'being' cannot be a genus, that is, in effect, that there must be irreducibly different kinds of being (*Metaphysics* 998b22). (2) Aristotle does not seem to doubt our ability to say what answers would be possible to given questions or to determine the correct unique definitions *per genus et differentiam* of any item we consider. When he looks for features peculiar to a given category (4a10, 6a26, 11a15) he does not do this to suggest criteria for categorial classification; his search presupposes that we already know what items fall into the category in question. He assumes also that we can tell which words or expressions signify *single* items rather than compounds of items from different categories. He does not explain the special role of words like 'species', 'predicate', etc., nor warn us against treating them, like 'animal' or 'generosity', as signifying items in categories. (3) Aristotle does not adopt or try to establish any systematic ordering of categories. Substance is, of course, prior to the rest; and he argues in the *Metaphysics* (1088a22) that what is relative is farthest removed from substance. (4) Aristotle does not in the *Categories* indicate the value of the theory of categories either for dealing with the puzzles of earlier thinkers or for investigating new problems. Nor does he, as elsewhere, develop the idea that 'is', 'being', etc. have different (though connected) senses corresponding to the different categories (*Metaphysics* 1017a22–30, 1028a10–20, 1030a17–27; *Prior Analytics* 49a7).

CHAPTER 5

2a11. The terms 'primary substance' and 'secondary substance' are not used in other works of Aristotle to mark the distinction between individual substances and their species and genera, though the distinction itself is, of course, maintained. The discussion of substance in *Meta-physics* Z and H goes a good deal deeper than does this chapter of the *Categories*. Aristotle there exploits the concepts of matter and form, potentiality and actuality, and wrestles with a whole range of problems left un-touched in the *Categories*.

Aristotle characterises primary substance by the use of terms introduced in Chapter 2. But he does not, as might have been expected, go on to say that secondary sub-stances are things said of a subject but not in any sub-ject. Instead he describes them as the species and genera of primary substances and only later makes the point that they are said of primary substances but not in any sub-ject. The reason for this may be that he is going to say (surprisingly) that the differentiae of substance genera, though not themselves substances, are nevertheless said of the individuals and species in the genera, and are not in them.

'Called a substance most strictly, primarily, and most of all': does Aristotle mean to suggest that 'substance' is used in two different *senses*? It would be difficult for him to allow that without upsetting his whole scheme of cate-gorial classification. Aristotle is no doubt aware that the distinction between primary and secondary substances is not like that between two categories or that between two genera in a category; 'Callias is a primary substance' is unlike both 'Callias is a man' and 'Callias is a substance'. But he fails to say clearly what type of distinction it is.

2a19. 'What has been said' presumably refers to 1b10–15, which is taken to explain why, if A is said of B, not only the name of A but also its definition will be predi-cable of B. The first part of the paragraph is important as showing very clearly that the relation 'said of . . . as subject' holds between things and not words. The fact that A is said of B is not the fact that 'A' is predicable of B. The fact that A is said of B is not even the fact that both 'A' and the definition of A are predicable of B. This is a fact about language that follows from that fact about the relation between two things.

The second part of the paragraph is also of importance.

It shows that Aristotle recognizes that, for example, 'generosity' and 'generous' do not serve to introduce two different things (we should say 'concepts'), but introduce the same thing in two different ways. In saying that usually the name of what is in a subject cannot be predicated of the subject he obviously means more than that, for example, one cannot say 'Callias is generosity'. He means that there is something else which one does say—'Callias is generous'—by way of ascribing generosity to Callias. His point would be senseless if 'generous' itself were just another name of the quality generosity or if it were the name of a different thing altogether.

2a34. Someone might counter the claim in the first sentence by pointing out that, for example, animal is said of man and colour is in body, and man and body are *secondary* substances. Aristotle therefore examines just such cases. It is somewhat surprising that he says: 'were it predicated of none of the individual men it would not be predicated of man at all.' For in view of the meaning of 'said of' he could have made the stronger statement: 'were if not predicated of *all* of the individual men. . . . However, what he does say is sufficient for the final conclusion he is driving at, that nothing else could exist if primary substances did not. As for colour, Aristotle could have argued to his final conclusion simply by using the definition of 'in' together with the fact, just established, that the existence of secondary substances presupposes the existence of primary substances: if colour is in body it cannot exist if body does not, and body cannot exist if no individual bodies exist. What is Aristotle's own argument? It was suggested earlier that to say that colour is in body is to say that every instance of colour is in an individual body. If so, Aristotle's present formulation is compressed and careless. For he does not mention individual instances of colour; he speaks as if, because colour is in body, colour is in an individual body. Strictly, however, it is not colour, but this individual instance of colour, that is in this individual body; for colour could exist apart from this body (though this instance of colour could not). Aristotle's use of a relaxed sense of 'in' may be connected with his almost complete neglect, after Chapter 2, of individuals in non-substance categories.

In drawing his final conclusion in the last sentence Aristotle relies partly on the definition of 'in' ('. . . cannot exist separately . . .'); partly on the principle that if A is said of B, A could not exist if B did not. The closest he comes to arguing for this principle is at 3b10–23, where he insists that secondary substances are just *kinds of* primary substance.

Aristotle's conclusion is evidently intended to mark out primary substances as somehow basic (*contra* Plato). But the point is not very well expressed. For it may well be doubted whether (Aristotle thinks that) primary substances could exist if secondary substances and items in other categories did not do so. But if the implication of existence holds both ways, from the rest to primary substances and from primary substances to the rest, the statement in the last sentence of his paragraph fails to give a special status to primary substances.

2b7. The two arguments given for counting the species as 'more a substance' than the genus—for carrying into the class of secondary substances the notion of priority and posteriority already used in the distinction between primary and secondary substances—come to much the same. For the reason why it is more informative (2b10) to say 'Callias is a man' than to say 'Callias is an animal' (though both are proper answers to the 'what is it' question, 2b31–37) is just that the former entails the latter but not vice versa: 'the genera are predicated of the species but the species are not predicated reciprocally of the genera' (2b20). The point of view is different at 15a4–7, where it is said that genera are always prior to species since they do not reciprocate as to the implication of existence: 'if there is a fish there is an animal, but if there is an animal there is not necessarily a fish'. For this sense of 'prior' see 14a29–35.

2b29. Here the connexion between the 'what is it' question and the establishment of categorial lines is made very clear.

The second argument (from 'Further, it is be-

cause . . .') is compressed. Primary substances are subjects
for everything else; everything else is either said of or in
them (2a34, 2b15). Aristotle now claims that secondary
substances are similarly related to 'all the rest', that is,
to all things other than substances. This must be because
all those things are *in* secondary substances. All Aristotle
says, to establish this, is that 'this man is grammatical'
entails 'a man is grammatical'. He means to imply that
any non-substance that is in a primary substance is necessarily in a secondary substance (the species or genus of
the primary substance). Since he has already argued that
all non-substances are in primary substances he feels entitled to the conclusion that all non-substances are in secondary substances. But it will be seen that a further re-
laxation in the sense of 'in' has taken place. It is now
implied, not only that generosity can be described as in
Callias (though generosity could certainly exist in the absence of Callias), but also that generosity can be described as in man simply on the ground that some one
man is generous (and not, as it strictly should be, on the
ground that all instances of generosity are in individual
men).

3a7. Why is it 'obvious at once' that secondary substances are not *in* primary substances? It is not that they
can exist separately from primary substances (2a34–b6).
Nor does Aristotle appear to rely on the fact that a given
secondary substance can exist separately from any given
individual, that there could be men even if Callias did
not exist, so that the species man can exist separately
from Callias and is, therefore, not in him. Aristotle seems
rather to be appealing to the obvious impropriety in ordinary speech of saying such a thing as 'man is in Callias'. It was suggested in the note on 1a24–25 that Aristotle made it a necessary condition of A's being in B that
it should be possible to say in ordinary non-technical discourse such a thing as 'A is in B' ('belongs to B', etc.).
Now Aristotle is pointing out that this condition is not
satisfied in the case of man and Callias. If this is his point
he could have extended it to other categories; no genus
or species in any category can naturally be described as

in (or belonging to or had by) any subordinate genus, species or individual. What distinguishes secondary substances from non-substance genera and species is not that they are not in the individuals, species, and genera subordinate to them but that they are not in any *other* individuals, species, or genera; virtue is not in generosity, but it is in soul, whereas animal is not in man and not in anything else either.

One cannot say 'hero is in Callias' or 'father is in Callias'; but if Callias is a hero and a father the definition of 'hero' and 'father' can also be predicated of him. So it might be suggested that the considerations advanced by Aristotle in this paragraph imply that hero and father are secondary substances. But Aristotle is not claiming that any predicate-word which can be replaced by its definition is the name of a secondary substance (or differentia of substance, see below), but that a predicate-word can be replaced by the definition of the item it introduces if and only if the item is a secondary substance (or differentia of substance). 'Generous' can be replaced by definitions of 'hero' and 'father', but not by definition of the item which 'generous' introduces, the quality generosity. Similarly, 'hero' and 'father' can be replaced by definitions of 'hero' and 'father', but not by definitions of the items they serve to introduce, heroism and fatherhood. Aristotle gives no explicit rules for deciding which common nouns stand for species and genera of substance (natural kinds) and which serve only to ascribe qualities, etc., to substances. He would presumably rely on the 'what is it' question to segregate genuine names of secondary substances from other common nouns; but the question has to be taken in a limited or loaded sense if it is always to collect only the sorts of answer Aristotle would wish, and an understanding and acceptance of the idea of natural kinds is therefore presupposed by the use of the question to distinguish the names of such kinds from other common nouns which serve merely to ascribe qualities, etc. Surely it would often be appropriate to say 'a cobbler' in answer to the quesion 'What is Callias?'.

3a21. The statement that something that is not substance is nevertheless said of substance is a surprising
one, which can hardly be reconciled with the scheme of
ideas so far developed. If the differentia of a genus is not
a substance (secondary substances being just the species
and genera of substance), it ought to belong to some other
category and hence be in substance. That an item in one
category should be said of an item in another violates the
principle that if *A* is said of *B* and *B* of *C* then *A* is said of
C. Aristotle, indeed, positively claims that the definition
as well as the name of a differentia is predicable of the
substance falling under it, but this too seems very strange.
In a definition *per genus et differentiam* the differentia is
commonly expressed by an adjective (or other non-sub-
stantive), and this should surely be taken to introduce an
item named by the corresponding substantive (as 'generous' introduces but is not the name of generosity). If
we say that man is a rational animal 'rational' brings in
rationality, but neither the name nor the definition of
rationality can be predicated of man. Thus the differentiating property satisfies a test for being *in* substance (cp.
2a19–34).

Aristotle is no doubt influenced by the following facts.
(1) Species and genera of individual substances are themselves called substances because 'if one is to say of the
individual man *what* he is, it will be in place to give the
species or the genus' (2b32). If we now consider the
question 'what is (a) man?' we shall be strongly inclined
to mention not only the genus animal but also the appropriate differentia. The differentia seems to be *part of*
the 'what is it' of a secondary substance, and this provides a strong motive for assimilating it to substance even
while distinguishing it from species and genera. (2) The
principle enunciated at 1b16 implies that mention of a
differentia-words words which function naturally in Greek
true classification of things) any mention of the genus.
To ascribe the differentia 'two-footed' to man is as good
as to say that he is a two-footed land animal. Thus the
differentia is, in a way, the *whole* of the 'what is it' of
a secondary substance. (3) Aristotle uses as examples of

differentia-words words which function naturally in Greek as nouns (though they are strictly neuter adjectives). At 14b33–15a7 he uses the same words when speaking explicitly of *species* (and so they are translated there by 'bird', 'beast' and 'fish'). Moreover, there are in Aristotle's vocabulary no abstract nouns corresponding to these neuter adjectives (as 'footedness', 'two-footedness'). Such facts are far from establishing that the definition as well as the name of a differentia is predicated of substances. For not all differentiae are expressed by nouns or words used as nouns, and abstract nouns corresponding to differentia-words are not always lacking. In any case, there are plenty of nouns (like 'hero') which Aristotle would insist on treating as mere derivatives from the names of the things they introduce ('heroism'); and the fact that there is no name for, say, a quality does not exclude the possibility that some predicative expression serves to ascribe that quality (though not, of course, paronymously: 10a32–b5). Thus, that 'footed' is (used as) a noun and no noun 'footedness' exists is not a justification for refusing to treat 'footed' in the same kind of way as 'hero' or 'generous', as introducing a characteristic neither the name nor the definition of which is predicable of that which is footed. Nevertheless, the above features of the examples he hit upon may have made it somewhat easier for him to say what he does about differentiae without feeling the need for full explanation. For deeper discussion of the relation of differentia to genus, and of the connected problem of the unity of definition (referred to at *De Interpretatione* 17a13), see especially *Metaphysics* Z 12.

3a33. 'All things called from them are so called synonymously': Aristotle is not denying that there are words which stand ambiguously for either of two kinds of substance (like 'animal' in Chapter 1). Things to which such a word applied in one sense would not be 'called from' *the same substance* as things to which it applied in the other sense; and Aristotle is claiming only that all things called from any given substance are so called synonymously, not that all things called by a given substance-word are necessarily so called synonymously.

Aristotle is drawing attention again to the following point (it will be convenient to assume that there is no sheer ambiguity in the words used). There are two ways in which something can be called from the quality virtue: generosity is a virtue, Callias is virtuous; neither the name nor the definition of virtue is predicable of Callias. There are two ways in which something can be called from the quality white: Della Robbia white is (a) white, this paper is white; the name but not the definition of white is predicable of this paper. There is only one way in which something can be called from man: Callias is a man, Socrates is a man, and so on; both the name and the definition of man are predicable of Callias and Socrates and so on.

It is not quite clear that Della Robbia white and this paper are homonymous with respect to the word 'white', in the meaning given to 'homonymous' in Chapter 1. For there the case was that the word (e.g. 'animal') stood in its two uses for two different things with two different definitions. Now, however, we have 'white' in one use standing for a thing (a quality) which has a certain definition, but in the other use not standing for a different thing with a different definition but introducing differently the very same thing. However, an easy revision of the account in Chapter 1 would enable one to say that 'synonymously' in the present passage contrasts with both 'homonymously' and 'paronymously': most non-substances (like generosity) generate paronymy, a few (like the quality white) generate homonymy; no substance generates either.

'From a primary substance there is no predicate': there is no subject of which Callias is said or in which Callias is. In the *Analytics* Aristotle speaks of sentences in which the name 'Callias' is in the predicate place, and says that this is only accidental predication (43a34; cp. 83a1–23). He does not make any thorough investigation of the different types of sentence in which a proper name may occur in the predicate place. Nor does he discuss such uses as 'he is a Socrates', 'his method of argument is Socratic'. He would no doubt allow that these are cases of genuine predication but deny that the predicates are 'from a primary substance': the connexion between the characteristics ascribed by '. . . is a Socrates' and '. . . is Socratic' and the individual Socrates is purely historical and contingent; we should not have used '. . . is a Socrates' as we do if there had been no Socrates or if Socrates had had a different character, but we could perfectly well have used a different locution to ascribe the very same characteristics. A similar answer would be available if someone claimed that there are after all two ways in which something may be called from a secondary substance since while Tabitha is *a cat* Mrs. So-and-so is *catty*. It is because of real or assumed characteristics of cats that the word 'cattiness' names the characteristics it does; but the characteristics themselves could have existed and been talked about even if there had never been any cats.

3b10. Aristotle has contrasted individual substances with their species and genera. He has labelled the latter 'secondary' and has argued that their existence presupposes that of primary substances. Nevertheless, much that he has said provides a strong temptation to thing of species and genera of substance as somehow existing in their own right like Platonic Forms. In the present passage Aristotle tries to remedy this. It is careless of him to speak as if it were substances (and not names of substances) that signify. More important, it is unfortunate that he draws the contrast between a primary substance and a secondary substance by saying that the latter signifies a certain qualification. For although he immediately insists that 'it does not signify simply a certain qualification, as white does', yet the impression is conveyed that secondary substances really belong in the category of quality. This, of course, Aristotle does not mean. 'Quality of substance' means something like 'kind' or 'character of substance'; it derives from a use of the question 'of what quality?' different from the use which serves to classify items as belonging to the category of quality. 'Of what quality is Callias?' (or 'what kind of person is Callias?') gets answers from the category of quality. But 'what quality of animal is Callias?' (or 'what kind of animal is Callias?') asks not for a quality as opposed to substance, quantity, etc., but for the quality-of-animal, the kind-of-animal. It is a result of the limitations of Aristotle's vocabulary that he uses the same word as a category-label and to convey the idea of a kind, sort or character of so-and-so. (Cp. *Metaphysics* 1020a33 – b1, 1024b5–6, where 'quality' refers to the differentia—in any category—not to the *category* of quality.) It is also clear that he is at a disadvantage in this passage through not having at his disposal such terms as 'refer', 'describe', 'denote', 'connote'; and that he would have been in a better position if he had from the start examined and distinguished various uses of expressions like '(a) man' instead of embarking at once upon a classification of 'things there are'.

3b24. Aristotle raises the question of contrariety in each of the categories he discusses. On the suggestion that large and small are contraries see 5b11 – 6a11.

3b33. The question of a more and a less is raised in each category. 'We have said that it is': 2b7. There is a certain ambiguity in 'more', since to say that a species is more a substance than a genus is to assign it some sort of priority but not to ascribe to it a higher degree of some feature as one does in saying that this is more hot than that.

The point Aristotle makes here about substances applies also, of course, to sorts which he would not recognize as natural kinds: one cobbler or magistrate is not more a cobbler or magistrate than another.

4a10. What Aristotle gives here as distinctive of substance is strictly a characteristic of *primary* substances. For he is not speaking of the possibility of man's being both dark and pale (of there being both dark men and pale men), but of the possibility of one and the same individual man's being at one time dark and at another time pale. (It will then be distinctive of secondary substances that the individuals of which they are said are capable of admitting opposites.) Correspondingly, Aristotle must be meaning to deny, not that species and genera in other categories may in a sense admit contraries (colour may be white or black), but that individual instances of qualities, etc., can admit contraries while retaining their identity. His first example is not convincing. An individual instance of colour will necessarily be an instance of some specific colour and will be individuated accordingly: if X changes from black to white we first have X's blackness and then X's whiteness, *two* individuals in the category of quality. (To this there corresponds the fact that one and the same individual substance cannot move from one species to another.) What is required is to show—not that X's blackness cannot retain its identity while becoming white, but—that X's blackness cannot retain its identity while having contrary properties at different times. The sort of suggestion Aristotle ought to rebut is, for example, the suggestion that one and the same individual instance of colour could be at one time glossy and at another matt, this variation not making it count as different instances of *colour*. Aristotle's second example is of the right kind, since the goodness or badness of an action does not enter into the identity-criteria for an individual action in the way in which the shade of colour does enter into the identity-criteria for an individual instance of colour. However, the example is still particularly favourable for him. For 'good' and 'bad' are commonly used to appraise an action *as a whole*, and for this reason one would not speak of an action as having been good at first and then become bad. There are clearly very many cases which it would be less easy for Aristotle to handle (cannot an individual sound sustain change in volume and tone?). The question demands a fuller scrutiny of cases and a more thorough investigation of usage than Aristotle attempts. It would seem that the power to admit contraries is not peculiar to individual substances but is shared by certain other continuants, so that a further criterion is required to explain why these others are not counted as substances.

4a22. Aristotle of course treats the truth and falsity of statements and beliefs as their correspondence and lack of correspondence to fact (4b8, 14b14–22; *Metaphysics*

1051b6–9). Here he first points out that it is not through a change in itself that a statement or belief at one time true is at another time false, whereas an individual substance itself changes; so that it remains distinctive of primary substances that they can admit contraries *by changing*. He next argues (4b5) that strictly a thing should be said to admit contraries only if it does itself undergo a change from one to the other; so that, strictly speaking, it is not necessary to qualify what was said at 4a10–11: only individual substances can admit contraries.

Aristotle might have argued that the alleged counterexamples, individual statements or beliefs which change their truth-value, fail, because my statement now that Callias is sitting and my statement later that Callias is sitting are not the same *individual* statement even if they are the *same statement* (just as 'a' and 'a' are two individual instances of the same letter). Thus they are not examples of the very same individual admitting contraries. Alternatively, Aristotle could have denied that the statement made by 'Callias is sitting' when uttered at one time *is* the *same statement* as that made by 'Callias is sitting' when uttered at another time. The sameness of a statement or belief is not guaranteed by the sameness of the words in which it is expressed; the time and place of utterance and other contextual features must be taken into account.

ARISTOTLE'S THEORY OF CATEGORIES

J. M. E. MORAVCSIK

In several of his writings Aristotle presents what came to be known as a "list of categories." The presentation of a list, by itself, is not a philosophic theory. This paper attempts a few modest steps toward an understanding of the theory or theories in which the list of categories is embedded. To arrive at such understanding we shall have to deal with the following questions: What classes of expressions designate items each of which falls under only one category? What is the list a list of? and What gives it unity? To show this to be a worthwhile enterprise, let us consider a few passages in which the list of categories is introduced or mentioned.

In *Topics* 103b20 ff. the list is introduced as containing certain kinds (*gené*) within which one can find the accidents, genus, properties, and definition of anything. Thus apparently all (simple?) elements of the nature of any entity are to be found in one of the categories. In *Metaphysics* 1028a10 ff. we are told that 'is' has as many senses as there are categories. Thus we see that Aristotle analyzes the ambiguity of 'is' with the list of categories as an assumed background. What he takes to be the systematic ambiguity of 'is' provides one of the cornerstones of his metaphysical speculations. In *Physics* 225b5 ff. Aristotle analyzes the concept of *kinésis* and concludes that instances of this can be found in three of the categories.

Each of these passages presents problems; some of these will be taken up later in this paper. This brief preliminary survey is intended only to show that the list of categories plays an important role in several of Aristotle's theories, and thus it is reasonable to assume that the list has constitutive principles and unity.

I

Which parts of language designate an item in one of the categories? In *Categories* 1b25 ff. the list of categories is introduced as containing the kinds (e.g. quality, quantity) of those items (e.g. white, grammatical, three cubits long) which are signified by "things said without any combination" (Ackrill's translation, contained in this volume). Chapters 2 and 4 of the *Categories* taken together make it quite clear that the "things" in question are linguistic items. Our first task is to determine which parts of language Aristotle is referring to in the passage under consideration. Earlier, in 1a16 ff. we read that "Of things that are said, some involve combination while others are said without combination. Examples of those involving combination are 'man runs', 'man wins'; and of those without combination 'man', 'ox', 'runs', 'wins'."[1] In view of the meagerness of the examples, the key term in this account is "combination." As Ackrill,[2] and a century ago Trendelenburg,[3] pointed out, the Greek term *sumploké* used here by Aristotle had been previously used by

[1] J. L. Ackrill's translation here is far superior to the old Oxford version, which renders the first part of this passage as: "Forms of speech are either simple or composite." This suggests, wrongly, that Aristotle is saying something about all forms of speech, and, equally wrongly, that the distinction to be drawn is a surface distinction between what is syntactically simple or analyzable.

[2] J. L. Ackrill, *Aristotle's Categories and De Interpretatione* (Oxford, 1963), p. 73. (See earlier in this volume p. 102.)

[3] A. Trendelenburg, *Geschichte der Kategorienlehre* (Hildesheim: Olms, 1846 [1963]), p. 11.

Plato to refer not to mere conjunction or juxtaposition, but rather to the interweaving of words and phrases into sentences.[4] This would suggest that the uncombined elements are parts of language from which sentences can be formed. This is confirmed by 2a4 ff., where Aristotle says that the combination of these items produces a true or false sentence. (Aristotle regards sentences as the bearers of truth-value.) There is an interesting parallel to this passage in *Topics* 101b26–28, according to which the key elements in a statement are property, genus, definition, and accident, and it is emphasized that none of these by themselves make up a statement. Thus as a reasonable first approximation we can say that Aristotle is interested in potential elements of sentences that are true or false, or definitions. One is tempted to add the qualification: "sentences of subject-predicate form," for neither in the examples given nor in the subsequent discussions are sentences expressing identity or existence treated. Their inclusion in the discussion would raise some interesting questions about the extent to which these types of sentence could be regarded as "interweaving," and about the senses of 'is' involved. The addition of this qualification would be in harmony with Trendelenburg's remark that Aristotle in this context seems to have in mind what Kant called judgments,[5] (a notion which carries similar limitations).

Having specified the relevant class of sentences, we should investigate whether the Aristotelian theory entails that every element of such a sentence designates an item, and whether every element that designates is supposed to designate an item falling into only one of

---

[4]On Plato's views on this see J. M. Moravcsik, *"Sumploké Eidoon,"* Archiv für die Geschichte der Philosophie, XLII (1960) 117–29; also "Being and Meaning in the *Sophist,"* Acta Philosophica Fennica, XIV (1962), especially pp. 61–65.

[5]Trendelenburg, op. cit., p. 12.

the categories. An affirmative answer to either question would place the theory in jeopardy. There is, however, evidence that:

(i) Aristotle does not think that every word or phrase which could be part of a sentence of subject-predicate form has the function of designating an entity.

As both Steinthal and Trendelenburg remarked,[6] Aristotle does not ascribe the same type of significance to every word within a sentence, and he does not think that every word has a designative role. In *Poetics* 1456b38 ff. he separates from nouns and verbs (to which he also assimilates adjectives) the so-called connectors or auxiliary expressions. These are said to include particles and prepositions, but in order to complement the theory of categories they ought to include a great deal more: logical constants, articles, and the ordinary language equivalents of quantifiers must also be members of this class. There is evidence to support the view that Aristotle intended the connectors to include a great deal more than he explicitly mentions. For one thing, what he says about them applies to a much larger group than his examples would suggest, for he says that these expressions (a) do not designate and (b) do not contribute to the content of a new (larger) linguistic unit, i.e. the sentence. These criteria are interesting, for they show that Aristotle did not mark off the connectors on purely syntactic grounds. The criteria can be taken as foreshadowing the characterization of what were later called the syncategorematic expressions. In any case, these conditions would allow all the above-mentioned types of expression to qualify. It is impossible to say how many of these Aristotle had in mind when he wrote the *Poetics*, but the

[6]Trendelenburg, op. cit., pp. 24 ff. and H. Steinthal, *Geschichte der Sprachwissenschaft* (Hildesheim: Olms, 1890 [1961]), Vol. I, pp. 263 ff.

fluidity of the classification is witnessed by *Rhetoric* III 5 where—as Steinthal saw—Aristotle blends articles, pronouns, and conjunctives into one class. Steinthal's interpretation of what Aristotle thought of as the main parts of speech is of further relevance here, for it is claimed that apart from nouns and verbs Aristotle recognized only one more class, i.e. the connectors.[7] None of this is direct evidence, but taken all together it renders plausible the interpretation of the class of connectors on the suggested broad basis.

With this we have narrowed down the candidates for the "uncombined elements" to the members of the class of designative expressions which can be elements of those sentences that are definitions or are of subject-predicate form. Still, further restrictions are obviously needed. Fortunately there is evidence to support additional qualifications.

(ii) Aristotle does not think that every noun or verb designates an item in one of the categories.

In *De Interpretatione* 16a13 ff. Aristotle lists as a necessary condition for the production of what is true or false the combination of verb and noun, and in this context treats "being" as a verb. We see, however, from his treatment of being in the *Categories* and the *Metaphysics* (see the reference in the beginning of this paper) that he does not construe being as falling into only one of the categories. His claim that being is not a genus, and the argument backing up this claim,[8] are sufficient ground on which to base the interpretation that 'being'—and similar terms like 'same', 'one', etc.— have either no designative role or a divided designative role.

---

[7]Steinthal, op. cit., pp. 260 ff.

[8]The most profound discussion of this argument is to be found in John Cook Wilson's paper "Categories in Aristotle and in Kant," *Statement and Inference*, Vol. II, pp. 696–706 [above, pp. 75–89].

Before we consider further qualifications, let us look briefly at the interesting status that definitions had for Aristotle. It is not clear whether he regarded definitions as true or false, and whether they counted as instances of combination. The passage quoted from the *Topics* above casts doubt on their counting as combinations. Now in *De Interpretatione*, chapters 4 and 5, he argues that what is true or false must contain such interweaving or combination. Again in *Poetics* 1457a25 ff. Aristotle says that, though definitions are sentences, they need not contain a verb. This passage, however, can be construed as saying only that no verb need appear explicitly in a definition; the same is true in Greek for many other types of sentences. Again in *De Anima* III 6 it is pointed out that a definition does not involve a mental task of synthesis as an assertion does. All of this together supports the interpretation according to which Aristotle did not regard definitions as true or false or as produced by combination. Nevertheless, we must assume that he thought of parts of definitions as falling under one category.

(iii) There are some noun- or verb-phrases (other than words like 'being', etc.) that designate items falling under more than one category.

An obvious example of a phrase designating a complex that spans two categories is the expression 'incontinent man'. In order to rule out such cases we have to introduce further qualifications. The restriction to be put forward here is not backed by direct textual evidence, but it is supported by what we took to be the significance of *sumploké* and the proposed broad delineation of the class of connectors: it is to rule out as not completely uncombined all those phrases which the mere addition of connectors can transform into a sentence. For though 'red colored' and 'incontinent man' are not sentences, they can be expanded into the sentences 'all red things are colored' and 'some men are incontinent' by the mere addition of connectors. Here one can see the importance of our previous qualification that only sentences of subject-predicate form are under consideration. Without it our current restriction would turn out to be so strict as to leave no word in the "uncombined" class, since the addition of "there are some ... things" will render 'white' or 'heavy' into sentences; yet 'white' and 'heavy' are known to be expressions which Aristotle regards as "in no way combined."

Throughout this discussion we have taken the notion of a sentence for granted. It is time to see what Aristotle has to say on this topic. But his account of a sentence as significant sound, some part of which is significant in separation as an expression (*De Interpretatione* 16b26 ff. and *Poetics* 1457a23 ff.), is obviously inadequate since it fails even to separate sentences from clauses. The reason for this seems to be that Aristotle finds himself in a curious predicament. He cannot accept the Platonic account of a sentence as the interweaving of noun and verb since he recognizes counterexamples to it. On the other hand, he knows that he cannot use the theory of categories to explain a sentence as an intercategorial connection, since he knows that a sentence like 'all men are animals' does not combine elements from different categories. Thus he lacks a conceptual framework that would enable him to give an adequate account of what a sentence is. In view of this, we shall have to continue in this discussion to take the notion of a sentence for granted.

We are not yet finished with the required restrictions, for we must admit the following:

(iv) Not all relevantly simple nouns and verbs designate items falling into only one category.

As Aristotle saw, one can simply define a word *x* as 'incontinent man' and thereby create a word which our previous restrictions allow as uncombined but which designates something that spans two categories. What is clearly needed is a further restriction that would rule out expressions like x as somehow ill-formed. There is evidence that Aristotle did have such a qualification in mind, for in *De Interpretatione*, chapters 8 and 11, he discusses the problem of the extent to which a predicate expression may or may not designate a "genuine unity." The discussions are sketchy and no adequate interpretations of them have so far been offered. Thus Ackrill wrote[9] that the difficulty of deciding what Aristotle regards as a genuine unity "corresponds" to the difficulty of deciding which simple phrases are supposed to designate items falling into only one category. Ackrill is quite correct in emphasizing the magnitude of the task facing the interpreter, but this should not keep us from seeing that the notion of a genuine unity could still be invoked by Aristotle in an account of the "uncombined" elements of language. For as 18a18 ff. shows, there are certain predicates, e.g. that which is the equivalent of 'horse and man', which designate items falling into one category only, which nevertheless Aristotle would not regard as having genuine unity. Thus whatever the correct account of genuine unity is, the passage under consideration shows that it does not presuppose the correlation between uncombined elements and the list of categories, and thus it could be invoked without circularity to place further restriction on what is to count as an uncombined element.

In view of these considerations it is not unreasonable to suppose that Aristotle could describe x defined as 'incontinent man' as an expression not designating a genuine unity; that he could do so without assuming anything about its correlation with any of the categories, and that he could on this ground rule that it is not one of the legitimate uncombined elements. This

[9]Ackrill, op. cit., p. 126.

final restriction leaves us with the following formulation of Aristotle's view:

(v) Those elements of sentences of subject-predicate form, or definitions, which (a) are not connectors; (b) are not, like 'being', otherwise non-designative in nature; (c) cannot be turned into sentences of subject-predicate form, by the mere addition of connectors; and (d) designate genuine unities, are "uncombined elements" of language, and designate items falling into one and only one category.

Intuitively restated, Aristotle's principle says that by what we would call semantic and syntactic analysis[10] we can discover certain basic units among the elements of sentences of subject-predicate form, and that these turn out to designate those simple elements of reality which fall into only one category. Thus the designative link between these simple parts of language and the simple parts of reality which fall into only one category is, according to Aristotle, the key link between the structure of language and the structure of reality.

This account is not without difficulties. The main problem is the as yet unexplained doctrine of genuine unity. Another problem is the fact that the restriction ascribed to Aristotle that rests on the possibility of expanding certain phrases into sentences with the help of connectors is not supported by direct evidence. But it is not a weakness of the interpretation that it seeks to connect what is said in the *Categories* with some of what is said in the *Poetics* and the *Rhetorics*. On the contrary, to show that under a certain interpretation these passages complement the views of the passages in the *Categories* is to give that interpretation added plausibility.

Given the difficulties, we might cast around for alternative interpretations. In this connection it is worth not-

---

[10]Aristotle, like Plato, did not distinguish between these.

ing that both the possible solutions listed by Ackrill,[11] and perceptively criticized by him, turn out to be inferior to the account presented in this paper. One of these solutions takes "without combination" to mean "designates an item falling into only one category." The main difficulty with this view is that—as Ackrill observes—it construes the statement introducing the list of categories in chapter 4 as analytic. If the statement that the elements which are in no way combined designate items falling into only one category is analytic, it is deceptively so; for this would imply that there is no way of sorting out the uncombined elements of a sentence except by observing whether their designata fall into only one category. Thus the beginning of chapter 4 could just as well have started: "some sentential elements designate ... and we regard these as being without any combination." Furthermore, according to this interpretation what Aristotle says about the combined and uncombined parts of language rests entirely on metaphysical grounds and thus cannot be connected with what he says elsewhere about the structure of language.

The other possible solution fares hardly better, since according to it the distinction between what is and what is not combined is identical with the distinction between simple words and more complex sentential elements. In order to accept this view we would have to assume that in chapter 4 of the *Categories* Aristotle forgets about the possibility of simple terms with complex meanings. However, we saw above that this possibility is discussed in *De Interpretatione*, and to suppose that Aristotle is not aware of this issue in a context in which it is vital is to accuse him of too gross a mistake. Moreover, this version suggests that Aristotle's distinction among different parts of language rests on purely superficial features, whereas the passages

[11]Ackrill, op. cit., pp. 73–74 [pp. 102–103 above].

quoted from the *Topics* and the *Poetics* assure us that this is not so.

To sum up, if we can regard the evidence presented in support of the interpretation argued for in this section as adequate, the interpretation recommends itself on the following grounds: it links Aristotle's metaphysical speculation with his view on the structure of language; it relates the *Categories* to what is said in other works on language; it helps to explore Aristotle's views on language, which turn out to be far from simple-minded; and it sketches the structure of an explanation that Aristotle would be likely to give as justification of the claim that there are certain "uncombined" elements in language with a—to him—vital designative role.

II

The unity and completeness of the list of categories. In the beginning of chapter 4 of the *Categories* we find a list of ten categories. The labels given to them are oddly heterogeneous. Some are philosophical constructs, some are ordinary questions, and some are lifted out of simple singular sentences of subject-predicate form.[12] Thus at first glance it is not clear whether the list is supposed to yield an ontological classification or an analysis of the structure of propositions. Some interpreters have gone as far as accusing Aristotle of having failed to give the list sufficient unity. Perhaps the most famous of these critics is Kant,[13] who assumes that Aristotle was interested in the same task that he was—i.e. to give a set of necessary conditions under which judgments are possible—and then concludes that Aristotle failed in this task. A comparison of Kant's categories with those of Aristotle, however, suggests the not too surprising alternative that Kant and

12Ackrill, op. cit., p. 73 and Trendelenburg, op. cit., p. 13.
13*Critique of Pure Reason* B 105–107.

Aristotle designed their categories with different purposes in mind. Many of Kant's categories must be construed as properties of judgments or ideas (e.g. universality or singularity). Aristotle's list, on the other hand, cannot be so construed. His items are either very general properties of objects or not properties at all. There is no reason why the two lists should coincide, and once the difference in their aims has been discerned, the two need not be regarded as conflicting.[14]

One way of explaining the heterogeneity of the labels is to assume that Aristotle is concerned primarily with the types to be designated, and not with the manner of designation. As we shall see, the adoption of this assumption is rewarding. We must note at this point, however, that it leads us to reject a claim like that made by Trendelenburg, according to which the list of categories is derived from grammatical considerations.[15]

Let us begin by considering one commonly accepted characterization of the categories, the one that describes them as the "highest predicables."[16] In order for this view to be even initially plausible, we must construe 'predicable' in a technical sense. For not only is the first category ambiguous between primary and secondary substance, but some of the examples given for the other categories, e.g. 'in the Lyceum' and 'yesterday', cannot be regarded as predicables in the ordinary sense of the term. What this technical sense of 'predicable' wide enough to embrace everything falling under each of the ten categories could be is far from clear. But

[14]For a different view of the relation between Aristotle and Kant see H. W. B. Joseph, *An Introduction to Logic* (Oxford, 1916), pp. 63–65. Also Cook Wilson, op, cit,, p. 704 [p. 85].
[15]Trendelenburg, op. cit., p. 33.
[16]As remarked but not endorsed by W. D. Ross in *Aristotle*, pp. 27–28. According to Joseph, op. cit., pp. 48–49, the Greek word for category (κατηγορία) means 'predicate,' but for counterexamples see H. Bonitz, *Über die Kategorien des Aristoteles* (Vienna, 1853), pp. 30–31.

even if such a sense could be found, further difficulties
arise in connection with the term 'highest'. There are
two ways in which the metaphorical value of this term
could be captured by logical analysis. On one interpretation predicate p′ is higher than predicate p″ if
and only if all members of the class which makes up
the range of application of p″ are also members of
the class which makes up the range of application of
p′, but not the other way around. In this sense *animal*
is higher than *man*. The other interpretation takes p′
as higher than p″ if and only if p′ is an attribute of p″.
In this sense *category* would be a higher predicate than
quality or *quantity*, and *colour, quality, category* would
constitute a hierarchy. It is clear, however, that Aristotle does not want such a pyramid. He denies the
ontological reality of the higher strata here indicated.
Not to do so would leave him far closer to Platonism
than he would find comfortable. Thus the sense in
which the categories would have to be "higher" is the
former sense—as Cook Wilson noted.[17] That is to
say, as we go to wider and wider genera, the particulars
contained in any one genera are on the same level as
the particulars contained in the wider genera. Given
this characterization of the categories, one is confronted
with the question: where must one stop? Why call
the categories the "highest" (actually the "widest")
genera? The only plausible Aristotelian reply is: "because by some principle the genera that would have
even wider comprehensions are not genuine genera; i.e.
they have no ontological status." Such a reply takes
us back to a metaphysical principle, and it is the ex-
plication of that principle, rather than the phrase
"highest predicables," that will shed light on the nature
of the categories.

Another current interpretation could be characterized

[17]Cook Wilson, op. cit., pp. 696 and 705 [pp. 75 and 86].

as the "linguistic view." Among its advocates are Ryle[18] and Anscombe.[19] According to this view Aristotle uses the list of categories to mark off the different kinds of fairly simple things that can be said about a substance. As such, the list could not be regarded as final or complete, since there may be an indeterminate number of ways in which one can raise questions about substances. The most important achievement of the list turns out to be—according to this interpretation—the anticipation of the concept of semantic category and the notion of a "category-mistake," a confusion which supposedly underlies a type of semantically deviant sentence. (E.g. an answer in terms of food to a question about the size of a substance allegedly does not make sense, even though the sentence expressing the answer is—on the surface at least—syntactically well formed.)

This is not the place to hold autopsy over the notion of a category-mistake as used by recent analytic philosophers. To show that this could not be the correct interpretation of Aristotle's theory will have to suffice. Three considerations prove fatal to this account. First, according to this view once the significance of the list is properly understood, questions about completeness could not arise. But, as some of the passages quoted at the beginning of this paper show, Aristotle committed himself to claims which entail that the list should contain mutually exclusive categories which are jointly exhaustive of reality. (More on this point below.) Thus either this interpretation is incorrect, or we must

---

[18]G. Ryle, "Categories," *Logic and Language,* second ser., ed. A. Flew (Oxford, 1955), pp. 65–81. Ryle—like Kant—thinks that Aristotle was really interested in what he, Ryle, is interested in doing but that he did not do it so well. I find deeply depressing this tendency of philosophers to think that the great men of the past tried to do what they are doing but that they did not do it so well.

[19]G. E. Anscombe, in *Three Philosophers* (Oxford, 1961), pp. 14–15.

suppose that Aristotle himself completely misunderstood the significance of his own theory. Such an assumption should be adopted by a historian only as a last resort. Secondly, the only basis for the individuation of the categories would be the linguistic intuition which allows us to detect category-mistakes. It is clear, however, that Aristotle does not leave the individuation of his categories to intuitions, linguistic or otherwise. He states their differentiating characteristics quite explicitly: e.g. quality is that in virtue of which things can be said to be similar; quantity is that which can be said to be equal or unequal.[20] These characteristics do not depend on the notion of semantic anomaly. Finally, it is difficult to suppose that had Aristotle been concerned with semantic anomaly, he would have missed the glaring fact that to describe a shape as red or blue is semantically odd, even though both shape and colour belong to the same Aristotelian category, i.e. that of quality. Thus the linguistic interpretation can be safely rejected.

Let us proceed to the consideration of the interpretation put forward by Professor Ackrill.[21] According to this view Aristotle arrived at the list of categories in two ways. One of these is the sorting out of the different types of question that can be asked about substances. The other is to start by asking what any given thing is and to continue by repeating that question with reference to whatever the previous answer revealed. Both these approaches are supposed to come to an end when irreducible genera are reached. Ackrill thinks that the two ways are exemplified in *Topics* I 9. He does not find it surprising that they should result in the same list, with the exception that only the second brings particulars into the classification. He leaves open the question of completeness, since he does not think

20*Categories* 11a15–20 and 6a26.
21Ackrill, op. cit., pp. 78–81 [pp. 109–12].

that Aristotle had any grounds, in the form of a general argument or principle, on which he could have concluded that his list includes all and only irreducibly different genera.

This summary shows that Ackrill's account has an element in common with the "linguistic view." Both interpretations assume that the list of categories is arrived at by the consideration of questions, or classes of properties, concerning substances. The only evidence in favour of this assumption is the fact that Aristotle's examples seem to be about a substance, i.e. man. We must remember, however, that Aristotle employed the category-structure in his attempt to show substances to be prior to all else. Thus if we accept this hypothesis, we must attribute to him the grand design of outlining a set of categories by classifying questions about substances, and then using this structure to show that substances are prior to all entities collected under the other categories. Such an outrageously question-begging procedure should not be attributed to any philosopher except in the face of overwhelming evidence. After all, the use of a pattern such as the one under consideration would make proofs of ontological priority surprisingly easy. For example, one could collect all the questions which can be raised about shadows, classify the relevant predicates gathered through the answers to these questions, and conclude that the items in the categories thus formed are posterior to shadows since they are specifications of shadows. As long as Aristotle's general account of his list and his characterizations of the several categories lend themselves to alternative accounts, which avoid such question-begging, these alternatives should be explored.

This objection leads to the observation that it would be surprising indeed if the two approaches described by Ackrill were to yield the same list. Why should the classification of the aspects of one kind of entity, e.g.

substance, coincide with an exhaustive classification of the essences of all entities that make up reality? Would this be true also of other types of entity, such as events, qualities, numbers, etc.? Such a correlation will not hold unless one views everything as a modification or relational accident of the type of entity preferred. These ways of viewing things are trivial.

Ackrill's second way of arriving at the list of categories also contains an inherent weakness. For there are an indeterminate number of ways in which we can classify things by the repeated asking of the question: What is it? Furthermore, how could one decide whether the highest genera have been reached? Intuitions, as we saw, are not enough. To take one of Aristotle's examples, why should one not arrive at change (*kinésis*) as one of the categories? It certainly answers a "what is it?" question. Yet, as we know, Aristotle does not think that this is one of the categories; on the contrary, he thinks that the list of categories must be presupposed by the adequate analysis of this concept which shows it to be cutting across three categories.

It does not, therefore, seem likely that Aristotle arrived at his list in either of the ways that Ackrill suggests. In view of this we should take a look at the passage in the *Topics* (103b22 ff.)—mentioned above —which Ackrill construes as containing the second way of arriving at the list. It states, among other things, that the essence of anything will be found in one of the categories. This statement does not entail Ackrill's second approach, but only that the categories make up such an exhaustive classification of reality that no real essence will cut across categories. Thus it is consistent with the possible claim that there are irreducible ultimate genera within the categories, or that the categories could be reduced in number. Most importantly, the statement is only a necessary condition for the correct list of categories; in itself it does not provide a procedure for arriving at the list. Nor does it give a principle of unity for the list of categories.

In turning to the more constructive task of spelling out a plausible alternative interpretation, let us begin by noting—partly on the basis of the negative discussion above—some necessary conditions for any adequate interpretation. These conditions arise out of the ways in which Aristotle employs the list of categories in his philosophizing.[22] The passages quoted previously from the *Topics*, *Physics*, and *Metaphysics*, together with *Metaphysics* 1017a, show that Aristotle uses the list in his analyses of key concepts such as being and change, and also in his claiming priority for substances. Thus the list has to be complete in the following ways: (i) It must be exhaustive of all that Aristotle takes to be existing. (ii) No reduction of the number of categories should be possible without violating the principle upon which the list is constructed. (iii) No further subdivision of the categories should be possible without violating the constitutive principle. Without these conditions Aristotle could not claim that *kinésis* can be found in exactly three categories, or that by saying that 'is' has as many senses as there are categories he is giving a significant characterization of being.

These conditions help in resolving the question whether the categories include only universals, or particulars as well. Underlying this issue is the debate whether there are particulars and universals in each category, or only universals in all but the first.[23] It is difficult to conceive of each category as containing universals; for example, what universal would correspond to 'in the Lyceum'? On the other hand, it is equally difficult to conceive of particulars falling under

[22]"Da endlich jede Lehre erst in ihren Folgen ihre Stärke und Schwäche offenbart, so wird es wichtig sein, die Kategorien in der Anwendung zu beobachten." Trendelenburg, op. cit., p. 11.

[23]See Ross, op. cit., p. 28, n. 20.

each category. What particulars would we find under the category of relation? The conditions laid down above do not entail that each category must contain both universals and particulars; they entail rather, that the categories jointly must contain all the universals and particulars that Aristotle would acknowledge as existing. This leaves open the possibility that in some categories there may be only universals, in some only particulars, and in some both. In any case, events, processes, and abstract entities such as numbers must be contained within the categories. The analysis of *kinésis*, and the explanation of the category of quantity reveals how Aristotle conceived of this inclusion.

The constitutive principle which we seek is likely to be one that shows how the categories make up classes of predicates (in a very wide sense of 'predicate') to each of which some type of entity must be related. Apart from the issue of question-begging, our conditions of completeness guarantee that the type in question cannot be that of substance; for in order to be a sensible substance an entity must have both shape and weight, and these two properties fall under the same Aristotelian category of quality. Thus if the categories are those classes of predicates of which substances must partake, then the list as we have it would have to be subdivided to put weight and shape into different categories, a violation of the completeness conditions.

A more adequate interpretation can be given, based partly on Bonitz's suggestion[24] that Aristotle's list yields a survey of what is given in sense experience, and that each entity thus given must be related to some item in each of the categories. According to this interpretation the constitutive principle of the list of categories is that they constitute those classes of items to each of which any sensible particular—substantial or otherwise—must be related. Any sensible particular, sub-

[24]Bonitz, op. cit., pp. 18, 35, and 55.

stance, event, sound, etc. must be related to some substance; it must have some quality and quantity; it must
have relational properties, it must be related to times
and places; and it is placed within a network of causal
chains and laws, thus being related to the categories
of affecting and being affected. The only categories of
the complete list of ten that cause difficulties for this
interpretation are those of "having" and of "being-in-
a-position." In this connection the following should
be noted. First, these two categories are not always
included in the list Aristotle gives. Secondly, 'have'
is taken by Aristotle—as chapter 15 of the *Categories*
shows—in a variety of senses, one of which is the sense
of "having" parts. Given this construction, all sensible
particulars relate to that category. The category of
"position" is an obscure one, and it causes difficulties
for any interpretation, including the ones surveyed
critically above.

This proposed interpretation meets the completeness
conditions stated above. Neither a reduction nor a further subdivision would leave the list as definitive of
that to which sensible particulars must be related. The
account also meets the exhaustiveness condition, at
least as far as Aristotle is concerned. For the Stagirite
believed that all properties, including the second-order
ones, are ultimately related to what is presented by our
senses. Finally, this account construes the list of categories as the proper background for Aristotle's investigations of being, change, and priority relations. If it is
question-begging, it is so only in the same way that
one might construe Aristotle's general preference for
what is presented to the senses—a preference never
defended—as question-begging. Thus this interpretation
fulfills the promise made at the beginning of this paper;
we have shown how the list of categories can be construed as part of a theory and how this in turn serves
as a background for other Aristotelian theories.

Conclusion. The theory of categories is partly a theory about language and partly a theory about reality. With regard to language it states that certain elements of a language have key-designating roles, the full understanding of which requires that we understand the designata as falling within those classes which jointly form the set definitive of that to which a sensible particular must be related. We can see from this that Aristotle did not think of the structure of language as mirroring the structure of reality. But he did believe that there are specific items of language and reality the correlation of which forms the crucial link between the two.

III. METAPHYSICS

ESSENCE AND ACCIDENT

IRVING M. COPI

The notions of essence and accident play important and unobjectionable roles in pre-analytic or pre-philosophical thought and discourse. These roles are familiar, and need no elaboration here. Philosophers cannot ignore them, but must either explain them or (somehow) explain them away. My interest is in explaining them.

If they are taken seriously, the notions of essence and accident seem to me most appropriately discussed within the framework of a metaphysic of substance, which I shall accordingly assume. The account of essence and accident that I wish to set forth and argue for derives very largely from Aristotle, although it is not strictly Aristotelian. Where it differs from Aristotle's account it does so in order to accommodate some of the insights formulated by Locke in his discussion of "real" and "nominal" essences. My discussion is to be located, then, against the background of a substance metaphysic and a realist epistemology. The theory of essence and accident to be proposed seems to me not only to fit the demands of the general philosophical position mentioned, but also to be consistent with the apparent requirements of contemporary scientific development. I wish to begin my discussion with some historical remarks.

From *The Journal of Philosophy*, LI (1954), 706–19. Reprinted by permission of the author and editor of *The Journal of Philosophy*.

The earliest Western philosophers were much concerned with change and permanence, taking positions so sharply opposed that the issue appeared to be more paradox than problem. If an object which changes really changes, then it cannot literally be one and the same object which undergoes the change. But if the changing thing retains its identity, then it cannot really have changed. Small wonder that early cosmologists divided into warring factions, each embracing a separate horn of their common dilemma, the one denying permanence of any sort, the other denying the very possibility of change.

Aristotle discussed this problem in several of his treatises, bringing to bear on it not only his superb dialectical skill but an admirable, common-sense, dogged insistence that some things do maintain their identity while undergoing change. To explain the observed facts he was led to distinguish different kinds of change. A man does retain his identity though his complexion may change from ruddy to pale, or though he may move from one place to another. He is the same man though he become corpulent in middle life or his sinews shrink with age. In these types of change, called *alteration, locomotion, growth,* and *diminution,* the changing thing remains substantially or essentially what it was before changing.

Another type of change, however, was admitted to be more thoroughgoing. To take, for example, an artificial substance, we can say that if a wooden table is not just painted or moved, but destroyed by fire, we have neither alteration, locomotion, growth, nor diminution alone, but *substantial* change. The characteristic mark of substantial change is that the object undergoing the change does not survive that change or persist through it, but is destroyed in the process. The ashes (and gas and radiant energy) that appear in place of the burned table are not an altered, moved, or larger or smaller table, but no table at all. In substantial change its essential property of being a table disappears.

It seems clear that distinguishing these different kinds of change involves distinguishing different kinds of attributes. The basic dichotomy between substantial change and other kinds of change is parallel to that between essential attributes or *essences*, and other kinds of attributes, which may be lumped together as accidental attributes or *accidents*. (Here we diverge rather sharply from at least one moment of Aristotle's own terminology, in ignoring the intermediate category of "property" or "proprium.")

Of the various bases that have been proposed for distinguishing between essence and accident, two stand out as most reasonable. The first has already been implied. If we can distinguish the different kinds of change, then we can say that a given attribute is essential to an object if its loss would result in the destruction of that object, whereas an attribute is a mere accident if the object would remain identifiably and substantially the same without it. This basis for distinguishing between essence and accident, although helpful heuristically, is not adequate philosophically, for it seems to me that the distinctions among these kinds of change presuppose those among the different kinds of attributes.

The other, more satisfactory basis for distinguishing essence from accident is an epistemological or methodological one. Knowledge of the essence of a thing is said to be more important than knowledge of its other attributes. In the *Metaphysics* Aristotle wrote: "... we know each thing most fully, when we know what it is, e.g. what man is or what fire is, rather than when we know its quality, its quantity, or its place...."[1] It is the essence that is intended here, for a subsequent passage explains that: "... the essence is precisely what

[1] 1028a37–1028b2. Quotations are from the Oxford translation.

something *is*. . . ."[2] It is perhaps an understatement to say that Aristotle held knowledge of essence to be "more important" than knowledge of accidents, for he later says explicitly that: ". . . to *know* each thing . . . is just to know its essence. . . ."[3] And if we confine our attention to scientific knowledge, Aristotle repeatedly assures us that there is no knowledge of accidents at all,[4] but only of essences.[5]

Aristotle was led to draw an ontological conclusion from the foregoing epistemological doctrine. If some attributes of objects are epistemologically significant and others are not, the implication is that the former constitute the real natures of those objects, whereas the latter can be relegated to some less ultimate category. I must confess that I am in sympathy with the realist position which underlies and justifies such an inference, but to expound it in detail would take us too far afield.

As a biologist Aristotle was led to classify things into genera and species, holding that things belong to the same species if and only if they share a common essence. In remarking this fact we need not commit ourselves to any position with respect to the systematic or genetic priority of either logic or biology in Aristotle's thought. He apparently believed these species to be fixed and limited, and tended to ignore whatever could not be conveniently classified within them, holding, for example, that "the production of a mule by a horse" was "contrary to nature,"[6] a curious phrase. Some modern writers have tended to regard this shortcoming as fatal to the Aristotelian system. Thus Susan Stebbing wrote: "Modern theories of organic evolution have

[2]1030a1.
[3]1031b20.
[4]1026b4; 1027a20, 28; 1064b30; 1065a4. Cf. also *Posterior Analytics* 75a18–22.
[5]75a28–30.
[6]1033b33. But cf. 770b9–13.

combined with modern theories of mathematics to destroy the basis of the Aristotelian conception of essence. . . ."[7] It seems to me, however, that the fixity of species is a casual rather than an integral part of the Aristotelian system, which in its broad outlines as a metaphysical framework can be retained and rendered adequate to the most contemporary of scientific developments. A not dissimilar objection was made by Dewey, who wrote that: "In Aristotelian cosmology, ontology and logic . . . all quantitative determinations were relegated to the state of *accidents*, so that apprehension of them had no scientific standing. . . . Observe by contrast the place occupied by measuring in modern knowledge. Is it then credible that the logic of Greek knowledge has relevance to the logic of modern knowledge?"[8] But the Aristotelian notion of essence *can* admit of quantitative determination, as is suggested by Aristotle himself in admitting ratio as essence.[9] Hence I do not think that this criticism of Dewey's can be regarded as any more decisive than that of Miss Stebbing.

Having set forth in outline an Aristotelian philosophy of essence and accident, I propose next to examine what I consider to be the most serious objection that has been raised against it. According to this criticism, the distinction between essence and accident is not an objective or intrinsic one between genuinely different types of attributes. Attributes are really all of the same basic kind, it is said, and the alleged distinction between essence and accident is simply a projection of differences in human interests or a reflection of peculiarities of vocabulary. Let us try to understand this criticism in as sympathetic a fashion as we can.

The distinction between different kinds of change,

---

[7] *A Modern Introduction to Logic*, p. 433.
[8] *Logic: The Theory of Inquiry*, pp. 89–90.
[9] 993a17–20.

on this view, is subjective rather than objective. We happen to be interested, usually, in some attributes of a thing more than in others. When the thing changes, we say that it persists through the change provided that it does not lose those attributes by whose possession it satisfies our interests. For example, our interest in tables is for the most part independent of their colors. Hence that interest remains satisfiable by a given table regardless of any alteration it may suffer with respect to color. Paint a brown table green, and it remains substantially or essentially the same; the change was only an accidental one. If our interests were different, the same objective fact would be classified quite differently. Were our interest to lie in *brown* tables exclusively, then the application of green paint would destroy the object of our interest, would change it substantially or essentially from something which satisfied our interest to something which did not. The implication is that attributes are neither essential nor accidental in themselves, but can be so classified only on the basis of our subjective interests in them. Dewey stated this point of view very succinctly, writing: "As far as present logical texts still continue to talk about essences, properties and accidents as something inherently different from one another, they are repeating distinctions that once had an ontological meaning and that no longer have it. Anything is 'essential' which is indispensable in a given inquiry and anything is 'accidental' which is superfluous."[10]

The present criticism lends itself easily to reformulation in more language-oriented terms. That we regard a table as essentially the same despite alteration in color or movement from place to place is a consequence of the peculiar nature and limitations of our vocabulary, which has a single word for tables, regardless of color, but lacks special words for tables of dif-

[10]Op. cit., p. 138.

ferent colors. Suppose that our language contained no word for tables in general, but had instead—say—the word "towble" for brown table and the word "teeble" for green table. Then the application of green paint to a towble would be said to change it essentially, it might be argued, for no towble would remain; in its place would appear a teeble. Or if there were a single word which applied indiscriminately to tables and heaps of ashes, say "tashble," with no special substantive denoting either of them univocally, then perhaps the destruction of a table by fire would not be regarded as an essential change. That which appeared at the end of the process would admittedly be in a different state from what was there at the start, but it would still be identifiably the same tashble. C. I. Lewis regards the difference between essence and accident to be strictly relative to vocabulary, writing: "Traditionally any attribute required for application of a term is said to be of the essence of the thing named. It is, of course, meaningless to speak of the essence of a thing except relative to its being named by a particular term."[11]

I think that for our purpose these two criticisms can be regarded as variants of a single basic one, for the connection between human interests and human vocabulary is a very intimate one. It is an anthropological and linguistic commonplace that the concern of a culture with a given phenomenon is reflected in the vocabulary of that culture, as in the several Eskimo words which denote subtly different kinds of snow. In our own culture new interests lead continually to innovations in vocabulary; and surely it is the decline of interest in certain things that leads to the obsolescence of words used to refer to them.

Both variants of this criticism were formulated long ago by Locke, and developed at considerable length in his *Essay*. Locke paid comparatively little attention

[11]*An Analysis of Knowledge and Valuation,* p. 41.

to the problem of change, but where he did discuss it his treatment was very similar to Aristotle's. Thus we are assured in the *Essay* that: "... an oak growing from a plant to a great tree, and then lopped, is still the same oak; and a colt grown up to a horse, sometimes fat, sometimes lean, is all the while the same horse...."[12] The oak "... continues to be the same plant as long as it partakes of the same life ..."[13] and the identity of animals is explained in similar terms. Personal identity is explained in terms of sameness of consciousness.[14] If we ignore the Cartesian dualism implicit in that last case, and if we are not too critical of the reappearance of the term "same" in the explanation of *sameness*, we can recognize these answers to be the Aristotelian ones, for according to Aristotle the soul is the principle of life,[15] the life of a plant is the nutritive soul,[16] that of an animal its sensitive soul,[17] and that of man his rational soul,[18] these souls constituting the substantial forms or essences of the respective substances.[19] On the other hand, in his brief discussion of identity as applied to non-living things, Locke construes it very strictly to apply only to things which "... vary not at all...."[20] But the following passage has a characteristically Aristotelian flavor: "Thus that which was grass to-day, is to-morrow the flesh of a sheep; and within a few days after becomes part of a man: in all which, and the like changes, it is evident their real essence, i.e. that constitution,

[12]Bk. 2, ch. 27, §3.
[13]Ibid.
[14]Bk. 2, ch. 27, §8, §9, §10, §16, §17, §23.
[15]*De Anima* 402a6, 415b8.
[16]432a29, 434a22–26; cf. also *De Plantis* 815b28–34.
[17]432a30.
[18]*Politics* 1332b5.
[19]*De Anima* 412a20, 412b13, 415b10.
[20]Bk. 2, ch. 27, §1.

whereon the properties of these several things depended, is destroyed, and perishes with them."[21]

Despite this partial similarity of their views, the bases for distinguishing between the essential properties and other properties of a thing are very different for Locke than for Aristotle. For Aristotle, the distinction is twofold: first, the essential properties of an object are those which are retained by it during any change through which the object remains identifiably the same object; and second, the essential properties of an object are most important in our scientific knowledge of it. For Locke, on the other hand, the *real* essence of a thing is a set of properties which *determine* all the other properties of that thing.[22] Since all other properties depend on its real essence, any change in an object entails a change in its real essence. Hence for Locke the essential properties of an object are *not* retained by it during any change. This view is very different from Aristotle's, on which the accidents of a thing are not bound to its essence but can change independently of it. The epistemological difference is equally striking. Whereas for Aristotle all scientific knowledge is knowledge of the essence, for Locke there is no knowledge of the real essences of things.[23]

Locke was more interested in what he called "nominal essences," which are more nearly analogous to the Aristotelian notion of essence. Our idea of a particular substance, according to Locke, is a complex idea composed of a number of simple ideas which are noticed to "go constantly together," plus the notion of a substratum "wherein they do subsist."[24] A general or abstract idea of a sort or species of substance is made

---

[21]Bk. 3, ch. 4, §19. But cf. Bk. 3, ch. 6, §4, §5.
[22]Bk. 3, ch. 3, §15.
[23]Bk. 3, ch. 3, §15, §17, §18; ch. 6, §3, §6, §9, §12, §18, §49; ch. 9, §12; ch. 10, §18.
[24]Bk. 2, ch. 23, §1.

out of our complex ideas of various particular substances that resemble each other by leaving out "that which is peculiar to each" and retaining "only what is common to all."[25] Such an abstract idea *determines* a sort or species,[26] and is called a "nominal essence,"[27] for "every thing contained in that idea is essential to that sort."[28]

The properties contained in the nominal essence of a thing can be distinguished from the other properties of that thing on the same basis as that on which the Aristotelian essence is distinguished from accidents. In the first place, a particular substance of a given species can change with respect to some property whose idea is *not* included in the nominal essence of that species, and will continue to be recognizably the same thing; whereas it must be regarded as a quite different thing if it changes with respect to some property whose idea *is* included in the nominal essence.[29] And in the second place, the nominal essence is more important in knowledge than other properties. To have knowledge of a thing is to know what sort of thing it is, and to know the nominal essence is to know the sort. Locke says, moreover, that the leading qualities of a thing, that is, the most observable and hence, for Locke, the most knowable, are ingredient in the nominal essence.[30] Finally, it is argued in the *Essay* that knowledge of nominal essences is required if we are ever to be certain of the truth of any general proposition.[31] Since Locke's nominal essences play so similar a role to that of Aristotle's essences, Locke's arguments intended to prove their subjectivity and relativity to human interests and vocabulary can be interpreted as applying to Aristotle's notion as well as his own.

[25]Bk. 3, ch. 3, §7.
[26]Bk. 3, ch. 3, §12.
[27]Bk. 3, ch. 3, §15.
[28]Bk. 3, ch. 6, §2.

[29]Bk. 2, ch. 27, §28.
[30]Bk. 3, ch. 11, §20.
[31]Bk. 4, ch. 6, §4.

One fairly minor difference should be noted before going on. Since Locke's nominal essences are abstract ideas, they are immediately subjective in a way that Aristotle's essences are not. But that difference is not decisive, for substances may well have objective properties that nominal essences are ideas of, or objective powers that correspond to them exactly.[32]

Locke urges that essences are subjective in a less trivial sense. Since they are "inventions"[33] or the "workmanship"[34] of the understanding, different persons in fashioning abstract ideas which they signify by the same term can and do incorporate different simple ideas into them. Acts of choice or selection are involved here, and people do make different choices, as proved by the disputes that so frequently arise over whether particular bodies are of certain species or not.[35]

That essences are relative to vocabulary is argued by Locke in terms of an example: "A silent and a striking watch are but one species to those who have but one name for them: but he that has the name watch for one, and clock for the other, and distinct complex ideas, to which those names belong, to him they are different species."[36]

That the "... boundaries of species are as men, and not as nature, makes them ...,"[37] proved by the verbal disputes already referred to, is explained by the fact that since we have "... need of general names for present use ..."[38] we "... stay not for a perfect discovery of all those qualities which would best show us their most material differences and agreements; but we our-

---

[32]Bk. 2, ch. 23, §7.
[33]Bk. 3, ch. 3, §11.
[34]Bk. 3, ch. 3, §12, §13, §14.
[35]Bk. 3, ch. 3, § 14; ch. 6, § 26, § 27; ch. 9, § 16; ch. 10, § 22; ch. 11, §6, §7.
[36]Bk. 3, ch. 6, §39.
[37]Bk. 3, ch. 6, §30.
[38]Ibid.

selves divide them, by certain obvious appearances, into species. . . ."[39] Nominal essences are made for use, and different intended uses or interests will determine different essences. Even the *noticing* of similarities between distinct particulars is relative to our interest in them, so our selection of simple ideas for inclusion in a nominal essence is relative to such interests. These determining interests are not scientific, for as Locke observed, ". . . languages, in all countries, have been established long before sciences."[40] The situation is rather that the terms of ordinary discourse ". . . have for the most part, in all languages, received their birth and signification from ignorant and illiterate people. . . ."[41] And for the purposes or interests of those practical people, the properties selected by them as essential to the objects they deal with are adequate enough. For "Vulgar notions suit vulgar discourses; and both, though confused enough, yet serve pretty well the market and the wake."[42]

Now do these arguments succeed in establishing that the distinction between essence and accident is subjective rather than objective, that is, relative to human interests and vocabulary?

I think that the objections are not utterly destructive of the Aristotelian doctrine, although they do call attention to needed modifications of it. Locke's case, it seems to me, depends upon his distinction between real and nominal essences, and his belief that real essences are unknowable. But his doctrine that real essences cannot be known flows from two peculiarities of his philosophy, which I see no reason to accept. One of the bases for his belief that real essences are unknowable is his view that the only objects of our knowledge are the ideas that we have in our minds.[43] Locke's

[39]Ibid.
[40]Bk. 3, ch. 6, §25.
[41]Ibid.

[42]Bk. 3, ch. 11, §10.
[43]Bk. 2, ch. 1, §1.

other basis for his belief that real essences are unknowable is his doctrine that experiment and observation
yield only "... judgment and opinion, not knowledge...."[44] Here the term "knowledge" is reserved for
what is *certain*.

I would reject these two doctrines on the following
grounds. The first of them, that knowledge is only
of ideas, is the germ of scepticism. Locke's premisses
lead necessarily to Hume's conclusions, and the partial
scepticism we find explicitly set forth in Locke is but
a fragment of the complete scepticism that Hume
later showed to be implicitly contained there. It seems
to me that if a philosophy denies the very possibility
of scientific knowledge, then so much the worse for
that philosophy. As for reserving the term "knowledge"
for what is certain, that usage has but little to com-
mend it. It seems more reasonable to accept the results
of experiment and observation, although probable
rather than demonstrative, as knowledge nonetheless.

It must be admitted that the doctrine of the unknowability of real essences was not an unreasonable
conclusion to draw from the relatively undeveloped
state of science in Locke's day. For chemistry, at least,
if we can believe what is said of it in the *Essay*, was
in a very bad way in the seventeenth century. Locke
tells us of the "sad experience" of chemists "... when
they, sometimes in vain, seek for the same qualities
in one parcel of sulphur, antimony or vitriol, which
they have found in others. For though they are bodies
of the same species, having the same nominal essence,
under the same name; yet do they often, upon severe
ways of examination, betray qualities so different one
from another, as to frustrate the expectations of very
wary chemists."[45]

Contemporary science, however, presents a quite dif-

44Bk. 4, ch. 12, §10; cf. also Bk. 4, ch. 3, §28.
45Bk. 3, ch. 6, §8.

ferent picture. Locke characterized the (allegedly un-knowable) real essences of things as the "...constitu-tion of their insensible parts; from which flow those sensible qualities, which serve us to distinguish them one from another...."[46] Now modern atomic theory is directly concerned with the insensible parts of things. Through the use of his Periodic Table, interpreted as dealing with atomic number and valency, "...Men-deléev was enabled to predict the existence *and proper-ties* ..." of half a dozen elements whose existence had not been previously known or even suspected.[47] And other scientists have subsequently been able to make similar predictions. Modern science seeks to know the *real* essences of things, and its increasing successes seem to be bringing it progressively nearer to that goal.

It must be granted that Locke's distinction between real and nominal essence is a helpful one, even though it is not absolute. The construction of nominal essences is usually relative to practical interests, and the or-dinary notion of the essence of a thing is relative to the words used in referring to it. I think that Locke (and Dewey and Lewis) are correct in that contention. Surely different interests lead different people to clas-sify or sort things in different ways, and thus to adopt different nominal essences, the more permanently use-ful of which receive separate names in ordinary lan-guage. Thus it is that: "Merchants and lovers, cooks and taylors, have words wherewithal to dispatch their ordinary affairs...."[48]

The distinction, however, is not absolute. Not every interest is narrowly practical. The interest of the scien-tist is in knowledge and understanding. The scientist desires to know how things behave, and to account

[46]Bk. 3, ch. 3, §17.
[47]J. D. Main Smith, in the *Encyclopaedia Britannica* (14th ed.; 1947), Vol. 17, p. 520 (my italics).
[48]Bk. 3, ch. 11, §10.

for their behavior by means of explanatory hypotheses or theories which permit him to predict what will occur under specified conditions. He is interested in discovering general laws to which objects conform, and the causal relations which obtain among them. The scientist's sorting or classifying of objects is relative to this interest, which is not well served by classifying things on the basis of properties which are either most obvious or most immediately practical. It is better served by classifying things in terms of properties which are relevant to the framing of a maximum number of causal laws and the formulation of explanatory theories. Thus a foodstuff and a mineral source of aluminum, common salt and cryolite, are both classified by the chemist as sodium compounds, because in the context of modern chemical theory it is this common characteristic which is most significant for predicting and understanding the behavior of these substances. In the sphere of scientific inquiry, the distinction between real and nominal essence tends to disappear. The scientist's classification of things is intended to be in terms of their *real* essences. And here, too, the process is reflected in vocabulary, not necessarily or even usually in that of the man in the street, but rather in the technical jargon of the specialist.

The essences which science seeks to discover, then, are real essences rather than nominal ones. Since the arguments for subjectivity or relativity to interest or vocabulary were concerned with nominal rather than real essences, they simply do not apply to real essences as either Locke or Aristotle conceived them.

In one passage of his *Essay*, though, Locke does make the further claim that even a real essence relates to a sort and supposes a species.[49] But on Locke's own account of real essence, the real essence of a particular must be that set of its properties on which all of its

[49]Bk. 3, ch. 6, §6.

other properties depend. And that can be investigated independently of any sorting or classifying we may do —although once its real essence is discovered, that will determine how we should classify it scientifically if the occasion for doing so arises.

At this point let me indicate the direction in which I think the Aristotelian doctrine of essence and accident might well be modified. Aristotle definitely held that there could be no scientific knowledge of accidents,[50] but contemporary science would admit no such limitation. It seems to me that both Locke's and Aristotle's views about unknowability should be rejected. Contrary to Locke, I should hold that real essences are in principle knowable, and contrary to Aristotle, I should hold that non-essential or accidental properties can also be objects of scientific knowledge.

It seems to me also that neither Locke nor Aristotle gives a satisfactory account of the relationship between essence and accident. For Locke, all (other) properties of a thing depend on its "real constitution" or real essence[51]; but it is not clear whether the dependence is supposed to be causal or logico-deductive. The former is obviously the more acceptable doctrine. Aristotle, on the other hand, held that some properties of a thing, namely, its accidents, do not in any way depend upon its essence. I think that Locke's view, understood as asserting a causal dependence of accident on essence, is the more plausible one, and that the Aristotelian doctrine ought to be so modified as to accord with that of Locke in this respect.

Now if both essences and accidents are scientifically knowable, on what basis are they to be distinguished from each other? I suggest that the epistemological or methodological distinction is still valid. For example,

[50]1064b30–1065a25.
[51]Bk. 3, ch. 3, §18.

common salt has many properties, some more obvious
than others, and some more important than others
relative to different practical interests. The scientist
singles out its being a compound of equal parts of
sodium and chlorine as its essential nature. In doing
so he surely does not mean to imply that its chemical
constitution is more easily observed than its other
properties, or more important to either cook, tailor,
merchant, or lover. He classifies it as sodium chloride
because, within the context of his theory, that property
is fundamental. From its chemical formula more of
its properties can be inferred than could be from any
other. Since the connection is causal rather than logical, the inference from essence to accident must make
use of causal law premises or modes of inference as
well as strictly logical ones. Hence to derive conclusions about *all* accidental properties of a substance, we
should need to know both its real essence and all relevant causal laws. That is an ideal towards which
science strives, rather than its present achievement, of
course. To the extent to which one small group of
properties of a substance can serve as a basis from
which its other properties can be causally derived, to
that extent we can be justified in identifying that group
of properties as its real essence. This view, it should
be noted, is in agreement with Aristotle's doctrine that
the definition of a thing should state its essence,[52] and
that definition is a scientific process.[53]

There is a certain relativity implied in this account,
although it is quite different from those previously
discussed. Our *notion* of what constitutes the real essence of a thing is relative to the science of our day.
Centuries hence, wiser men will have radically different
and more adequate theories, and their notions will be
closer approximations than ours to the real essences

[52]91a1, 101b21, 38.
[53]1039b32.

of things. But it will still be the real essences of things that are destined to be known by Peirce's ultimate community of knowers.

There is one other and more radical sense of accident that I would agree to be relative. Each separate science is concerned with only some of the properties or aspects of things which it studies. Those left out will be accidental relative to the special science which ignores them. They will not be derivable from what that science considers to be the real essences of those things, although a different special science might be much concerned with them, and even include them in *its* notion of the thing's real essence. But as (and if) the sciences become more unified, no properties of a thing will be wholly accidental in this sense, and all will be causally derivable from the real essence.

In closing, I should like to refer once again to the topic of change. If all of a thing's properties depend on its real essence, then it would seem to follow that every change is an essential one. In my opinion, that unwelcome conclusion can be evaded in two ways. In the first place, with respect to common-sense, practical usage, our ordinary sortings will continue to be based on nominal rather than real essences, so that changes can continue to be classified as accidental or essential in the traditional way. And in the second place, with respect to scientific usage, we can say the following. The real essence of a thing will consist very largely of powers or, in modern terms, dispositional properties. An essential change in a thing will involve the replacement of some of its dispositions or powers by other dispositions or powers. But a change which is non-essential or accidental would involve no such replacement; it would rather consist in differently actualized manifestations of the same dispositional property or power. Unfortunately, lack of space prevents an adequate development of this suggestion.

ΤΙΘΕΝΑΙ ΤΑ ΦΑΙΝΟΜΕΝΑ

G. E. L. OWEN

The first part of this paper tries to account for an apparent discrepancy between Aristotle's preaching and his practice on a point of method. The second part reinforces the first by suggesting a common source for many of the problems and methods found in the *Physics*.

I

There seems to be a sharp discrepancy between the methods of scientific reasoning recommended in the *Analytics* and those actually followed in the *Physics*. The difference is sometimes taken to lie in the fact that the *Posterior Analytics* pictures a science as a formal deductive system based on necessary truths whereas the *Physics* is more tentative and hospitable both in its premisses and in its methods. But this is too simple a contrast. It is true that for much of the *Physics* Aristotle is not arguing from the definitions of his basic terms but constructing those definitions. He sets out to clarify and harden such common ideas as change and motion, place and time, infinity and continuity, and in doing so he claims to be defining

From *Aristote et les problèmes de la méthode* (Symposium Aristotelicum; Louvain, 1961), pp. 83–103. Reprinted by permission of the author and Editions Nauwelaerts, S.P.R.L., Louvain.

his subject matter.[1] But after all the *Analytics* shows interest not only in the finished state of a science but in its essential preliminaries; it describes not only the rigorous deduction of theorems but the setting up of the ἀρχαί, the set of special hypotheses and definitions, from which the deductions proceed. And the *Physics*, for its part, not only establishes the definitions of its basic concepts but uses them to deduce further theorems, notably in books VI and VIII. The discrepancy between the two works lies rather in the fact that, whereas the *Analytics* tries (though not without confusion and inconsistency) to distinguish the two processes of finding and then applying the principles, the *Physics* takes no pains to hold them apart. But there seems to be a more striking disagreement than this. It concerns the means by which the principles of the science are reached.

In the *Prior Analytics* Aristotle says: "It falls to experience to provide the principles of any subject. In astronomy, for instance, it was astronomical experience that provided the principles of the science, for it was only when the *phainomena* were adequately grasped that the proofs in astronomy were discovered. And the same is true of any art or science whatever."[2] Elsewhere he draws the same Baconian picture: the *phainomena* must be collected as a prelude to finding the theory which explains them. The method is expressly associated with φυσική and the φυσικός,[3] and from the stock example in these contexts—astronomy—it seems clear

[1]*Phs.* III 1, 200b12–21.
[2]*An. Pr.* I 30, 46a17–22: διὸ τὰς μὲν ἀρχὰς περὶ ἕκαστον ἐμπειρίας ἐστὶ παραδοῦναι, λέγω δ' οἷον τὴν ἀστρολογικὴν μὲν ἐμπειρίαν τῆς ἀστρολογικῆς ἐπιστήμης (ληφθέντων γὰρ ἱκανῶς τῶν φαινομένων οὕτως εὑρέθησαν αἱ ἀστρολογικαὶ ἀποδείξεις), ὁμοίως δὲ καὶ περὶ ἄλλην ὁποιανοῦν ἔχει τέχνην τε καὶ ἐπιστήμην.
[3]*De Part. Anim.* I 1, 639b5–10 with 640a13–15; *De Caelo* III 7, 306a5–17.

that the *phainomena* in question are empirical observations.[4] Now such a method is plainly at home in the biological works and the meteorology;[5] equally plainly it is not at home in the *Physics*, where as Mgr. Mansion observes "tout s'y réduit en général à des analyses plus ou moins poussées de concepts,—analyses guidées souvent et illustrées par des données de l'expérience, plutôt qu'appuyées sur celle-ci."[6] In this sense of "*phainomena*" it would be grossly misleading for Aristotle to claim that he is establishing the principles of his physics upon a survey of the *phainomena*. And there his critics are often content to leave the matter.

But in other contexts similarly concerned with methods of enquiry "*phainomena*" has another sense.[7] In the *Nicomachean Ethics* Aristotle prefaces his discussion of incontinence with the words: "Here as in other cases we must set down the *phainomena* and begin by considering the difficulties, and so go on to vindicate if possible all the common conceptions about these states of mind, or at any rate most of them and the most important."[8] Here Sir David Ross translates φαινόμενα by "observed facts," a translation evidently designed to bring Aristotle's programme into conform-

[4]Cf. further *An. Po.* I 13, 78b39 with 79a2–6; *De Caelo* II 13, 293a23–30; 14, 297a2–6; *Met.* A 8, 1073b32–38; Bonitz, *Index*, 809a34 ff.

[5]*De Part. Anim.* II 1, 646a8–12, referring to *Hist. Anim.* I 7, 491a7–14; *Meteor.* III 2, 371b18–22 with Olympiodorus' scholium (217.23–27 Stueve. Olympiodorus' reference to *De Gen. et Corr.* is to I 5, not II 8 as Stueve and Ideler think).

[6]*Introduction à la physique aristolélicienne²*, p. 211.

[7]There is a temptation to distinguish this sense as what φαίνεται εἶναι by contrast with what φαίνεται ὄν. But this overstates the difference; see pp. 174–76 below. Aristotle is ready to use φαίνεσθαι with the infinitive even of empirical observations, *De An.* I 5, 411b19–22.

[8]*NE* VII 1, 1145b2–6:   δεῖ δ', ὥσπερ ἐπὶ τῶν ἄλλων, τιθέντας τὰ φαινόμενα καὶ πρῶτον διαπορήσαντας οὕτω δεικνύναι μάλιστα μὲν πάντα τὰ ἔνδοξα περὶ ταῦτα τὰ πάθη, εἰ δὲ μή, τὰ πλεῖστα καὶ κυριώτατα.

ity with such passages as those already cited. But this can hardly be its sense here. For, in the first place, what Aristotle proceeds to set out are not the observed facts but the ἔνδοξα, the common conceptions on the subject (as the collocation of φαινόμενα and ἔνδοξα in his preface would lead us to expect). He concludes his survey with the words τὰ μὲν οὖν λεγόμενα ταῦτ' ἐστίν,[9] and the λεγόμενα turn out as so often to be partly matters of linguistic usage or, if you prefer, of the conceptual structure revealed by language.[10] And, secondly, after this preliminary survey Aristotle turns to Socrates' claim that those who act against their own conviction of what is best do so in ignorance, and says that this is plainly in conflict with the *phainomena*.[11] But he does not mean that, as Ross translates it, "the view plainly contradicts the observed facts." For he remarks later that his own conclusion about incontinence seems to coincide with what Socrates wanted to maintain,[12] and in reaching it he takes care to answer the question that he had named as a difficulty for Socrates, namely what kind of ignorance must be ascribed to the incontinent man.[13] So Socrates' claim conflicts not with the facts but with what would commonly be said on the subject, and Aristotle does not undertake to save everything that is commonly said. He is anxious, unlike Socrates, to leave a use for the expression "knowing what is right but doing what is wrong," but he is ready to show a *priori* that there is no use for the expression "doing what is wrong in the full knowledge of what is right *in the given circumstances*."[14] It is in the same sense of the word that

9Ibid. 2, 1145b8–20.
10Especially Ibid. 1145b10–15, 19–20.
11NE VII 3, 1145b27–28.
12Ibid. 5, 1147b14–15.
13Ibid. 3, 1145b28–29; 5, 1147b15–17.
14Ibid. 5, 1146b35–1147a10, 1147a24–b14. But Ross's translation of φαινόμενα in the two passages 1, 1145b3 and 3,

all dialectical argument can be said to start from the *phainomena*.[15]

This ambiguity in φαινόμενα, which was seen by Alexander,[16] carries with it a corresponding distinction in the use of various connected expressions. Ἐπαγωγή can be said to establish the principles of science by starting from the data of perception.[17] Yet ἐπαγωγή is named as one of the two cardinal methods of dialectic[18] and as such must begin from the ἔνδοξα, what is accepted by all or most men or by the wise;[19] and in this form too it can be used to find the principles of the sciences.[20] Similarly with the ἀπορίαι. When the φαινόμενα are empirical data such as those collected in the biology and meteorology, the ἀπορίαι associated with them will tend to be questions of empirical fact[21] or of the explanation of such facts,[22] or the problem of squaring a recalcitrant fact with an empirical hypothesis.[23] In the discussion of incontinence, on the other hand, where the φαινόμενα are things that men are inclined or accustomed to say on

---

1145b28 is at any rate consistent and so superior to that adopted by most scholars from Heliodorus to Gauthier-Jolif, who see that at its first occurrence the word must mean ἔνδοξα (τοὺς δοκοῦντας περὶ αὐτῶν λόγους. Heliodorus *Paraphr.* 131.16 Heylbut) but suppose that at its occurrence 25 lines later it means the unquestionable facts (τοῖς φανεροῖς, ibid. 137.29–30).

[15]*An. Pr.* I 1, 24b10–12; *Top.* VIII 5, 159b17–23. Cf. *Ph.* IV 1, 208a32–34, where the *phainomenon* is the theory as contrasted with the facts (τὰ ὑπάρχοντα). At *De Caelo* II 5, 288a1–2; 12, 291b25; IV 1, 308a6; *De Part. Anim.* I 5, 645a5, it is the speaker's own view.

[16]*Meteor.* 33.6–9 Stueve.

[17]*An. Po.* II 19, 100b3–5; I 18, 81a38–b9.

[18]*Top.* I 12, 105a10–19.

[19]*Top.* I 1, 100b21–23.

[20]*Top.* I 2, 101a36–b4.

[21]*Meteor.* II 3, 357b26–30.

[22]*Meteor.* I 13, 349a12–14 with a 31-b2; II 5, 362a11–13; *De long. et brev vitae* 1, 464b21–30; *De Gen. Anim.* IV 4, 770b 28–30 with 771a14–17; *Hist. Anim.* VI 37, 580b14–17.

[23]*Meteor.* II 2, 355b20–32.

the subject, the ἀπορίαι that Aristotle sets out are not unexplained or recalcitrant data of observation but logical or philosophical puzzles generated, as such puzzles have been at all times, by exploiting some of the things commonly said. Two of the paradoxes are veterans, due to Socrates and the sophists.[24] The first of the set ends with the words "If so, we shall have to say that the man of practical wisdom is incontinent, *but no one would say this*" (not that it happens to be false, but that given the established use of the words it is absurd).[25] The last ends "But we say (i.e. it is a common form of words) that some men are incontinent, without further qualification."[26]

Now if the *Physics* is to be described as setting out from a survey of the φαινόμενα it is plainly this second sense of the word that is more appropriate. Take as an example the analysis of place. It opens with four arguments for the existence of place of which the first states what δοκεῖ (it appeals to established ways of talking about physical replacement),[27] the third states what certain theorists λέγουσι,[28] the fourth quotes what Hesiod and the majority νομίζουσι,[29] and the remaining one relies on the doctrine of natural places which is later taken as an ἔνδοξον.[30] Of the ἀπορίαι which follow, one is due to Zeno, one is due to an equally rich source of logical paradoxes of which I shall say more in a later section, and all ultimately depend on the convictions or usage of the many or the wise. Nor are these arguments merely accessory to the main

[24]*NE* VII 3, 1145b23–27, 1146a21–31.
[25]Ibid. 1146a5–7.
[26]Ibid. 1146b4–5.
[27]*Ph*. IV 1, 208b1, 5.
[28]Ibid. 208b26.
[29]Ibid. 208b32–33.
[30]*Ph*. IV 1, 208b8–25; 4, 211a4–6 with Ross's note on 5, 212b29–34 (*Aristotle's Physics*, p. 580).

analysis: those of the δοκοτῦνα which survive the preliminary difficulties are taken over as premises for what follows.[31] "For if the difficulties are resolved and the ἔνδοξα are left standing," as Aristotle says in both the *Physics* and the *Ethics*, "this in itself is a sufficient proof."[32] As for ἐπαγωγή, when it is used in the argument it proves to be not a review of observed cases but a dialectical survey of the senses of the word "in."[33]

By such arguments the *Physics* ranks itself not with physics, in our sense of the word, but with philosophy. Its data are for the most part the materials not of natural history but of dialectic, and its problems are accordingly not questions of empirical fact but conceptual puzzles. Now this reading of the work is strikingly reinforced, as it seems to me, when we recognize the influence of one other work in particular on the argument of the *Physics*. In a following section of this paper I shall try to show that in the *Physics* Aristotle over and again takes his start, not from his own or others' observations, but from a celebrated set of logical paradoxes that may well have appeared during his own early years in the Academy. Far more than that overmined quarry the *Timaeus*, it is the *Parmenides* which supplies Aristotle in the *Physics* not only with many and perhaps most of his central problems but with the terminology and methods of analysis that he uses to resolve them. But before turning to this evidence let us see whether we are yet in a position to explain the discrepancy from which we set out.

---

[31]*Ph*. IV 4, 210b32–211a7. Thus for instance the common conception of place as a container which is not part of what it contains (1, 208b1–8; 2, 209b28–30) must be rescued from Zeno's puzzle (1, 209a23–26; 3, 210b22–27) by a survey of the senses of "this is in that" (3, 210a14 ff.) and can then be taken as secure (4, 210b34–211a1).

[32]*NE* VII 1, 1145b6–7; *Ph*. IV 4, 211a7–11. The verb for proof in each case is δεικνύναι.

[33]*Ph*. IV 3, 210b8–9 (ἐπακτικῶς σκοποῦσιν) with 210a14–24.

Can we appeal to this ambiguity in Aristotle's terminology in order to explain how such a generalization as that quoted from the *Prior Analytics* could be taken to cover the methods of the *Physics?* By now the ambiguity seems too radical for our purpose. Even within the second sense of φαινόμενα, the sense in which it is equated with ἔνδοξα and λεγόμενα, some essential distinctions lie concealed. For an appeal to a λεγόμενον may be an appeal either to common belief about matters of fact[34] or to established forms of language[35] or to a philosophical thesis claiming the factual virtues of the first and the analytic certainty of the second.[36] And the broader ambiguity between the two senses of the word was one which Aristotle himself had the means to expose. For when he wishes to restrict φαινόμενον to its first sense he calls it expressly a perceptual φαινόμενον and distinguishes it from an ἔνδοξον.[37] And in the *De Caelo* it is this more precise form of words that he uses to describe the criterion by which the correctness of our principles in physics must ultimately be assessed.[38]

I think such considerations show that it is a mistake to ask, in the hope of some quite general answer, what function Aristotle assigns to φαινόμενα, or to ἀπορίαι, or to ἐπαγωγή; or they show how the function can vary with the context and style of enquiry. But we have pressed them too hard if they prevent us from understanding how Aristotle could have taken the formula in the *Analytics* to apply to the *Physics* as well as to the *Historia Animalium*. If there is more than one use for the expression φαινόμενα, the uses have a great deal in common. Thus for example it is not a

34E.g. *NE* I 11, 1101a22–24.
35E.g. Ibid. VII 2, 1145b19–20; 3, 1146b4–5.
36E.g. Ibid. I 8, 1098b12–18.
37 τῶν φαινομένων κατὰ τὴν αἴσθησιν, *De Caelo* III 4, 303a 22–23.
38Ibid. 7, 306a16–17.

peculiarity of φαινόμενα in the second sense that they may fail to stand up to examination; for so may the φαινόμενα of perception,[39] and within this latter class Aristotle is careful to specify only the reliable members as a touchstone for the correctness of physical principles.[40] As for his favourite example, astronomy, Aristotle knew (or came to realize) how inadequate were the observations of the astronomers.[41] And of the biological "observations" many were bound to be hearsay, λεγόμενα, to be treated with caution.[42] Such φαινόμενα must be "properly established," ascertained to be "true data."[43] In the same fashion the ἔνδοξα must pass the appropriate scrutiny, but in doing so they too become firm data.[44] Nor, if Aristotle associates the φαινόμενα with ἐμπειρία, as he does in the text from the *Analytics*, must it be supposed that his words are meant to apply only to φαινόμενα in the first sense. Ἔνδοξα also rest on experience, even if they misrepresent it.[45] If they did not Aristotle could find no place for them in his epistemology; as it is, an ἔνδοξον that is shared by all men is *ipso facto* beyond challenge.[46]

Nor is it in the least surprising if Aristotle, writing in the tradition of Parmenides and Protagoras, tended to assimilate these different senses of φαινόμενα.

[39]*De Caelo* II 8, 290a13–24 and esp. *Met.* Γ 5, 1010b1–11. (On Protagoras cf. p. 176 below.)

[40]*De Caelo* III 17, 306a16–17: τὸ φαινόμενον ἀεὶ κυρίως κατὰ τὴν αἴσθησιν, "the perceptual *phainomenon* that is reliable when it occurs," *not*, as Tricot translates, "l'évidence toujours souveraine de la perception sensible": for κυρίως here cf. *Met.* Γ 5, 1010b14–19.

[41]*De Part. Anim.* I 5, 644b24–28.

[42]E.g. *Hist. Anim.* II 1, 501a25–b1.

[43]*An. Pr.* I 30, 46a20, 25.

[44]*Ph.* IV 4, 210b32–34, 211a7–11, *NE* VII 1, 1145b6–7.

[45]E.g. *De Div. per Som.* 1, 462b14–18.

[46]*NE* X 2, 1172b36–1173a1; cf. VII 14, 1153b27–28, *EE* I 6, 1216b26–35.

For Parmenides, the δόξαι βροτεῖαι include not only
the supposed evidence of the senses but the common
assumptions (and specifically the common uses of
language) which form men's picture of the physical
world.[47] As for Protagoras, both Plato and Aristotle
represent his theory as applying indifferently to perceptual phenomena and ἔνδοξα, and use φαίνεσθαι
in describing both these applications.[48] It is the same
broad use of the word that is to be found in the formula from the *Prior Analytics*. In the *De Caelo*, it is
true, Aristotle observes that it is the φαινόμενα of
perception by which we must ultimately test the adequacy of our principles in physics;[49] but this is said of
φυσική as a whole, a body of science in which the
analyses of the *Physics* proper are preliminary to other
more empirical enquiries and consequently must be
justified, in the last resort, by their success in making
sense of the observations to which they are applied.
But this is not to say (and it does not commit Aristotle
to supposing) that in the *Physics* proper the analyses
either start from or are closely controlled by our inspections of the world. Nor in fact is he liable to consider his analyses endangered by such inspections: if
his account of motion shows that any unnatural movement requires an agent of motion in constant touch
with the moving body, the movement of a thrown
ball can be explained by inventing a set of unseen
agents to fill the gap.[50] The *phainomena* to which the
Physics pays most attention are the familiar data of
dialectic, and from the context in the *Prior Analytics*
it seems clear that Aristotle's words there are meant
to cover the use of such data. For in concluding the

[47]A conflation helped by talking as though data of perception
were themselves arbitrary assumptions (B 8, 38–41 Diels-Kranz).
On the "common uses of language" see B 8, 53; B 9; B 8, 38.
[48]*Crat.* 386a1; *Met.* Γ 5, 1010b1, 1009a38–b2.
[49]*De Caelo* III 7, 306a16–17.
[50]*Ph.* VIII 10, 266b27–267a20.

passage and the discussion in which it occurs Aristotle
observes that he has been talking at large about the
ways in which the premisses of deductive argument
are to be chosen; and he refers for a more detailed
treatment of the same matter to the "treatise on dialectic."[51] He evidently has in mind the claim made in
the *Topics* that the first premisses of scientific argument can be established by methods which start from
the ἔνδοξα.[52]

II

I turn to the part played by the *Parmenides*, and
specifically by the arguments in which "Aristotle" is
the interlocutor, in shaping the *Physics*. Perhaps it is
by misreading the *Physics* as a confused and cross-bred
attempt at empirical science that critics have been led
to look for its antecedents elsewhere and so to make
excessive claims for its originality. So it is worth dwell-
ing on this particular Platonic influence, partly for
the light that it throws on the methods and interests
of Aristotle's work, partly to call in question the claim
that "the discussions in books III–VI ... attack a series
of problems for which there was little in Plato's teaching to prepare the way,"[53] and partly to establish, if
this needs establishing, that the *Parmenides* was not
read by the Academy either as a joke or as a primer
of fallacies.[54] What the positive aims of the dialogue

[51]*An. Pr.* I 30, 46a28–30.

[52]*Top.* I 2, 101a36–b4. Ross seems to mistake the sense of the
An. Pr. text (46a28–30) when he writes: "It is of course only the
selection of premisses of *dialectical* reasoning that is discussed in
the *Topics*; the nature of the premisses of scientific reasoning is
discussed in the *Posterior Analytics*" (*Aristotle's Prior and Posterior Analytics*, p. 396). But in this passage Aristotle is concerned with finding the principles of scientific reasoning, and
must be thinking of the claim made in the *Topics* to find such
principles dialectically.

[53]Ross, *Aristotle's Physics*, p. 9.

[54]In this respect what follows can be read as complementary

may have been does not concern us; the present enquiry is a necessary preliminary to settling such questions.

Consider the celebrated account of the point. It is Plato in the *Parmenides* who argues first that what is indivisible (viz. the One, which cannot be plural and so has no parts) cannot have a location. For to have a location is to have surroundings i.e. to be contained in something; and this is to be contained either in something other than oneself or in oneself. But to be contained in something other than oneself is to have a circumference and to be in contact with that other thing at various points, and an indivisible thing cannot have various points or a circumference distinct from its centre. Nor can a thing without parts be contained in itself, for this would entail dividing it into container and contained, and no such division of it is possible. "Hence it is not anywhere, since it is neither in itself nor in another."[55] This concept of place as surroundings is normal in Greek philosophy, as the arguments of Zeno and Gorgias show (and in ordinary conversation, which has small use for plotting objects by Cartesian co-ordinates, it still is so). Aristotle took it over as an ἔνδοξον and made a more sophisticated version of it in the fourth book of the *Physics*. And one problem that he raises at the start of his argument depends on the assumption that if a point has any location it must be its own location, an assumption that flatly conflicts with the received view that place is a container distinct from the thing contained.[56] Aristotle does not argue the assumption; plainly he is drawing on Plato's argument that an indivisible cannot be contained in something else, nor yet can there be any distinction within it between container and

to Professor D. J. Allan's essay in *Aristotle and Plato in the Mid-fourth Century* (*Aristotle and the Parmenides*).

[55]*Parm.* 138a2–b6 (Burnet's lineation). The lack of shape and circumference is proved in 137d8–138a1.

[56]*Ph.* IV 1, 209a7–13.

contained. And he concludes that a point cannot be said to have a location.[57]

On the way to this conclusion, and as a preface to his general account of place, he lists the different senses in which one thing can be said to be in another,[58] and follows this with an argument to show that a thing cannot be said to be in itself except in the loose sense that it may be a whole having parts present in it.[59] This sense is sharply distinguished from the "strictest sense of all," that in which a thing is said to be in a place.[60] Why does he spend so much time on this? Because of further arguments in the *Parmenides*. Having maintained, in the first arm of his argument about the One, that an indivisible cannot be contained in itself, Plato goes on in the second arm to reduce his subject to a whole of parts and so, by dubious steps, to reimport the notion of place. For (a) since the subject is in itself in the sense that all its parts are contained in it,[61] it is always "in the same thing," i.e. in the same place and hence at rest;[62] and (b) since the subject is not in itself, in the sense that as a whole it is not contained in any or all of its parts, it must be always in something else[63] and so never at rest.[64] Among other eccentricities, the argument clearly relies on (and I think is clearly out to expose) an ambiguity in the form of expression "being in so-and-so": it shows that any sense of the phrase in which a thing can be said to be in itself cannot be the appropriate sense for talking of location, otherwise paradoxes result. Anaxagoras had traded on this ambiguity,[65] and no doubt

[57]*Ph.* IV 5, 212b24–25.
[58]*Ph.* IV 3, 210a14–24.
[59]Ibid. 210a25–b22.
[60]Ibid. 210a24.
[61]*Parm.* 145b6–c7.
[62]*Parm.* 145e7–146a3.
[63]*Parm.* 145e7–e3.
[64]*Parm.* 146a3–6.
[65]*Ph.* III 5, 205b1–5.

Plato wrote with Anaxagoras in mind; but that Aristotle's arguments are framed primarily with a view to those of the *Parmenides* is shown by the fact that he mentions Anaxagoras' thesis not in this context but elsewhere and by the clear echoes of Plato's language in his own.[66]

Points, then, cannot have location. And it is Plato who first proves the corollary, that something without parts cannot be said to move. But his reason is not just that what has no location cannot be said to change location. It is that to move to a certain place is a process, and there must be some intermediate stage of the process at which the moving body has arrived partly but not altogether.[67] And it is just this argument that Aristotle in the *Physics* takes over and generalizes, so that it applies to other forms of change besides locomotion.[68] Again, Plato prefaces his proof that an indivisible thing cannot change place by showing that it cannot even rotate in one place, since rotation entails a distinction between a centre and other parts;[69] and with this in mind Aristotle prefaces *his* argument by noticing the case in which a point might be said to move if it were part of a rotating body, but only because the whole body, which has a distinct centre and circumference, can be said to move in the strict sense.[70] Since it is often mistakenly said that Aristotle accepted the

---

[66]E.g. *Ph*. IV 3, 210a25–26 = *Parm*. 145d7–e1; *Ph*. IV 3, 210a27–29 = *Parm*. 145c4–7. Notice too that by μέρη here Plato means attributes of the subject, i.e. its being and unity and their derivatives (cf. 142d1–5); and that in the corresponding context of the *Physics* Aristotle corrects this use of the word by pointing out that attributes may be contained κατὰ μέρη in the subject not as being μέρη themselves (which he rejects, *Cat*. 2, 1a24–25) but as being attributes of μέρη (*Ph*. IV 3, 210a29–30).
[67]*Parm*. 138d2–e7.
[68]*Ph*. VI 10, 240b8–241a6.
[69]*Parm*. 138c7–d2.
[70]*Ph*. VI 10, 240b15–20.

definition of a line as the path of a moving point,[71] it is worth stressing how thoroughly he accepts Plato's reduction of this idea to absurdity—a *reductio* which no doubt counted as part of Plato's "war against the whole class of points."[72]

Again, consider the account of a connected concept, continuity. In the *Parmenides* Plato defines "contact" (ἅπτεσθαι) in terms of "succession" (ἐφεξῆς) and "neighbouring position" (ἐχομένη χώρα).[73] These terms Aristotle takes up in the fifth book of the *Physics*. "Contact" he defines as holding between terms whose extremities are together, i.e. in one and the same place;[74] an unhappy suggestion, since in themselves extremities can have no magnitude and so no position. And then, changing Plato's order of definition, he defines "neighbouring" (ἐχόμενον) in terms of "contact" and "succession."[75] From both accounts, it is clear, the same implication can be derived: Plato, by defining contact in terms of neighbouring *position*, and Aristotle, by defining it in terms of things having *extremities*, preclude the attempt to talk of a series of points as having contact with each other and so making up a line or any other magnitude. But this result only follows from Plato's definition if it is coupled with the argument that an indivisible thing cannot have position; and no doubt it was this that determined

[71]E.g. by Heath, *Mathematics in Aristotle*, p. 117; he cites *De An*, I 4, 409a4–5, where Aristotle is reporting someone else's theory. Of other passages which seem to imply this view *Ph*. IV 11, 219b16–20 can be read otherwise and *Ph*. V 4, 227b16–17 may represent an objector's view. But Aristotle does inconsistently credit points with location at *An. Po*. I 27, 87a36; 32, 88a33–34; *Met*. Δ 6, 1016b25–26, 30–31, and perhaps with the possibility of being in contact at *Ph*. V 3, 227a27–30 (but this seems to depend on the unaristotelian thesis in lines 27–28).

[72]*Met*. A 9, 992a19–22.

[73]*Parm*. 148e7–10.

[74]*Ph*. V 3, 226b23. "Together" (ἅμα) is defined in 226b 21–22.

[75]*Ph*. V 3, 227a6–7.

Aristotle to reform the definition so that the conclusion would follow directly from the simple premiss that a point has no parts or extremities. This reordering of the definition would not have served Plato's purpose, for in this particular chain of reasoning in the *Parmenides* he reserves the right to treat his subject as indivisible[76] without committing himself to the conclusion that it can therefore have no location. His definition allows him to talk of an indivisible thing as having contact with something else, and when he proves that it cannot have contact with itself it is on other grounds than the mere lack of location.[77] As a result his proof is valid for all things and not merely for indivisibles. But it is plain that his definition of contact, taken together with his denial of location to indivisibles, produces exactly the conclusions which Aristotle draws from his own definitions at the beginning of the sixth book of the *Physics*,[78] namely that there is no sense in saying that lines are collections of points in contact. It was in the *Parmenides* that Aristotle found not only the general approach to his problem but the special ideas in terms of which he treats it.[79]

There is another point in these contexts at which Aristotle corrects Plato. For Plato, contact requires *immediate* (εὐθύς) succession in the contiguous terms,

[76]*Parm.* 147a8–b2; but earlier in the same movement he has treated it as divisible into parts and continues to do so later.

[77]*Parm.* 148e10–149a3.

[78]*Ph.* VI 1, 231a21–b10.

[79]Another such term in the same context is χωρίς (*Parm.* 149a5), taken over and defined by Aristotle. And there are other reminiscences of Plato's treatment of these ideas. One is the comment at *Ph.* I 2, 185b11–16, which Aristotle admits to be irrelevant to the argument in hand. Why does he introduce it? Because he has just mentioned continuity, and this reminds him to Plato's argument in this connexion that, since the parts can be distinguished from the whole, the whole can have contact with itself (*Parm.* 148d6–7, 148e1–3).

and this immediacy he explains by saying that they must occupy neighbouring positions.[80] But a little later he explains this requirement in turn by saying that there must be no third thing between the two terms;[81] and Aristotle is anxious to find room for this condition too in his definitions. He cannot use it to define "neighbouring," since he has another definition of that concept in view; so he uses it to define "successive,"[82] and in doing so he adds an important qualification: there must be nothing between the terms *of the same kind as themselves.*[83] If A B C are consecutive sections of a straight line, C cannot follow ἐφεξῆς after A, but it evidently can do so if B is merely a point. In correcting Plato here Aristotle may have in mind the treatment of limits in one passage of the *Parmenides* as parts of a thing, logically comparable with what lies between them;[84] but this is a treatment that Plato's own argument enables Aristotle to reject.

There is an embarrasing wealth of examples of this influence in the *Physics*, and I shall not bore you with them all. But one group is too important to omit. We saw earlier that, in arguing that an indivisible thing cannot move, Plato (and Aristotle after him) treated movement as a process taking time and having intermediate stages. As Aristotle would say, it is a continuous change, divisible into parts which are themselves changes taking time. But later in the *Parmenides* Plato argues that if a change is construed as the passage from not-A to A the change must be instantaneous; for there is no time in which a thing can be neither A nor not-A, neither at rest (for instance) nor in motion.[85] And this introduction of changes which are not

[80]*Parm.* 148e7–10.
[81]*Parm.* 149a6.
[82]*Ph.* V 3, 226b34–227a4.
[83]*Ph.* V 3, 227a1; cf. VI 1, 231b8–9.
[84]*Parm.* 137d4–5.
[85]*Parm.* 156c6–7: the whole context is 155e4–157b5.

processes is carefully prepared by some earlier arguments. Twice—once in each of the first two chains
of argument about the One—Plato discusses the logic
of growing older. In the first argument[86] he considers
it as a special case of becoming different; and he argues
that if X is becoming different from Y it cannot be
the case that Y already is different from X, since otherwise X would already be different from Y and not
merely becoming so. All that follows from "X is becoming different from Y" is another proposition about
becoming, "Y is becoming different from X." The
conclusion is applied forthwith to the particular case,
to show that if X is becoming older than itself it is at
the same time becoming younger. But on a later page
the same example is taken up again.[87] Now Plato argues
that at any moment during the process of growing
older the subject must be older; at any stage of becoming different, the thing must already be different. For
to say that it is becoming different is to say something
about its future as well as its present; but so far as the
bare present is concerned, it must already be something that it was becoming, given that the process of
change is under way at all. Thus the argument relies
heavily on the law of excluded middle: either the
changing thing is already different, or it is not. If it is
not, the process of change is not yet under way. And
if it is, then the old conclusion, that from "X is becoming different from Y" we can infer only what X
and Y are becoming and not what they are, breaks
down. The old conclusion relied on inserting a *tertium
quid* between "X is different" and "X is not different,"
namely "X is becoming different," something tem-
porally intermediate between the first two; but such
a *tertium quid* is ruled out by the law of excluded
middle. Yet it is just this law that leads to the problem

[86]*Parm.* 141a6–c4.
[87]*Parm.* 152a5–e3.

of instantaneous change with which we began; for Plato goes on to argue that, if there is no time in which a thing can be neither A nor not-A, neither still nor moving, it baffles us to say when it makes the change from the one to the other.[88] When it changes from rest to motion it cannot be either at rest (for then the change would be still to come) or moving (for then the change would be past). Yet the change is not to be talked away: "if a thing changes, it *changes*."[89]

Here then is the problem, and the whole context of argument, taken over by Aristotle. It is generally held that Plato's purpose was to show that there can be no period of time during which a thing is neither A nor not-A, and consequently that the change from one to the other must occur at a moment of time.[90] But Aristotle evidently thought the puzzle more radical, and I think he was right. For by the same law of excluded middle not only is there no period but there is no point of time at which a thing can be neither A nor not-A. At any rate, whether Aristotle is enlarging or merely preserving Plato's problem, he gives it considerable space in the *Physics*. He agrees that some changes take no time at all.[91] Among other instances he cites the recovery of health, which is "a change to health and to nothing else";[92] in other words, although the process towards recovery may take time, the actual

[88]*Parm.* 156c1–7.

[89]*Parm.* 156c7–8: 'Αλλ' οὐδὲ μὴν μεταβάλλει ἄνευ τοῦ μετα-βάλλειν. Cornford (*Plato and Parmenides*, p. 200, n. 2) mistakes the sense, insisting that the statement is "intelligible only if we suppose that Plato shifts here from the common use of μεταβάλλειν for 'change' in general to the stricter sense of 'transition' or passing from one state to another." What Plato means is like our truism "business is business"—sc. it mustn't be taken for anything else or explained away. He would probably regard Aristotle as explaining such changes away.

[90]Cornford goes so far as to call it a "businesslike account of the instant" (Ibid., p. 203).

[91]*Ph.* VIII 3, 253b21–30; cf. I 3, 186a13–16.

[92]*Ph.* VIII 3, 253b26–28.

recovery is simply the change from not-A to A.[93] In any process of change to a given state there will be a similar completion of the change, and this will take no time:[94] the argument at once recalls Plato's discussion of the transition from movement to stillness. Later, in the eighth book, Aristotle faces the problem squarely. It will not help, he argues, to postulate a time-atom between the period in which something is not white and the subsequent period in which it is white, with a view simply to providing a time for the change to occur from not-white to white. For one thing, time-atoms cannot be consecutive to periods of time or to other time-atoms, just as points cannot have contact either with lines or with other points. Moreover the suggestion would set a regress on foot. For when we have postulated one time-atom to house the change from not-white to white, there will be another change to be accommodated in the same way: the change from changing to being white.[95] In brief, Aristotle takes the puzzle to show that it is a mistake to look for a special time-reference such that the subject is then neither white nor not-white. The primary moment at which the subject becomes (or, as Aristotle prefers to say, has become) white is the first moment at which it is white.[96] And, given this moment, it becomes improper to talk of the last moment at which

[93]Ross explains it otherwise; but for the treatment of ὑγίανσις as the limit of a κίνησις cf. *Met.* Θ 6, 1048b18–23.

[94]*Ph.* VI 5, 235b32–236a7.

[95]*Ph.* VIII 8, 263b26–264a1.

[96]Ibid. 263b9–26, 264a2–4, cf. the earlier argument in VI 5, 235b32–236a7. The solution of Plato's puzzle given in *Ph.* VIII 8 is more trenchant than the earlier reply in VI 9 (240a19–29): there Aristotle suggested that even between not-A and A a *tertium quid* could be inserted, viz. when the subject is neither *wholly* not-A nor *wholly* A; but this is easily defeated by reformulating the contradictions as "wholly A" and "not wholly A." Just as the reply to Zeno which is given in VI 9 is admitted to be inadequate in VIII 8 (263a15–18), so the reply to Plato's puzzle given in VI 9 is superseded in the same later chapter.

the subject was *not* white, for the two moments would have to be consecutive.[97] Equally, given a last moment of stability there cannot be a first moment of change.[98] And Aristotle, having thus saved the situation and the law of excluded middle, can take over without qualms the moral of Plato's second analysis of growing older: namely that at any time during the period in which a thing is becoming different, it has already completed a change and to that extent is different from what it was.[99]

His reply to Plato's puzzle has side-effects on other discussions. To underline the paradox, Plato had called all change from not-A to A "sudden" change (ἐξαίφνης).[100] Aristotle restores the word to its proper use: it is used of what departs from its previous condition in an imperceptibly short time.[101] But all change, he adds, involves departing from a previous condition; and his motive for adding this is clear. He has in mind that because of this characteristic Plato had tried to reduce all change to sudden change, and he implies that this was a misleading extension of the word's use. There is nothing physically startling in most changes and nothing logically startling in any of them.

There is no need to go on. It might indeed be objected that the evidence does not necessarily show that Aristotle was indebted to the *Parmenides;* both Plato and Aristotle may have been drawing on a lost source. These problems were surely discussed in the Academy,[102] and the Academy in turn must surely have

[97]*Ph.* VIII 8, 264a3–4.
[98]*Ph.* VI 5, 236a7–27.
[99]*Ph.* VI 6, 236b32–237a17.
[100]*Parm.* 156d1–e3.
[101]*Ph.* IV 13, 222b14–16.
[102]We know for instance that others had tried to define continuity (*Ph.* III 1, 200b18–20), though they did not make use of the nexus of ideas common to Plato's and Aristotle's treatments

drawn on earlier arguments, in particular those of Zeno and Gorgias. The general purposes of this paper would be as well served by such a theory, but it cannot account for the intricate correspondence that we have seen in our two texts. Gorgias' part in the matter is guesswork: the evidence for his sole adventure into abstract thought has been contaminated, probably beyond cure, by traditions to which both the *Parmenides* and the *Physics* contributed. Of Zeno luckily we know more; we know that Plato does echo some arguments of Zeno, but that he transforms them radically for his own ends.[103] The *Parmenides* was not an historical anthology, and when Aristotle's words and ideas coincide closely with those of the dialogue he is under the spell of a work of astonishing brilliance and originality. A work, moreover, of logic or dialectic, not in the least a piece of empirical science; and the *Physics* is in great parts its successor.

This is not to say, of course, that Aristotle would call his methods in the *Physics* wholly dialectical. He, and his commentators on his behalf, have insisted on the distinction between "physical" and "dialectical," or "logical," or "universal," arguments; and no doubt

---

of the subject; hence Aristotle can take over their definition at the start of the *Physics* (I 2, 185b10–11) before producing his own revision of Plato's account.

[103]The *Arrow* underlies *Parm.* 152b2–d2, and the argument of B 1 and 2 in Diels-Kranz (the resolution of a thing into its fractions without ever reaching ultimate units) underlies *Parm.* 164c 8–d4 and 165a5–b6. I have not been convinced by Hermann Fraenkel's interpretation of B 3, nor therefore by his claim that it underlies the last-mentioned passages of the dialogue ("Zeno of Elea's Attacks on Plurality," *American Journal of Philology*, LXIII [1942], pp. 6, 198–99 = *Wege und Formen*, pp. 203, 227–28). Fraenkel is also inclined to see the Arrow behind *Parm.* 145–46 (art. cit., p. 13, n. 33 = *Wege und Formen*, p. 210, n. 1), where others will more readily detect Anaxagoras (cf. p. 94 above); and he sees B 4 behind *Parm.* 156c–d ibid. pp. 11–13 = pp. 207–9). He says all that is necessary for my purpose when he observes that in such echoes "Plato modifies the argument and ... transfers it, as it were, to a higher order."

some of the reasoning in the *Physics* falls within the first class. Yet even if the distinction were (as it seldom is) sharp and fundamental in sciences where a knowledge of particular empirical fact is in question,[104] we need not expect it to be so in such an enquiry as the *Physics*. This is clear from the one major example of the contrast that is offered in the work, the dialectical and physical proofs that there can be no infinite physical body.[105] The dialectical proof is evidently distinguished by the fact that it proves too much: starting from a definition that applies to mathematical as well as to physical solids, it reaches conclusions that apply to both sciences.[106] Yet immediately after his promise to turn to physical arguments Aristotle produces a proof that no complex body can be infinite, and this proof shares the characteristics of its predecessor. It relies partly on quite general definitions of "body" and "infinite,"[107] partly on a treatment of the ratio between finite and infinite terms which could be formulated quite generally[108] and which in fact is later given a different application to speed and resistance;[109] and partly, perhaps, on the argument against an infinite number of elements which occurs in the first book and relies largely on quite general premisses.[110] Certainly there are other arguments in the context which seem

[104]E.g. *De Gen. Anim.* II 8, 747b27–748a16.

[105]*Ph.* III 5, 204b4–206a8. There is a second use of the same distinction (unnoticed by Bonitz s.v. λογικῶς) at VIII 8, 264a-7–9, and here too it proves elusive. The "logical" arguments can hardly be marked by their generality (the λόγος μᾶλλον οἰκεῖος at 264b1–2 itself applies to kinds of change other than movement) nor the "physical" by their reliance on the special theorems of physics (the "logical" also may do this, 264a24).

[106]*Ph.* III 5, 204b4–7, cf. Ross's notes on 204b4, 204b6.

[107]Ibid. 204b20–21.

[108]Ibid. 204b11–19: a particularly clear case of the artificial restriction of a general theorem of proportion so as to bring it within "physics."

[109]*Ph.* IV 8, 215b10–216a11.

[110]*Ph.* III 5, 204b12–13; I 6, 189a12–20.

to depend on special empirical claims, such as the
unfortunate hypothesis of natural places.[111] But the
impulse throughout the work is logical, and the restriction of its subject-matter to movable bodies and their
characteristics does not entail a radical difference of
method from other logical enquiries. It makes for better understanding to recall that in Aristotle's classification of the sciences the discussions of time and movement in the *Parmenides* are also physics.

[111]*Ph*. III 5, 205a10–12; but for the treatment of this too as an
ἔνδοξον see n. 30 above.

MATTER AND PREDICATION
IN ARISTOTLE

JOSEPH OWENS, C. SS. R.

§1 INTRODUCTION

In describing the basic matter of things, Aristotle removed from it all determinations and so all direct intelligibility. Yet he regarded the basic matter just in itself as a subject for predication. You can say things about it. You can say, for instance, that it is ingenerable and indestructible, and that it is the persistent substrate of generation and corruption. Still more strangely, Aristotle means that a substance or substantial form, like that of a man, of a plant, of a metal, can be predicated of matter.[1] How can this be, if matter is in itself wholly undetermined and entirely unintelligible?

From *The Concept of Matter in Greek and Medieval Philosophy*, ed. E. McMullin (Notre Dame, Ind., 1963), pp. 99–115. Reprinted by permission of the University of Notre Dame Press.

[1]See Aristotle *Met.* Z 3, 1029a20–30. The technical term used by Aristotle for matter was the Greek *hylê* or 'wood'. He seems to have been the first to coin a term for this notion, though the philosophic use of *hylê* for materials in general was prepared by Plato at *Ti.* 69A, and *Phlb.* 54C. In modern times the overall approach to the scientific notion of matter is hardly different; e.g.: "By the building materials I mean what we call matter, . . . ordinary matter is constructed out of two types of ultimate things called 'electrons' and 'protons.' " C. G. Darwin, *The New Conceptions of Matter* (London, 1931), p. 8. Aristotle, however, is approaching the question on a level that does not lead to electrons and protons but to very different principles; cf. Appendix. For texts, see Bonitz' *Index Aristotelicus*, 652b49–51, 785a5–43.

How can matter even be indicated, if it exhibits nothing that can halt the gaze of the intellect?

The above observations envisage two ways in which characteristics may be predicated of matter. One is essential (*per se*) predication. Matter is of itself ingenerable and indestructible, somewhat as man is animal and corporeal. The other way is through added forms. Matter is metallic, bovine, human through the forms of a metal, a cow, a man. But these forms are substantial, not accidental. Yet their predication in regard to matter resembles accidental predication, just as the specific differentia in the category of substance is predicated of the genus as though it were a quality. As changes within the category of substance are called by Professor Fisk in the present volume "qualified-like changes," this type of predication may correspondingly be designated "quality-like" predication. It is one type of the medieval *predicatio denominativa*.

In ordinary predication, as treated in Aristotelian logic, the ultimate subject is always actual and concrete. The universal, from a metaphysical viewpoint, is potential (*Met.* M 10, 1087a15–22). The concrete singular always retains its actuality as its various features are universalized and made potential. It cannot be treated as an undetermined residue that remains after its predicates have been removed. Logical analysis of predication, therefore, leads ultimately in Aristotle to the actual, and not to something wholly potential like matter. Ultimate matter is arrived at through the reasoning of the *Physics*. So reached, it poses problems for metaphysics. How does it have being, and how are forms predicated of it? The Stagirite had here to grapple with a refined concept attained by his scientific thinking and established to the satisfaction of that technical procedure itself, but which broke through the systematized logic presupposed by him for every theoretical science.

The solution reached by Aristotle in this question may or may not provide light for other disciplines when in the course of their reasonings they arrive at concepts that cannot fit into the grooves of the logic they have been using. Such new concepts may well appear self-contradictory when stretched on the Procrustean bed of a closed logical system. Certainly in metaphysics pertinent help for understanding the notion of essence can be obtained from studying Aristotle's procedure in establishing the notion of matter. Whether or not such help may be extended to other disciplines has to be left a question for investigators who specialize in them. But the contingency is one that can be encountered when any discipline pushes its concepts far past the experiences in which human thought commences. Concepts taken from immediate experience sometimes have to be refined in peculiar ways if they are to function in very remote areas of inquiry. The procedure of a first-rate thinker in meeting such a contingency belongs to the common treasury of achievements in the history of thought, and hardly deserves to be forgotten. Aristotle's method in this problem seems, then, *prima facie*, a subject worthy of investigation and critique.

§2 THE SUBJECT OF PREDICATION

First, what is the basic subject of predication in Aristotelian logic? As is well enough known, this ultimate subject of predication is the highly actual concrete singular thing. It is the individual man, or the individual horse, or the individual tree, according to the examples used in the Aristotelian *Categories*.[2] In a logical context, the real individual thing was called "primary substance" by the Stagirite. In Greek the term was *prôtê ousia*, primary entity. The term characterized the concrete singular thing as absolutely basic

2See *Cat.* V 2a13–14, 2b13.

among the subjects with which logic deals, and as the fundamental being that received the predication of all other perfections. Secondary substances, in that logical context, were *man, animal, body,* and the like, taken universally. They were all predicated of a primary substance, of a concrete individual man like Socrates or Plato, or of an individual horse or stone. Accidental characteristics, like *white, large, running,* and so on, were predicated of substances and ultimately of an individual substance. There was nothing more fundamental of which they could be predicated. For Aristotelian logic the concrete individual was the basic subject of predication. It was the primary entity upon which all logical structure was raised. In a logical context it was primary substance in the full sense of the expression.[3]

This doctrine of predication functioned without special difficulty when applied throughout the world of common sense thought and speech. Quite obviously the ultimates with which ordinary conversation deals are shoes and ships and sealing-wax and cabbages and kings, individual pinching shoes and flat-tasting cabbages and uncrowned office kings, as one meets them in the course of everyday life. These are all concrete individual things or persons. Aristotelian logic, it should be kept in mind, was expressly meant as a propaedeutic to the sciences. It did not presuppose knowledge of any theoretical science. Rather, it had to be learned before any theoretical science could be approached.[4] There should be little wonder, then, that Aristotelian logic was not geared to function smoothly in situations brought into being solely through the results of scien-

---

[3]*Cat.* V 2b4–6, 15–17. In a metaphysical context, on the other hand, the form and not the composite was primary substance, as at *Met.* Z 7, 1032b1–14; 11, 1037a28. On the category mistake occasioned by this twofold use of 'primary substance' in Aristotle, see my article "Aristotle on Categories," *The Review of Metaphysics,* XIV (1960), 83–84.

[4]See Aristotle *Met.* Γ 3, 1005b2–5.

tific analysis and construction. Yet those situations have to be expressed in concepts and in language. Logic has to be applied to them as they occur. Aristotle, as may be expected, could not go very deeply into any theoretical science without encountering situations that broke through the logical norms presupposed in his hearers. Was he prepared to meet such situations? Was he able to adapt his logic to them as they presented themselves in the course of his scientific investigations?

§3 THE PROBLEM OF MATTER

An instance that could hardly be avoided was that of matter. Matter quite obviously did not come under the notion envisaged for an ultimate subject of predication in a logic where that ultimate subject is the concrete singular thing. In the everyday universe of discourse the material or stuff out of which things are said to be made is always of the concrete individual stamp. The wood of which a house is constructed consists of individual pieces. The bronze in which a statue is cast is a piece of bronze in definite dimensions in a definite place at a definite time. In the later Scholastic vocabulary these concrete materials out of which more complex things were made received the designation, *materia secunda*, or 'secondary matter.' Bronze and wood and stone were indeed matter, in the sense that things were made out of them. But they were not the basic or ultimate matter out of which those things were made. That was signified by calling them secondary matter. The designation implied that there was a still more basic matter that was not concrete nor individual. Aristotle had not finished the first book of his *Physica* or philosophy of nature before he had established in sensible things a subject still more fundamental than the concrete individual. A visible, tangible, or mobile thing, the Stagirite showed, was necessarily composite. It was literally a *con-cretum*. It was composed of more fundamental elements. These ultimate constituents of sensible things, according to the Aristotelian reasoning, were form and matter. Matter played the role of ultimate subject, and a form was its primary characteristic.

The absolutely basic matter of the Aristotelian *Physics* became known in Scholastic terminology as *materia prima*, 'primary matter'. By Aristotle himself it was simply called matter. However, Aristotle uses the term 'matter' regularly enough to designate the concrete materials out of which artifacts are made, materials like bricks and stones and wood. So there was ground for the Scholastic insistence on the use of two expressions, 'primary matter' and 'secondary matter,' to mark the important distinction. For convenience in the present study the term 'materials' or 'material' will be used wherever possible to denote what the Scholastics called 'secondary matter', and the term 'matter' without any qualification will be used regularly for the absolutely basic substrate of things as established in the Aristotelian *Physics*. By 'matter', then, will be meant what the mediaeval vocabulary designated as 'primary matter'.

With matter in this sense established as subject, and form as its immediate though really distinct characteristic, you may readily expect to hear that the form is considered to be predicable of matter. You will not be disappointed; Aristotle actually does say that substance, in the sense of substantial form, is predicated of matter: "... for the predicates other than substance are predicated of substance, while substance is predicated of matter."[5] That is his express statement. What does it mean? At the very least, it means that matter is the ultimate subject with which predication is concerned. Everything other than substance you can predicate of substance. But what is intelligible about

[5]*Met.* Z 3, 1029a23–24; Oxford tr.

substance can in turn be predicated, denominatively of course, of matter. The principle of intelligibility in a substance is its form, and its form is the primary characteristic of its matter, from the "quality-like" viewpoint.

At first sight, perhaps, nothing could seem more natural than to predicate a form of its corresponding matter. Characteristics are regularly predicated of subjects. A new subject has been unearthed by the Aristotelian philosophy of nature. The substantial characteristic of that subject has been isolated. What is more normal, then, than to say that here as in other cases the characteristic is predicable of its subject?

Yet as soon as one tries to express this type of predication in any definite instance, linguistic and conceptual difficulties arise. How would you word a sentence in which a substance, or a substantial form, is predicated of matter? The first part of Aristotle's assertion was clear enough: "Predicates other than substance are predicated of substance." The predicates other than substance are the accidents. They are quantity, qualities, relations, activities, time, and place. They are predicated without difficulty of a concrete, individual substance. You may indicate a particular tree and say without hesitation that it is large, green, near to you, growing in the yard at the present moment. Each of these accidents is obviously predicated of a substance, the individual tree. But, the Aristotelian text continues: "the substance is predicated of matter." How would you express this in the case of the tree? You would have to say that matter is this particular tree. You would have to say that matter is likewise Socrates, or is Plato, or is this particular table or that particular stone. Such predication is unusual, and requires considerable explanation even to make sense.

Some light may be obtained from the way in which for Aristotle a thing may be defined in terms of the materials of which it is composed. If asked what a house is, you may answer that it is "stones, bricks, and timbers."[6] If that may be called a definition, it is surely the least perfect type of definition possible. But Aristotle does refer to it as a definition in terms of the materials that are able to be made into a house. From that viewpoint the house is the materials that constitute it, and conversely the materials are the house insofar as definition and thing defined are convertible. In general, then, in the way in which a thing may be said to be its materials, the materials themselves may be said to be the thing. Awkward though this predication is, what prevents it from being applied in the case of the basic matter of which things are composed? In each particular case it should allow you to say that matter is this individual man, this individual stone, this individual tree. Substance, even the individual substance, would in this way be predicated of matter.

The context in which the present doctrine occurs is one of the central books of the Aristotelian *Metaphys-*

---

[6]*Met.* H 2, 1043a15; Oxford tr. On this doctrine, and Aristotle's use of the expression 'primary matter' in connection with it, see W. D. Ross, *Aristotle's Metaphysics* (Oxford, 1924), II, 256–57. 'Primary matter' is found in various senses at *Ph.* II 1, 193a29; GA I 20, 729a32; and *Met.* Δ 4, 1015a7–10. 'Matter' in its chief or primary sense, however, meant for Aristotle the substrate of generation and corruption (GC I 4, 320a2–5), even though the designation 'primary matter' never seems to have been limited by him to that sense. The therapy required by the concept's genesis has to be kept applied in representing the absolutely undetermined matter as that of which things are composed. Such matter is not individual, like any of the materials of which a house is composed. Still less is it something universal, for the universal is subsequent to the individual in Aristotelian doctrine. Rather, it is below the level at which individuality and universality appear. Considered just in itself, it has nothing to distinguish it as found in one thing from itself as found in another. From this viewpoint it parallels the common nature of Duns Scotus, which of itself had nothing to distinguish it as found in Socrates from itself as found in Plato (see Duns Scotus, *Quaest. Metaph.*, 7, 13, No. 21; ed. Vivès, 7, 421b. In contrast to the Scotistic

ics. In a metaphysical context, the universal is not substance. When in this context substance is said to be predicated of matter, it can hardly mean just another instance of universal predicated of particular. From the viewpoint of logic, the secondary substance or the substance taken universally is predicated of the particular substance. Even though present as a condition, that logical doctrine can scarcely be what Aristotle meant in saying in the *Metaphysics* that substance is predicated of matter. It is not just another case of predicating universal of singular, as in the assertion: 'Socrates is a man.' Subject and predicate are really the same when a universal substance is predicated of a particular substance. If you say: "Matter is a man," however, you have a different type of predication. Matter does not coincide in reality with a man in the way Socrates does. A really distinct principle, the form of man, is added. From this viewpoint the predication resembles rather the assertion of an accidental form in regard to sub-

---

common nature, however, the Aristotelian basic matter lacks all formal determinations, and so not only individual determinations). The absolutely undetermined matter is accordingly one through the removal of all distinguishing characteristics. It is wholly formless in the *Physics* (I 7, 191a8–12) as well as in the *Metaphysics*. In this sense only, may it be regarded as common. When actuated, it differentiates by its very nature in making possible the spread of the same form in parts outside parts and the multiplication of singulars in a species. In that way it is an individuating principle without being of itself individual. As the substrate of substantial change, it may be said—with the appropriate therapy—to change from one form to another. So doing, it shows itself to be really distinct from its forms, since it really persists while the forms really replace each other. But it is not therefore a really distinct being from the form. In the individual there is but the one being derived from the form to the matter and the composite. Thus any single thing is differentiated from a "heap" (*Met.* Z 17, 1041b7–31). Subsidiary forms, for instance those indicated in water by the spectra of hydrogen and oxygen, would accordingly be accidental forms for Aristotle, and in a substantial change would be replaced by new though corresponding accidental forms.

stance, as when one says that a man is pale, or fat. The accidental form is really distinct from the substance, as the substantial form is really distinct from its matter. Such predication will be of the "quality-like" type.

That indeed is the way in which Aristotle presents the situation. As an accidental form, for instance quantity, is predicated of substance, so substance is predicated of matter. What is predicated of matter, accordingly should be the substantial form or act, and not the composite. Later in the same part of the *Metaphysics* it is stated in exactly that manner: "... as in substances that which is predicated of the matter is the actuality itself, in all other definitions also it is what most resembles full actuality."[7] As accidental forms are predicated of substances, then, so the substantial form is what is predicated of matter within the category of substance.

The doctrine clearly enough is that form in the category of substance may be predicated of its matter as of a subject. You may accordingly apply the form of man to matter, the form of iron to matter, and so on, and call it predication. But how can you express this in ordinary language? It can hardly be done. Ordinary language has not been developed to meet this contingency. The best you can do, perhaps, is to say that matter is humanized, equinized, lapidified, and so on, as it takes on forms like those of man, horse, and stone. To say that matter is human, equine, lapideous, or that it is a man, a horse, a stone, may be true enough in this context; but with all its linguistic oddity the way of speaking hardly brings out the full import of the situation. It tends to give the impression that matter is of itself these things. The Aristotelian meaning, on the contrary, is that matter is not of itself any of these things, but becomes them by receiving the appropriate substantial forms. As their real subject it

[7]*Met.* H 2, 1043a5–7; Oxford tr.

remains really distinct from them, somewhat as a substance remains really distinct from its accidents. The assertion that matter is humanized, equinized, lapidified by the reception of different substantial forms expresses the predication with less danger of being misunderstood, though with still less respect for linguistic usage.

The linguistic difficulties, however, turn out to be mild in comparison with the conceptual. The immediate context of the Aristotelian passage that gave rise to this discussion is enough to cause doubts about the very possibility of the predication. Matter had just been defined as "that which in itself is neither a particular thing nor of a certain quantity nor assigned to any other of the categories by which being is determined."[8] Matter is not anything definite. It is not a particular thing. It is not a "what" nor at all an "it." It exhibits nothing that could provide a direct answer to the question "What is it?" It has in itself none of the determinations by which a thing can be or be recognized or indicated or known or understood. The text states explicitly that it has no quantitative nor other categorical determination. Of itself, therefore, it has no length nor breadth nor thickness nor number nor parts nor position. It cannot at all be conceived in the fashion of the Cartesian concept of matter. In this concept, matter was identified with extension.[9] Nor can the Aristotelian matter be represented as anything capable of detection by means of a pointer-reading. There is nothing about it, in itself, that could register in quantitative terms. It belongs to a level on which neither quantitative nor qualitative physics has any means of functioning. It eludes quantitative and qualitative and other accidental determinations, as well as all substantial determinations.

[8]*Met.* Z 3, 1029a20–21; Oxford tr.
[9]See Descartes, *Principia Philosophiae*, 2, 4–9; A–T 8, 42.4–45.16 (9^2, 65–68).

Yet it cannot be expressed by negations of known characteristics, as for instance non-being is expressed negatively in terms of being.[10] The nature of matter cannot be represented in terms of what it is not. The same Aristotelian text continues:

> Therefore the ultimate substratum is of itself neither a particular thing nor of a particular quantity nor otherwise positively characterized; nor yet is it the negations of these, for negations also will belong to it only by accident.[11]

All categorical determinations are first denied to matter. They are outside its nature, and in that sense "belong to it only by accident." This has been expressed in the preceding paragraphs of the present study by saying that the forms are really distinct from matter somewhat as accidents are really distinct from substances. But, the Aristotelian text insists, the negations of all the different determinations are just as accidental to matter. None of them can express its nature, as the term 'nature' is used of matter in the *Physics* (II 1, 193a28–30; 2, 194a12–13). It eludes even negations. You can indeed say that matter is not something, or better still, that it is a "not-something." What you say is true. But you have not thereby expressed the nature of matter, even negatively. Negations are just as accidental to it as are the determinations it takes on in the actual world. You are still only skimming its accidental manifestations. You have not penetrated to its proper nature. Its nature eludes the negations.

In a word, matter as reached by Aristotle escapes in itself both determinative and negative characterizations.

---

[10]For Aristotle, predication of being is made through reference to the primary instance of being. Even the negation of being, namely "non-being," is asserted in this way. See *Met.* Γ 2, 1003b5–10.

[11]*Met.* Z 3, 1029a24–26; Oxford tr. 'Positively' refers here to determination; cf. a21.

It cannot be conceived or described in any direct fashion, either determinatively or negatively. It is not even a "what" nor an "it" that is capable of being indicated. In terms of modern logic, it is not the "referent" of any "demonstrative" (i.e. monstrative) symbol, because it cannot be presented directly to one's cognition. Nor can the referent be any property or set of properties, because such determinations are lacking to matter in itself.[12]

How, then, is the Aristotelian matter to be conceived and represented? How can it be set up as a subject for predication? Quite obviously, from the above considerations, no direct method, either affirmative or negative, is capable of grasping what Aristotle meant in this regard. The concept will have to be that of a positive subject, able to receive predication. No negation is able to express the nature of matter. Yet from that notion of positive subject every determination will have to be removed, even, or rather especially, the determination expressed by "something." Matter is explicitly not a "something" nor a "what" nor an "it." All determination, even the most elementary, has to be drastically eliminated from the notion of the positive in this concept. The concept that expresses the Aristotelian notion of matter will have to be the concept of a positive object that is wholly indeterminate. Is the human mind able to form such a concept? If so, upon what referents will it be based?

Presumably Aristotle could not have spoken so cogently about matter if he had not worked out its concept to his own satisfaction. The most likely way to

---

[12]"The referend of a demonstrative symbol (i.e. a word used demonstratively) is *the object directly presented to* the speaker. The referend of a descriptive phrase is a *property*, or *set of properties*." L. Susan Stebbing, *A Modern Introduction to Logic* (6th ed.; London, 1948), p. 499. On the technical term 'referend,' cf.: "We shall find it convenient to use the word 'referend' to stand for *that which is signified*." Ibid., p. 13.

learn how the concept is formed, accordingly, should be to follow the steps by which the originator of the concept reasoned to the presence of matter in sensible things. In this context, of course, the referents will be sensible things in themselves, and not Kantian phenomena.

§4 SUBSTANCE AND CHANGE

How, then, did Aristotle arrive at the notion of matter as a real subject, and as a subject denominatively characterized by forms that remained really distinct from it? In the first book of the *Physics*, the Stagirite surveyed the teachings of his philosophic predecessors on the basic principles of natural things. Things in the world of nature were known by observation to be capable of motion or change. In the course of his survey, attention is focused upon the universal requirements for change. Any change whatsoever needs three principles. It has to have a subject that loses one form and acquires another. The three principles necessarily involved are therefore the form that is lost, the form that is acquired, and the subject that undergoes the loss of the old form and the acquisition of the new.[13]

The Aristotelian examples meant to illustrate this doctrine are clear enough. They are concrete individual materials that lose and acquire different forms. Bronze is the subject that becomes a statue. At first the bronze

---

[13]See *Ph.* I 7, 189b30–191a7. The analysis of change or motion is made by Aristotle without dependence on the notion of time. Rather, motion is first defined, and then the notion of time is worked out in terms of motion, that is, as the numbering of motion in respect of prior and subsequent (*Ph.* IV 11, 219b1–2). Since Kant the tendency has been first to establish the notion of time, and then to describe motion in terms of relation to time; e.g.: "Change thus always involves (1) a fixed entity, (2) a three-cornered relation between this entity, another entity, and some but not all, of the moments of time." Bertrand Russell, *Principles of Mathematics* (Cambridge, Eng., 1903), 1, 469.

has a nondescript form or shape. Then it is cast into the form of a statue, say of the Greek god Hermes. It is the subject that changes from one form or shape to another. The notion of form in this example is readily understood from its ordinary English use. It is the external shape of the bronze. Another Aristotelian example, however, uses 'form' in a more esoteric way. A man from an uneducated state comes to be educated. The man is the subject that changes from uneducated to educated. 'Uneducated' describes the quality of the man who has not had proper schooling. 'Educated' means the quality of adequate instruction and cultural training. Both 'educated' and 'uneducated' mean qualities; and in the Aristotelian vocabulary qualities are forms.

As can be seen in these examples, the original form from which the subject changes is more properly regarded from the viewpoint of a privation of the form to be acquired in the change. It is expressed in a privative way, as in the term 'uneducated.' Any of the Aristotelian categories, like the thing's quantity, its place, its time of occurrence, or any of its relations, is a form in this technical Aristotelian sense. Change can take place in any of the categories of being.[14] But in its very notion, as has emerged from the foregoing analysis, it involves indispensably the three principles —a subject that changes, a form that is lost, a form that is acquired.

This essential notion of change is reached from the changes that are observed in the accidental categories, like change from place to place, from size to size, from color to color. But the analysis of the notion establishes it as a general concept that will hold wherever change is found, regardless of the particular category. It is accordingly applied by Aristotle in the category of sub-

[14]*Ph.* III 1, 201a8–9.

stance. In all other categories the subject of the change is observable. You can see the man who changes from uneducated to educated. You can touch the bronze that is cast from a nondescript form into a statue. You can handle the wood that is made into a bed. But with change in the category of substance you cannot observe the subject that changes, even in principle. This means that you cannot observe the subject changing. Change in the category of substance is accordingly not observable, even in principle.

There need be little wonder, then, that Aristotle is sparing in examples of change in the category of substance. Without too much enthusiasm he accepted the tradition of the four Empedoclean elements as the basic simple bodies, and admitted as generation the change of any one of these bodies into another.[15] But he is very circumspect in determining just where substance is found. Earth, air, and fire, three of the traditional elements, do not seem to him to have sufficient unity in their composition to be recognized as substances. Living things seem to have that unity, yet just where the unity is cannot be located too easily.[16] The one instance that he does mention definitely, though only in a passing way, is the change to plants and animals from seed.[17]

Today this Aristotelian example may not seem any too happy an illustration of substantial change. Without having to call the fertilized ovum of a rhinoceros a little rhinoceros, one may argue either for or against the position that an embryo is the same substance as the fully developed animal. To say that a tadpole is not a frog does not commit you to the stand that the

[15]See *Cael.* I 2, 268b26–29; GC II 1, 329a2–8; 8, 334b31–335a23.

[16]*Met.* Z 16, 1040b5–16.

[17]*Ph.* I 7, 190b4–5. Cf. GA I 18, 722b3–5, and St Paul's simile, I Cor. 15:36.

one is a different substance from the other. In general, it may be easy enough to claim that the change from something non-living to something alive is a change in substance. But in regard to pinpointing the change from non-living to living substance, or even to showing definitely that there was change from the truly non-living, are we today in any noticeably further advanced position than was Aristotle? Similarly, with modern chemical knowledge, it is easy to show definitely that air, fire, and earth are not substances in the Aristotelian sense. We no longer share the Stagirite's hesitations in that regard. With respect to water, however, can a definite decision be given? In the higher kinds of living things, Aristotle's criterion was a unity that distinguishes the complex organism from a heap. It is the same criterion that enables us now to consider the ant a different thing from the sandpile. In man, consciousness adds a still more profound criterion of unity. Every man considers himself a different being from other men, a different being from the substances he absorbs in nutrition and from those into which he will be dissolved when he dies. Apart from preconceived positions arising out of conclusions in metaphysics or in modern physics, and illegitimately transferred to the domain of natural philosophy, the difference of one being from another and the change of one sensible being into another may in general be admitted. *The evidence of pertinent bearing either for or against, though, is scarcely any greater now than it was in Aristotle's day.*

However, the plurality of things in the universe will hardly be contested any more today in a properly physical context than in the Stagirite's time.[18] As long as a plurality of beings in the sensible universe is admitted without subjecting the term 'beings' to intol-

[18]See *Ph.* I 2, 184b25–185a16.

erable strain, the plurality of substances required for
the Aristotelian demonstration of matter is present.
'Substance' in Aristotle's terminology meant the entity
or *ousia* of things. Wherever you have a being, simply
stated, you have an *ousia*, a substance. Nor should there
be too much difficulty about the change of one thing,
macroscopically speaking, into another. Molecular compounds are changed into other compounds, transmuta-
tion of the elements is no longer a dream. The one
real difficulty might lie in the proposal to locate the
individuality of things in sub-atomic particles. In that
case might not all the changes taking place in the
physical universe be merely new combinations of the
particles, as in Democritean atomism? There would be
only accidental change, not substantial change.

The denial of any unifying principle in things over
and above the sub-atomic particles would leave the
behavior of every particle wholly unrelated to that of
the others. A cosmic puppeteer would have to cause
the regularity of the world processes. A principle of
unity in each thing itself, on the other hand, would
have to be deeper than the division into particles and
into quanta, and indeed would have to be of a different
order. It would have to function on a more profound
level, in order to dominate the polarity of the sub-
atomic particles and to maintain the statistical regularity of the quanta. Such a principle would function exactly as the Aristotelian substantial form. It would be
the deepest principle of unity in a thing, and so would
make a thing "a being" simply and without qualification. It would be the principle that rendered the thing
intelligible. It would be the thing's basic determinant,
making the thing one kind of thing and not another.
It would be deeper than the entire qualitative and
quantitative or measurable orders in the thing, and so
would enable the thing to exist and function as a unit
in spite of the common patterns of atomic and sub-

atomic motion that it shares with other things. When this formal principle gave way to its successors in changes like nutrition or death, a radically new thing or things would come into being, in spite of common spectra before and after the change and in spite of the equality of the total weight before and after. It would enable the thing to function as a nature and not just artificially at the hands of a cosmic puppeteer. In a word, this principle would coincide entirely with the Aristotelian form in the category of substance.

The argument for the change of one substance into another, accordingly, seems neither stronger nor weaker in any notable way than it was in fourth century Greece. If you grant that you are a different thing or a different being from the food you absorb in nutrition and from the substances into which you will dissolve in death, you have recognized the data necessary to understand the Aristotelian demonstration. When one substance changes into another, what disappears is the most basic principle of determination and knowability, the principle that most radically made food one thing and man another thing. Without it, nothing in the thing could be knowable or observable. It is of course immediately succeeded by the form of the new thing. But the change of the one thing into the other requires a common subject, according to the very notion of change. Such a common subject will be unobservable both in principle and in fact, because it is what loses and acquires the most basic of forms and so of itself has not even the most rudimentary principle of knowability or observability. It has to be known in virtue of something else. That "something else," quite naturally, will be the observable subject in accidental change, like the wood that becomes a bed or the bronze that becomes a statue. Some corresponding subject has to be present for substantial change. In that analogous way, then, the subject of substantial change, namely matter, is indirectly known. It is known as the conclusion of scientific reasoning in the Aristotelian sense of 'scientific'. In Aristotle's own words:

> The underlying nature is an object of scientific knowledge, by an analogy. For as the bronze is to the statue, the wood to the bed, or the matter and the formless before receiving form to any one thing which has form, so is the underlying nature to substance, i.e. the "this" or existent.[19]

The presence of matter is proven stringently from the requirements for change, while the nature of matter is established through analogy with the subject of accidental change. The demonstration presupposes the universal notion of change and the two terms, but not the substrate, of substantial change.

The original referent upon which the Aristotelian concept of matter is based is therefore the subject of accidental change, like wood or bronze. From that notion of "subject," however, all determinations are removed, with the proviso that the negations as well as the determinations are accidental to it. In its own nature, then, this refined notion of subject remains as positive as ever. It was a positive notion from the start, as seen in a positive subject like wood or bronze, and all determinations were denied it under the express condition that none of these pertained to its own nature. In this way the notion *positive* is shown to be independent of *determinate*. For Aristotle, 'actual' was a synonym for 'determinate'. What lacked actuality, or in technical language the potential, could therefore be positive. By establishing the concept of the potential as positive even though non-actual or indeterminate, Aristotle has been able to set up matter as a positive though entirely non-actual subject of predication. Because the potential is positive without being

[19]*Ph.* I 7, 191a7–12; Oxford tr.

determinate, this concept of matter is possible to the human mind. Its referent is any sensible thing considered potentially as substance. It is the concept of a principle wholly undetermined, yet necessarily posited in reality by any form that is extended, multiplied in singulars, or terminating substantial change.

§5 CONCLUSION

As should be clear from the foregoing considerations, matter in the category of substance can be an object of scientific inquiry only on the level of natural philosophy. It cannot at all be reached by qualitative or quantitative procedures like those of chemistry and modern physics. What is predicated of it, in itself, does not belong to the order of the measurable or the directly observable, even in principle. Its predicates are notions like *purely potential, unknowable of itself, incorruptible,* and so on. Its presence is still necessary to explain substantial change, if such change is admitted. In any case, its presence is absolutely required to account for the extension of a formally identical characteristic in parts outside parts, and for the multiplication of the characteristic in a plurality of individuals, without any formal addition whatsoever. The Aristotelian matter has not been superseded nor even touched by the stupendous progress of modern physics. Nothing that is measurable can perform its function in explaining the nature of sensible things, and by the same token it cannot be brought forward to account for anything that requires explanation in measurable terms. Any type of matter dealt with by chemistry or modern physics would in comparison be secondary matter, and not matter that is a principle in the category of substance. "Matter" in the basic Aristotelian sense is therefore in no way a rival of the "matter" that can be measured or of the mass that can be transformed into energy, but is rather a very different means of explanation for sensible things on another scientific level, the level of natural philosophy.

In distinguishing his two tables, the solid one he wrote on and the "nearly all empty space" table he knew as a physicist, Eddington failed to stress that his knowledge of his scientific table was constructed from his knowledge of the ordinary table.[20] The scientific construct was the result of understanding the ordinary table in quantitative terms. The same ordinary table can also be understood scientifically (in the traditional sense of knowledge through causes) in terms of substantial principles, form and matter, as is done in natural philosophy. It can also be understood in terms of entitative principles, essence and being, as is done in metaphysics. They are all different accounts of the same thing, given on different levels of scientific (again, in the centuries-old meaning of "scientific") investigation. All these different accounts are necessary for a well-rounded understanding of sensible things. None of these accounts can afford to despise any of the others, nor seek to substitute for any of them, nor to interfere with any of them. Each has its own role to play, a role that only itself can play. The Aristotelian matter is a principle for explaining things on the level of natural philosophy. On that level it has its own predicates, predicates that still have to be used today in the properly balanced explanation of nature.

[20]See Arthur Stanley Eddington, *The Nature of the Physical World* (Cambridge, Eng., 1928), pp. ix–xi. Cf.: "The whole reason for accepting the atomic model is that it helps us to explain things we could not explain before. Cut off from these phenomena, the model can only mislead, . . ." Stephen Toulmin, *The Philosophy of Science* (New York, 1953), p. 12.

APPENDIX

On the independence of these different scientific procedures, see my paper "Our Knowledge of Nature," *Proceedings of the American Catholic Philosophical Association*, XXIX (1955), 80–86. A widely accepted view at present is to regard natural philosophy as a sort of dialectic that prepares the way for genuine physics; e.g.: ". . . frontier physics, natural philosophy. It is analysis of the concept of matter; a search for conceptual order amongst puzzling data." Norwood Russell Hanson, *Patterns of Discovery* (Cambridge, Eng., 1958), p. 119. "Not so very long ago the subject now called physics was known as "natural philosophy". The physicist is by origin a philosopher who has specialized in a particular direction." (Arthur S. Eddington, *The Philosophy of Physical Science* [Cambridge, Eng., 1939], p. 8.) It is true that before physics was developed through quantitative procedure as a special science, its problems had in point of historical fact been given over to the non-mathematical treatment of natural philosophy. That way of dealing with its problems was entirely illegitimate. The specific *differentiae* of natural things remain unknown and impenetrable to the human mind. They cannot be made the source for scientific knowledge of the specific traits of corporeal things. For this reason any new attempt to treat the experimental sciences as a continuation of natural philosophy, e.g. C. de Koninck, "Les Sciences Expérimentales sont-elles Distinctes de la Philosophie de la Nature?" *Culture*, II, (1941), 465–76, cannot hope to be successful. On the other hand, the view that natural philosophy consists only in "a search for conceptual order amongst puzzling data" seems continuous with the trend that has given rise to the conception of philosophy in general as linguistic analysis, concerned with words and concepts and not with things. Similarly, the notion that natural philosophy is a frontier investigation rather than a full-fledged science in its own right, seems to stem from Comte's law of the three stages, in which speculative philosophy in general was but an immature stage in the unilinear development towards positive science. In this view, philosophical treatment "will naturally be expected to deal with questions on the frontier of knowledge, as to which comparative certainty is not yet attained." Bertrand Russell, *Introduction to Mathematical Philosophy* (London, 1930), p. v. This is nothing but a cavalier dismissal of natural philosophy as a science.

Theoretically, it is indifferent whether the substantial principles (matter and form) used for the explanation of things through natural philosophy are reached by way of substantial change, or of extension, or of individuation. In point of fact, the way used by Aristotle himself was through substantial change. To show that the same two principles are required to explain extension and multiplication of singulars, is not a *tour de force* to safeguard the principles against someone who does not admit substantial change. It is rather a global view of the whole approach, from a theoretical standpoint, to the problem of matter.

May I express my thanks to Msgr. G. B. Phelan for many helpful suggestions, and to Fr. Ernan McMullin for carefully reading the first draft of this paper and pointing out a number of deficiencies. These I have tried to remedy in the final draft. This draft, of course, benefits from the other papers and the discussions at the conference, and in particular from the clear statement of the issues in Professor Fisk's contribution. Friedrich Solmsen's recently published work, *Aristotle's System of the Physical World* (Ithaca, N.Y., 1960), with its illuminating discussion (pp. 118–26) on the historical background of Aristotle's wholly undetermined matter, reached me too late to be of help in preparing the present paper.

PROBLEMS IN
METAPHYSICS Z, CHAPTER 13

M. J. WOODS

The purpose of this paper is to attempt a clarification
of the theory of substance which Aristotle had developed at the time when he wrote books Z, H, and θ of
the *Metaphysics*, by considering a passage where he
puts forward a number of arguments against a certain
doctrine about substance. Some of my conclusions
could, I think, be supported by an examination of certain other passages in Z. But in this paper I confine
my discussion to Z 13.

As Ross points out in his edition of the *Metaphysics*, chapters 13–16 form a single section, the
main upshot of which is summed up in 1041a3–5:[1]
ὅτι μὲν οὖν τῶν καθόλου λεγομένων οὐδὲν οὐσία
οὔτ᾽ ἐστὶν οὐσία οὐδομία ἐξ οὐσιῶν, δῆλον*

The suggestion that τὰ καθόλου λεγόμενα have
claims to be regarded as substances is raised at the
beginning of chapter 13, a discussion to which Aristotle
looks forward in chapter 3 at 1028b34. It is in the
course of these four chapters that the main, though

---

[1]Line references are all to Jaeger's Oxford text of *Metaphysics*.
[For the convenience of the reader, translations of some Greek
passages appear in footnotes. The translations used are those of
W. D. Ross and J. L. Ackrill.—Ed.]

*"Clearly, then, no universal term (τῶν καθόλου λεγομένων
οὐδέν) is the name of a substance, and no substance is composed
of substances."

not the only, criticism of the Theory of Forms occurs in this book.

To turn to detailed discussion of chapter 13: the exact course of the argument is difficult, and at some points the text is disputed. However, it is fairly clear that the main part of the chapter ends at 1039a14. an appendix. Beginning ἔχει δέ τό συμβαῖνον ἀπορία a dilemma is presented; it is a firmly held doctrine that it is substance which is the object of definition; but the earlier arguments tend to show that no actual substance is composite (σύνθετον). So substances appear to be indefinable. This dilemma is clearly before Aristotle's mind in the succeeding three chapters.

It is important to make clear exactly *what* doctrine Aristotle was attacking in these chapters. He was opposing the view that a correct answer to the question, "What is οὐσία?" would be given by saying that it is τὸ καθόλου. Thus he is denying that something καθόλου is *as such* an οὐσία. To deny this is not to claim that *nothing* καθόλου is an οὐσία, only that being καθόλου is not by itself a sufficient ground for so describing something. I wish to argue that Aristotle was in fact maintaining that only some things properly described as καθόλου are to be regarded as οὐσίαι; something καθόλου iis an οὐσία only if it is not predicated universally (καθόλου λεγόμενον). That is, the main purpose of these chapters is to deny that anything καθόλου λεγόμενον is an οὐσία. I will return to the distinction between being a universal and being predicated universally later.

We notice that he begins his discussion by saying (1038b3 f.) that some have regarded τὸ καθόλου as an αἴτιον or ἀρχή,* and it therefore needs investigation. No indication of who holds this is given, but it is difficult to believe that Aristotle would not have regarded

---

*"Cause" or "principle."

the Platonic Theory of Forms as an example of the sort of theory he had in mind.[2] I shall refer to Aristotle's opponent for convenience as "the Platonist," without intending to beg any question by the use of this label.

He continues (1038b8–9) with the remark that it is impossible for anything which λέγεται καθόλου to be an οὐσία. For that which is predicated universally is necessarily something which can be common to many things (ὃ πλείοσιν ὑπάρχειν πέφυκεν) whereas the οὐσία of something is that which is peculiar (ἴδιος) to it. Τὸ καθόλου cannot therefore be the οὐσία of all the set of objects of which it is predicated; equally it cannot be the οὐσία of nothing. But if it is the οὐσία of one of them, then all the other members of the set will have to be identical with this one, which is absurd; for things which share one οὐσία and τί ἦν εἶναι are one.

According to Ross,[3] the argument has to be interpreted as follows: the Platonist seeks to satisfy the requirement that the universal be ἴδιον to a single thing of which it is the οὐσία by supposing it to be the οὐσία of just one of its particulars; but unfortunately it has as good a claim to be the οὐσία of the other particulars of which it is predicated; so if the requirement of uniqueness is to be fulfilled, these others must be identical with the one selected, which is absurd. (From now on I shall call the requirement that an οὐσία be ἴδιος to that of which it is the οὐσία "the uniqueness requirement.")

This interpretation, which requires us to supply a good deal, seems untenable. It is, of course,

[2]Cf. H 1042a15–16: Τῷ δὲ καθόλου καὶ τῷ γένει καὶ αἱ ἰδέαι συνάπτουσιν (κατὰ τὸν αὐτὸν γὰρ λόγον οὐσίαι δοκοῦσιν εἶναι) ["And with the universal and the genus the Ideas are connected (συνάπτουσιν); it is in virtue of the same argument (κατὰ τὸν αὐτὸν λόγον) that they are thought to be substances"].

[3]*Aristotle's Metaphysics* (Oxford, 1924), Vol. II, p. 210.

true that if the Platonist said that the universal
animal were the οὐσία of only one particular
ζῷον (say, Socrates), not of Callias, Bucephalus,
and Fido, his position is vulnerable and indeed
absurd. Any such selection would be arbitrary. But
nothing in the text suggests that Aristotle regarded
the argument as vulnerable in just this way. Moreover,
the very absurdity and indeed lunacy of the position
put into the mouth of the Platonist may be thought
to be an argument against the view that he is toying
with the possibility of satisfying the uniqueness requirement in this way. Also, as reconstructed by Ross,
the argument seems to beg the question. The Platonist
begins by supposing that a universal like ζῷον is the
οὐσία of just one animal, e.g. Socrates; he is then told
that he will be committed to regarding τὰ ἄλλα as
identical with him, since τὰ ἄλλα will also have τὸ
καθόλου as their οὐσία. But this is precisely what the
Platonist is desperately denying. Τὰ ἄλλα must, on
this view, refer to those particulars of which τὸ
καθόλου is predicated other than the one of which it
is the οὐσία; and the Platonist will not agree that *they*
have τὸ καθόλου for their οὐσία without argument,
for the position he has just taken up is the denial of
this. As the passage stands he is represented as agreeing
without argument that *all* particulars of which τὸ
καθόλου is predicated have it for their οὐσία, and not
simply one of them. So Ross's interpretation does not
really find any argument in the passage at all.

Cherniss interprets the passage in a different way.[4]
According to him, the sentence ἑνὸς δ' εἰ ἔσται, καὶ
τἆλλα τοῦτ ἔσται* provides a reason for the dis-
junction stated in the first half of the previous sentence

---

[4]*Aristotle's Criticism of Plato and the Academy* (Baltimore,
1944), p. 318, n. 220.
*"If it is to be the substance of one, this one will be the others
also."

("either τὸ καθόλου is the οὐσία of *all* the particulars falling under it or of none of them"); while ὧν γὰρ μία ἡ οὐσία καὶ τὸ τί ἦν εἶναι ἕν, καὶ αὐτὰ ἕν* provides a reason for saying that it cannot be the οὐσία of all of them. This interpretation avoids the difficulty mentioned just now in Ross's interpretation: that no argument is presented which could lead the Platonist to abandon his suggestion that τὸ καθόλου might be the οὐσία of one thing. On the other hand, it is hard not to take 11, 14–15 (ὧν γὰρ μία . . .) as providing a reason for what is asserted immediately before, especially as it is readily intelligible as a reason for it. But even if we accept Cherniss' view, the passage concerned (11, 9–15) seems best interpreted, as I shall argue, not as an argument which is decisive as it stands, but as one which shows what a Platonist is committed to if he insists on regarding τὸ καθόλου as οὐσία. He will be committed to accepting it as the οὐσία of all its particulars, and treating these as identical with one another.

In order to see how this and later passages in these chapters are to be interpreted, we need to raise a major problem which immediately faces anyone who reads this passage in the light of Aristotle's criticism of Plato. Aristotle's answer to the question, "What is οὐσία?" is that what is οὐσία in the fullest sense is the εἶδος or τὶ ἦν εἶναι of something. This comes out very clearly in chapter 17, but it is already present as a doctrine in the chapters of Z before chapter 13. It emerges from the identification of εἶδος with τί ἦν εἶναι and of this with πρώτη οὐσία at 1032b1–2. Thus Aristotle is presumably committed to holding that the form of the species *man* is a substance. But this seems incompatible with the doctrine that nothing καθόλου can be a substance: for *man*

---

*"For things whose substance is one and whose essence is one are themselves also one."

is surely predicated universally of Socrates, Callias, etc. How can the species *man* be an οὐσία, if any οὐσία has to belong ὡς ἴδιον to that of which it is the οὐσία? It is clearly of no use to seek to avoid this difficulty by saying that, when discussing the suggestion that τὰ καθόλου are οὐσίαι, Aristotle has in mind only the higher genera into which species fall. For his own theory of substance may obviously still be open to the objections he makes to the claims of τὰ καθόλου λεγόμενα to be substances even if he himself only uses these arguments against the claims of higher genera to be οὐσίαι.

One way of escaping these difficulties is to suppose that in Z Aristotle, where he says that οὐσία is εἶδος, has in mind not the form common to all members of a species but something peculiar to an individual member. Thus the οὐσία of Socrates will be peculiar to him and will not be something predicated of anything universally. The thesis that, as well as the form of species, there is a form peculiar to each member of a species to be found, almost certainly, in Λ, and furthermore, the doctrine that in the case of animate objects their form is their soul is difficult to interpret without presupposing some such view as this. If this view can be found independently in Z, we shall have some grounds for interpreting chapter 13 along these lines. There will then be no conflict between the requirements for being an οὐσία stated at the beginning of 13 and the doctrine that οὐσία is form.

This question has been discussed in an article by Professor R. Albritton.[5] Albritton finds clear evidence that Aristotle believed in a distinct form for each individual substance in Λ and M of the *Metaphysics* and in the *De Anima*; but in Z and H of the *Metaphysics* the most he can find is some evidence that

---

[5]"Forms of Particular Substances in Aristotle's *Metaphysics*," *Journal of Philosophy*, Vol. LIV, No. 22 (October 1957).

Aristotle accepted that there was a distinct form for each *living* substance. This evidence lies in the passages in which the doctrine that the form and οὐσία of a man is his soul occurs. So whether or not these passages be regarded as evidence for the doctrine of particular forms depends on whether we regard the doctrine that the soul is the form of the body as intelligible only with such a view. But, in any case, the most that these passages could be said to point to is the doctrine that there is an individual form for each *living* individual. However, if Z 13, the passage with which we are immediately concerned, be interpreted as showing that Aristotle thought that there was a distinct form for each individual substance, it would show that Aristotle regarded the doctrine as holding for *all* individual substances, and not merely those with a ψυχή; for the argument would be a general one. Since nothing καθόλου λεγόμενον can be an οὐσία, and the form of the species is predicated of the plurality of individuals in the species, the οὐσία of each individual substance, whether animate or inanimate, must be a form which is peculiar to it.

Albritton considers the suggestion that chapter 13 implies a doctrine of particular forms and argues that there is nothing in the chapter which forces us to interpret Aristotle in that way. To quote Albritton (p. 706): "One might distinguish, as Aristotle does, ways of being 'one' and agree that things whose substance is one need not be one in every way but only in that of their substance. These are many in number. It follows that nothing one in number can be their substance. But the universal form of man is *not* one in number. . . . It is only one in form. And men are one in form. The one form of man may, therefore, be their substance."

This interpretation is very attractive, and I agree with the general approach. But as it stands, it seems to allow the Platonist a very obvious rejoinder. If the form of a species can be said to be an οὐσία, compatibly with the uniqueness condition, because the particulars are ἕν εἴδει, one might equally hold that the genus could be said to be an οὐσία also, in spite of being predicated of many things, since these things (species and particulars) though not ἕν ἀριθμῷ nor ἕν εἴδει are ἕν γένει.* Now it may be thought that the sense in which a group of things which belong to the same genus can be said to be one is weaker than the sense in which things in the same species can be so described, and that therefore the Platonist would at least have to admit that genera like *animal* are less fully entitled to be called οὐσίαι than species like man. But at least this defense would seem to show that τὰ καθόλου have some claim to be regarded as οὐσίαι; and this is something which Aristotle seems firmly to reject in this chapter. He insists roundly that nothing καθόλου λεγόμενον is a substance, and these assertions are difficult to reconcile with the position that they are substances of a sort, though less fully than certain other items. If he were prepared to concede that both *man* and *animal* qualify as οὐσίαι though the latter less than the former, we should have a position like the one he takes up in the *Categories* (2b7 f.: τῶν δὲ δευτέρων οὐσιῶν μᾶλλον τὸ εἶδος τοῦ γένους).† But it seems clear that this view is now abandoned. So we have the position that if we interpret the chapter along the lines that Albritton suggests, and make the fact that *man* is the οὐσία of many individuals compatible with the uniqueness requirement, the Platonist will be able, apparently, to find a comparable sense in which *animal* can be said to be

---

*"One in number," "one in form," "one in genus."

†"Of the secondary substances the species is more a substance than the genus, since it is nearer to the primary substance."

an οὐσία: and that is something Aristotle will not accept.

Although Albritton does not consider this way out for the Platonist, the next paragraph of his article suggests an answer that Aristotle might have made to the position. He says: "The argument would not allow any universal of species to be the substance of its species. The species of a genus, for example, are precisely many in *form*, not in number, and therefore this genus, which is one in form cannot be their substance." But where does Aristotle say that a genus is one in form? In order to find the argument acceptable we need to know that the genus *animal* is one in form in precisely the same way as that in which the species or individuals of which *animal* is predicated are *not* one in form. Only if that is so can we regard the argument as establishing a difference in the relation between *man* and the members of this species on the one hand and the relation between *animal* and the species and individuals of which it is predicated on the other.

Albritton does not mention any passage in which Aristotle says that a genus is one in form. But he draws attention a little earlier, amongst other passages, to the beginning of Book I of the *Metaphysics*. There Aristotle says that those things are one ὧν ἡ νόησις μία, τοιαῦτα δ᾽ ὧν ἀδιαίρετος, ἀδιαίρετος δὲ τοῦ ἀδιαιρέτου εἴδει ἢ ἀριθμῷ (1052a30).* Again, a little later he says τὸ ἑνὶ εἶναι τὸ ἀδιαιρέτῳ ἐστὶν εἶναι.† Since he does not in this passage explicitly mention γένη as examples of things which are ἕν εἴδει we must consider whether he would in fact have allowed a γένος to be something which was

---

*". . . the other things that are one are those whose definition is one. Of this sort are the things the thought of which is one (ὧν ἡ νόησις μία) i.e. those the thought of which is indivis-indivisible (ἀδιαίρετος); and it is indivisible if the thing is indivisible in kind (εἴδει) or number."

†" 'To be one' means 'to be indivisible'."

ἀδιαίρετον εἴδει. It seems to me that he would not.
When he says that something is ἕν εἴδει if it is
ἀδιαίρετον εἴδει, he seems to have in mind the same
idea that he expressed Z 1034a8 (for example). There
he says that Socrates and Callias are ταὐτὸ δὲ εἴδει
(ἄτομον γὰρ τὸ εἶδος).* An εἶδος is ἄτομον in the
sense that it is not capable of further differentiation.
This is precisely what is not the case with γένη. If
ἄτομον in this passage means the same as 'ἀδιαίρετον'
in Book I, then it seems that we are forbidden to treat
a γένος as being ἕν εἴδει in the sense distinguished in
that passage. Moreover, even if passages can be found
in which a genus is described as ἕν εἴδει, this will
presumably be in a wider sense of εἶδος in which it
is not contrasted with 'γένος', and therefore not that
sense in which the various species of a genus are not
ἕν εἴδει. Again, if it is the case that a γένος is correctly
described as ἕν εἴδει, presumably, derivatively from this,
there will a sense in which the different species of the
genus can themselves be ἕν εἴδει, which could be ex-
ploited by the Platonist.

I conclude that Albritton's suggestion does not provide Aristotle with a way of meeting the argument we
have put in the Platonist's mouth: that if the form
of a species can be allowed to be a substance compatibly
with the uniqueness requirement, so can a higher genus.
The difficulty seems to be that the suggestion does
not take seriously enough Aristotle's several times
repeated statement that nothing predicated universally
(καθόλου λεγόμενον, κατηγορούμενον, ὕπαρχον) is
an οὐσία. On the view we have just criticized, Aristotle
is saying simply that nothing that is predicated universally can be a substance, unless the plurality of objects
of which it is predicated can themselves be said to be
one in a certain sense. This runs into the difficulty

---

*"The same in form; for their form is indivisible."

that the Platonists can provide a sense in which the things of which a genus is predicated can be said to be one. Albritton's suggestion implicitly makes the predication of a universal of many things compatible with the satisfaction of the uniqueness requirement. But what Aristotle says is that since τὸ καθόλου is common to many objects, it cannot be ἴδιον to one. He does not restrict himself to saying that nothing can be a substance which is common to plurality of objects, unless the many are also one. The suggestion under discussion waters down Aristotle's remarks considerably, since it treats the doctrine that nothing καθόλου λεγόμενον is a substance as one accepted by Aristotle only with considerable qualification.

If we take these remarks as they stand and wish still to hold that when Aristotle says that the εἶδος is οὐσία he has in mind a form common to all numbers of a species, we must suppose that he would have denied that the form man is predicated universally of Socrates, Plato, Callias. If genera, by contrast are predicated of a plurality of objects, we have found a way of interpreting chapter 13 which allows Aristotle, consistently with his own doctrine that substance is form, to deny that anything predicated universally is a substance. For the remarks about τὰ καθόλου λεγόμενα will have application only to genera. I wish to claim that this is precisely the position that Aristotle adopts in *Metaphysics Z*.

This doctrine that the form of a species is not predicated universally of the members of the species involves an obvious departure from the sort of view advanced in, for example, the *Categories*. Indeed it might be said that the theory rejected in chapter 13 is as much the theory held by Aristotle himself earlier as it is that of Plato, though it is probable that in Z 13 Aristotle has Plato mainly in mind, in view of the contents of the succeeding chapters.

In saying that Aristotle denied that a species may properly be said to be predicated universally of its members, I am not of course denying that Aristotle might have allowed that the *name* of a species was predicated of its members. Nor, perhaps, would he have said that it was for *all* purposes impermissible to speak of the form of a species as being predicated universally of its members. What he seems to have thought is that, for the problems with which he is concerned in Z, it is incorrect to say that a species form is predicated universally of a plurality of individuals. It may be helpful at this stage to specify exactly what Aristotle thought could properly be said about species and what could not, on the view that I am advancing. Firstly, he appears to be denying that a species could be predicated universally of its members, and he expresses this in various ways. No οὐσία (and therefore no species) is καθόλου λεγόμενον (1038b9): again (1038b35) none of the things καθόλου ὑπάρχοντα is an οὐσία; the reason given in the next line is that none of the things κοινῇ κατηγορομενα* is τόδε τι, earlier (1038b11) the claims of the Platonist are rejected because he allows to be a substance something which is κοινόν; it is κοινόν because πλείοσιν ὑπάρχειν πέφυκεν. At the end of the whole discussion in these chapters (16, 1041a4), his conclusion is restated: τῶν καθόλου λεγοθένων οὐδὲν οὐσία. An οὐσία is not common to a plurality of objects; it is τόδε τι. A genus is not τόδε τι but τοιόνδε (1039a1). So there is a clear contrast between the things that Aristotle is willing to say about species-forms and the things that can, in his view, be said of genera.

It is interesting to note that in the *Categories* he is unwilling to say that a secondary substance (in the

---

*"Common predicates."

terminology he then used) properly speaking signified
τόδε τι (3b14 f.). At that time he did not object to
the notion that a species was predicated of a plurality
of objects. A secondary substance is then described as
ποῖόν τι,* and the reason given is that κατὰ πολλῶν
ὁ ἄνθρωπος λέγεται καὶ τὸ ζῶον.† Thus, already at
the time when he wrote the *Categories*, he regarded
being predicated of a plurality as strictly incompatible
with being τόδε τι. In *Metaphysics Z*, where the title
πρώτη οὐσία is given to an εἶδος, he rejected the idea
that an εἶδος is predicated of a plurality along with the
idea that it cannot strictly be called τόδε τι. It is characteristic of the *Categories* to regard the difference between genus and species, in respect of right to the name
οὐσία, as merely a matter of degree; and this, I suggest,
goes with a view which regards the relation between a
species and the particulars belonging to it as essentially
the same as that between a genus and its species. In
the *Metaphysics* he thought of genera as κοινῇ
κατηγορούμενα; and this is regarded as incompatible
with saying that a genus is τόδε τι. However, in *Metaphysics Z* 13 he no longer says, as he does in the *Categories* that a genus is not τόδε τι but ποῖον; instead
he says (1039a1): οὐδὲν σημαίνει τῶν κοινῇ κατηγο-
ρουμένων τόδε τι ἀλλὰ τοιόνδε.‡ The word τοιόνδε
replaces ποῖον as the other term of the contrast with
τόδε τι. As the use of the term ποῖον in connection
with something which belongs in the category of substance is obviousy potentially very misleading, it is not
difficult to see why he should have felt the need to use
another word. But I suggest that the reasons he has in
Metaphysics Z for regarding a genus as not τόδε τι but
saying that an εἶδος is strictly not τόδε τι but ποιόν.

Another passage in Z which is worth noticing is the

---

*"A certain qualification."
†"For both *man* and *animal* are predicated of many things."
‡"No common predicate indicates a 'this', but rather a 'such'."

well-known passage explicitly about the Theory of
Forms in 16, 1040b27: ἀλλ' οἱ τὰ εἴδη λέγοντες τῇ
μέν ὀρθῶς λέγουσιν χωρίζοντες αὐτά, εἴπερ οὐσίαι
εἰσί, τῇ δ' οὐκ ὀρθῶς, ὅτι τὸ ἕν ἐπὶ πολλῶν εἴδος
λέγουσιν.* It is the last phrase I am concerned with.
When Aristotle says that the Platonists went wrong in
describing, τὸ ἕν ἐπὶ πελλῶν as an εἴδος he says something which it would be difficult to square with a
view that εἴδη in one sense are properly described as
ἕν ἐπὶ πολλῶν. Admittedly, Aristotle's conception of
εἴδη was different from Plato's. But in a passage where
Aristotle tells us what is right about the Theory of
Forms as well as what is wrong, it would be strange
if he singled out as the fault in the theory that it calls
something which is 'one over many' an εἴδος if he
himself were ready to use the word εἴδος of something which was ἕν ἐπὶ πολλῶν. I suggest that Aristotle would have denied that the species man was
something 'ἐπὶ' individual men. His complaint against
Plato is that the Theory of Forms treats species and
genera as if they were alike; genera which are correctly described as ἕν ἐπὶ πολλῶν are being treated as
if they were εἴδη and therefore substances. The denial
that an εἴδος is ἕν ἐπὶ πολλῶν goes with the denial
that anything κοινῇ κατηγορούμενον is a substance.
This interpretation fits in well with the context, when
it is clear that he still concerned himself with the
evaluation of the claim of things predicated universally
to be substances.

Before I return to a detailed discussion of chapter
13, I ought to deal with a possible objection. It may
be said that Aristotle could not have denied that the
form of a species was something καθόλου and there-

---

*"But those who say the Forms exist, in one respect are right,
in giving the Forms separate existence, *if* they are substances; but
in another respect they are not right, because they say the one
over many is a Form."

fore the denial that any universal is a substance is incompatible with the view that it is εἴδη which are οὐσίαι, if the εἴδη he has in mind are εἴδη of species and not εἴδη distinct for each individual member of a species. Apart from the inherent implausibility of denying that εἴδη are καθόλου, Aristotle himself commits himself to this in Z. At 1035b27 f., he speaks of ὁ δ' ἄνθρωπος καὶ ὁ ἵππος καὶ τὰ οὕτως ἐπὶ τῶν καθ' ἕκαστα, καθόλου δέ etc.* The context is full of difficulties, but it is clear that what he has in mind in this passage are the forms of the species to which men and horses belong. Again, it is substances which are capable of definition in the strict sense, but definition is only of τὸ καθόλου (cf. 1035b34, and elsewhere).

As I have indicated earlier, my reply to this is that a distinction has to be made between the question whether an item is something καθόλου and the question whether it is καθόλου λεγόμενον. What he is concerned to deny is that that which is predicated universally is a substance. He is not denying that something which is καθόλου may be an οὐσία; he is saying that nothing which λέγεται καθόλου or is κοινῇ κατηγορούμενον is an οὐσία. Thus I think that when, early in chapter 13 (1038b11–12) he says: τοῦτο γὰρ λέγεται καθόλου ὃ πλείοσιν ὑπάρχειν πέφυκεν, we should regard him as saying, not that something is called a universal if it is such as to belong to several things, but that something is predicated univesally if it is such as to belong to several things. Again, when he sums up the whole discussion at the end of chapter 16, he states his conclusion by saying not simply that nothing universal is a substance, but that nothing predicated universally is one.

---

*"But man and horse and terms which are thus applied to (ἐπί) individuals, but universally, are not substance but something composed of this particular formula and this particular matter treated as universal."

It is time now to return to a detailed consideration
of chapter 13. This general discussion arose out of a
difficulty in seeing how 1038b8–15 provide an argument
against the Platonist. I shall return to this passage
later. In 11, 15–16, he offers another brief argument
against his opponent. An οὐσία is something which
is not said of a ὑποκείμενον, whereas the universal is
always said of ὑποκειμένον τι. The last statement will
have to be regarded, on the view I am defending as
claiming, not that everything universal is said of
ὑποκειμένον τι, but that everything predicated universally is said of ὑποκειμένον τι. If the sentence is taken
in context, this reading is, I think, possible. If this is
correct, Aristotle must deny that an εἶδος λέγεται
καθ’ ὑποκειμένου τινός if it is to be regarded as an
οὐσία. This conflicts, apparently, with what is said in
chapter 3, at 1029a23–24: τὰ μὲν γὰρ ἄλλα τῆς
οὐσίας κατηγορεῖται, αὕτη δὲ τῆς ὕλης.* But I think
that the conflict need not worry us greatly. Since the
word ὑποκείμενον is used in several senses, the question whether something λέγεται καθ’ ὑποκειμένου
τινός will also have a number of senses, and when
asked about a given item, will have different senses
according to how it is taken. The statement in chapter
13 that no οὐσία λέγεται καθ’ ὑποκειμένου τινός
is to be regarded as equivalent to the denial that an
οὐσία is, properly speaking, predicated of the individuals which belong to it. This will not prevent Aristotle
from saying that an εἶδος is, in a sense, predicated of
matter.

Before returning to the argument with which we
started, I will now consider the next section, 1038b16–
30. These are taken by Ross and others to be a series
of further arguments offered by Aristotle against the
view that any universal is a substance. The first argu-

*"For the predicates other than substance are predicated of
substance, while substance is predicated of matter."

ment is rather obscure; in 1, 19 ἔστι is corrected by Jaeger in the Oxford Classical Text to 'ἔσται', to bring it into line with ἔσται in 1, 22. This passage, 11, 16–23, is interpreted by Ross as follows: The Platonist concedes that something καθόλου cannot be regarded as an οὐσία in the way a τί ἦν εἶναι is; none the less a genus is an element in a τί ἦν εἶναι, and thus ought to have some claim to be regarded as an οὐσία. But it itself will have to be the τ.η.ε. of something in just the way that the τ.η.ε. in which it occurs as an element is. Thus the amended suggestion of the Platonist amounts to the same as the already rejected suggestion that something καθόλου can be an οὐσία through being a τ.η.ε.; it is subject to the objections raised earlier in the chapter.

At first sight this is plain sailing. The Platonist amends his position to meet the difficulties raised by Aristotle; Aristotle then shows that the amended position is really the same as the original one. But if we look at the actual reasons for saying that the new position is the same as the old, the passage becomes more and more puzzling. The reason given is that it will be ἐκείνου οὐσία ἐν ᾧ εἴδει ὡς ἴδιον ὑπάρχει* (if we follow Jaeger and excise 'οἷον τὸ ζῷον'). But surely if it is conceded that it is the οὐσία of something to which it belong ὡς ἴδιον, then this undermines the reasons given earlier for saying that nothing καθόλου λεγόμενον can be said to be an οὐσία. The argument given earlier was that nothing which did not satisfy what I called the uniqueness requirement can be regarded as an οὐσία. But now Aristotle appears to be saying that it does after all satisfy the uniqueness requirement. It is no use to appeal to the earlier established conclusion that nothing καθόλου λεγ. is an οὐσία in the way that a τ.η.ε. as if the reason for saying

---

*"The substance of that in which it is present as something peculiar to it."

that it is after all a τ.η.ε. is that it belongs to a unique
εἶδος; it was precisely because this condition is not
fulfilled in the case of καθόλου λεγόμενα that it was
denied that anything καθ. λεγ. can be an οὐσία in the
earlier argument. If it now turns out that something
καθ. λεγ. can be the οὐσία of a single εἶδος, the
earlier argument is called into question. The way out
of this difficulty that I suggest is that 1038b22–23 not
only does, but is intended to, undermine the earlier
argument. The words in question are not used by
Aristotle *propria persona* but are part of a set of arguments which he represents the Platonist as advancing
in favour of his position. I think we should regard the
whole passage from lines 16 to 30 as put into the mouth
of Aristotle's opponent. Aristotle's own objections to
the position begin at line 30: 'ὅλως δὲ συμβαίνει ...'
On the usual interpretation, only 11. 16–18 are attrib-
utable to the Platonist, and from 'οὐκοῦν δῆλον'
onwards there are three arguments against his amended
position. But it seems to me that much better sense
can be made of the whole passage down to line 30
if we suppose that it is the Platonist who is speaking.
The first argument, in 11. 16–23, can then be interpreted as follows: The Platonist concedes that it is
not an οὐσία in the way that τὸ τί ἦν εἶναι is. This
concession is temporary; what he means is that it is
not an οὐσία in the way that what are agreed to be
οὐσίαι, namely species, are; it will nevertheless be an
element in a substance-species. It will have a λόγος;
the fact that the λόγος of ζῷον is not a complete
λόγος of the οὐσία *man* makes no difference; since it
has a λόγος, this λόγος will define a unique class of
species of which it is the οὐσία in just the way that
ἄνθρωπος is the οὐσία of individual men. In other
words, the Platonist is insisting that the very same
reasons that enable one to regard ἄνθρωπος as an
οὐσία consistently with the uniqueness requirement

can also enable ζῷον to be regarded as an οὐσία. He insists that species and genera be treated on the same footing. It is noticeable that in 1038b23 he says, ἐν ᾧ εἴδει ὡς ἴδιον ὑπάρχει. This would be an odd remark if Aristotle were talking in his own person; the plurality of species of which ζῷον is predicated do not fall into a single εἶδος but a single γένος. But the universalist is naturally happy to say that the various species of animal fall into a single εἶδος just as much as single men do, since he wishes to assimilate the relation of a genus to its species to the relation of a species to the individuals belonging to it.

Finally, on this section, one point of translation: Ross has to translate 'ἔστι' both in 1. 19 and in 1. 20 existentially: "It makes no difference if not all the elements in the substance have a definition." He thinks that Aristotle has in mind the difficulty that if the elements of a substance revealed in a definition are themselves substances, we shall be forced to allow indefinable substances, when the process of analysis is carried to its limit, if an infinite regress is to be avoided. On the view I am taking, 'ἔστι' is to be construed in 1. 20 as a copula: "It makes no difference if it (sc. the λόγος of ζῷον) is not a λόγος of everything in the substance (sc. man)." Cherniss[6] takes 'ἔστι' in 1. 19 and in 1. 20 as a copula; on my interpretation, it has to be taken existentially in 1. 19, and as a copula in 1. 20.

The next argument, beginning with ἔτι in 1. 23 also seems to make more sense if it is treated as an argument advanced by the Platonist. The point is that if the elements of a substance which are revealed by a definition are prior to the whole in which they occur, then, if they are not substances, they must be (e.g.) qualities; so quality will be prior to substance. Regarded as an argument in the mouth of the Platonist the

[6]Op. cit.

argument makes good sense. No doubt the way in which the dilemma is presented is a little simple-minded; it does not follow from the fact that genera are not, properly speaking, οὐσίαι that they belong in some other category. Aristotle's own solution, which is admittedly not easy to understand, is to invoke the notion of potentiality. He says later in the chapter that ἀδύνατον γάρ οὐσίαν ἐξ οὐσιῶν εἶναι ἐνυπαρχουσῶν ἐντλεχεία (1039a4).* Still later he invokes the matter-form model to explain the relation of genus and differentia (1045a33 f.). However, the objection that if the elements of substance are prior to the whole, they must be substances is exactly the sort of objection that might occur to someone who had read Z 10, where Aristotle is quite happy about saying that some of the parts of a λόγος (by which, presumably, he means the εἶδος) are prior to the whole; and this might readily make someone wonder how the parts of a substance can fail to be substances themselves.

To turn briefly to the third argument in this section, at 1038b29–30, he says that τῷ Σωκράτει ἐνυπάρξει οὐσία, ὥστε δυοῖν ἔσται οὐσία. Ross[7] glosses this as follows: " 'In Socrates, himself a substance, there will be present as an element a substance (sc. animal), which will therefore be a substance of two things (sc. of the class of animals and also of Socrates)'." I think this is correct; but it makes sense in the context only if we regard it as an argument advanced by the Platonist. It cannot be an objection to regarding something καθόλου λεγόμενον as a substance that it would have to be the οὐσία of two things; for in that sense the species man is the οὐσία of two things, viz. the class of men and also Socrates. Regarded as an argument

---

*"A substance cannot be composed of actually existing substances. . . ."

[7]Op. cit., p. 211.

used by the Platonist, it makes sense. Just as the εἶδος man is the οὐσία of the class of men and, derivatively from that, of Socrates, so the genus *animal* is the οὐσία of the class of animals and also, derivatively from that, of Socrates. Considered as member of the class of men, the οὐσία of Socrates is the species *man*; considered as a member of the class of animals, his οὐσία is the genus ζῷον.

We are now in a position to explain the earlier argument in chapter 13 with which we began. It is not intended as a refutation of the Platonist's position; what Aristotle does is to draw out a consequence of it, which makes his opponent formulate it more clearly. Starting with the class of men, it is suggested that, despite appearances, if the species *man* can be said to be the οὐσία of them, so can ζῷον; Aristotle points out that if it is to be the οὐσία of the class of man, since *animal* is predicated of non-men, then other animals must be shown in some way to be identical with men. This leads the Platonist to formulate his position more carefully. Although *animal*, in relation to the class of men is not an οὐσία in quite the way the species *man* is, it is the τ.η.ε., and therefore οὐσία of a larger class. There is an εἶδος ἐν ᾧ ὡς ἴδιον ὑπάρχει.

Aristotle's own refutation of the Platonist begins at 1. 30. He says, in effect, that if we allow that species are substances, then no element of a species revealed by a definition is. His reasons for this are, firstly, that no ζῷον exists χωρὶς, παρὰ τὰ τινά. (As Ross remarks,[8] when he says that there is no ζῷον παρὰ ἃ τινά, he has in mind the point that there is no animal apart from the particular *species* of animal, not that there is no ζῷον apart from the individual animals.) Secondly, nothing predicated in common is a τόδε τι but only τοιόνδε. I have already discussed this passage. If I am

[8]Op. cit.

right, he is concerned here to deny that ζῷον is genuinely predicated of a plurality of objects.

He ends by saying that if these propositions are not
accepted, ἄλλα τε πολλὰ συμβαίνει καὶ ὁ τρίτος
ἄνθρωπος.* I end my discussion of this chapter by
considering how he thought that the denial of the
doctrines led to the Third Man. We noticed a little
before that in order to refute the Platonist he makes
use of the fact that no genus exists apart from its
species. This doctrine is not argued for in chapter 13
but in chapter 12. (This, incidentally, explains why
chapter 12 comes where it does in Z; he needed to
establish this in order to disallow the claim of things
καθόλου λεγόμενα to be substances.) The idea that
no genus exists apart from its species raises many problems of interpretation, but I take it that part of what
he is saying can be stated quite simply; he is saying
that nothing can be an animal without being a particular species of animal. This may seem platitudinous but
it is certainly un-Platonic; for in our version of the Theory of Forms, Forms are construed as paradigms or ex-
emplars with only one characteristic; so the form *animal* would have to be an animal without being a
particular kind of animal, and would thus be a counter-
example to the doctrine that there is no ζῷον παρὰ
τὰ τινά in a sense which can be precisely stated. We
are by now familiar with the arguments by which
Aristotle sought to derive the Third-Man regress from
the Theory of Forms thus construed. Can we find
anything analogous relevant to the present passage?

I think we can. The Platonist, who maintains that
the genus which is an element in a species like man is
an οὐσία, is committed to holding that the word ζῷον
is predicated in the same sense both of the species *man*
and the supposed οὐσία which is an element in the

---

*"If not, many difficulties follow and especially the 'third
man' ."

species *man*. But the common element which is present in all species of animal cannot of course itself be regarded as belonging to any animal-species. So he has to reject the doctrine that there is no ζῷον παρὰ τὰ τινά. It is not difficult to see that Aristotle could have developed a regress similar to the traditional Third-Man regress against this position; the first step would be to ask how the word ζῷον came to be used in the same sense of the species man and the supposed common element it shared with other animal species. Something very like this argument seems to be adumbrated in 14, 1039a30 f.

I have argued that the arguments of chapter 13 against those who say that things καθόλου λεγόμενα may be substances are not incompatible with Aristotle's own doctrine that εἴδη are substances. Εἴδη are things which are not λεγόμενα κατὰ πολλῶν. However, it may be thought that this remains no more than a verbal maneuver unless some justification is offered for treating species differently from genera. What justification is there for Aristotle's denial that man κατὰ πολλῶν λέγεται? The answer, I think, is along the following lines: It is the species-form *man* which supplies us with a principle for individuation for man: it is only in virtue of possessing the form *man* that bits of matter which constitute men are marked off from one another. To speak of a plurality of objects I need some means of marking off each member of the set from other things; I do this, according to Aristotle, by recognizing occurrences of a certain form in matter. Thus I must already regard things as possessing the form before I can think of objects as a genuine plurality. In so far as the statement that the form of a species is predicated universally of its members implies the contrary of this, it is incorrect. Aristotle refused to say that ἄνθρωπος was καθόλου λεγόμενον because that would suggest that you could distinguish men independently of their possession of the form—as if you could first distinguish individual substances and then notice that the predicate applied to them which supplied a basis for distinguishing them in the first place. With species in relation to genera, on the other hand, it is the other way round. The genus does not itself supply a basis for distinguishing species; the species are distinguished by appropriate differentia; in Z a species is virtually equated with its differentia (e.g. at 1038a19), so that species are in a certain sense self-individuating; hence the genus to which they belong *is* predicated universally of them.

IV. ETHICS

THE MEANING OF 'ΑΓΑΘΟΝ
IN THE *ETHICS* OF ARISTOTLE

H. A. PRICHARD

I have for some time found it increasingly difficult to resist a conclusion so heretical that the mere acceptance of it may seem a proof of lunacy. Yet the failure of a recent attempt to resist it has led me to want to confess the heresy. And at any rate a statement of my reasons may provoke a refutation.

The heresy, in brief, is that Aristotle (in the *Nicomachean Ethics*, except in the two discussions of pleasure—where ἀγαθόν is opposed to φαῦλον and μοχθηρόν) really meant by ἀγαθόν conducive to our happiness, and maintained that when a man does an action deliberately, as distinct from impulsively, he does it simply in order to, i.e. from the desire to, become happy, this being so even when he does what is virtuous or speculates. Of this heresy a corollary is the view that Aristotle, being anxious to persuade men first and foremost to practise speculation and secondarily to do what is virtuous, conceived that, to succeed, what he had to prove was that this was the action necessary to make a man happy. This corollary, how-

From *Moral Obligation* (Oxford, 1949), pp. 40–53. Reprinted by permission of the Clarendon Press, Oxford. Originally published in *Philosophy*, Vol. X, No. 37 (January 1935). For the convenience of the reader, the editor of this volume has added some translations in footnotes, using the Ross version current at the time the essay was written.

ever, which may seem only a further heresy, I propose
to ignore. The heresy, in my opinion, is equally at-
tributable to Plato, and for much the same reasons.
But for simplicity's sake I propose to confine consideration to Aristotle, with, however, the suggestion
that the same argument can be applied to Plato.

In attributing this view to Aristotle I do not mean
to imply that he does not repeatedly make statements
inconsistent with it. Nor do I mean to imply that the
question of the consistency of these statements with
the view simply escapes him; it seems to me that it
does not, but that owing to a mistake he thought
they were consistent with it. Nor do I mean to imply
that his acceptance of this view appears on the surface;
but rather that it becomes evident once we lay bare
certain misleading elements in his account of the motive of deliberate action.

The first two chapters of the *Ethics*, and especially
its opening sentence, are undoubtedly puzzling. Aristotle begins by saying: πᾶσα τέχνη καὶ πᾶσα μέθοδος,
ὁμοίως δέ πρᾶξίς τε καὶ προαίρεσις, ἀγαθοῦ τινὸς
ἐφίεσθαι δοκεῖ διὸ καλῶς ἀπεφήναντο τἀγαθόν οὗ
πάντ' ἐφίεται. 'Every art and every inquiry, and similarly every action and purpose, is thought to aim at some
good; and for this reason the good has rightly been
declared to be that at which all things aim'. Then after
pointing out that certain aims or ends are subordinate
to others, he contends that there must be one final end
to which all others are subordinate, and that this will be
τἀγαθόν, the good, and that, consequently, knowledge
of this final end will have great influence on our lives,
since if we have it, we shall have a definite mark or goal
to aim at. And he goes on to say that, this being so, his
object in the *Ethics* is to discover what this final end is.

Here, as the rest of the first book shows, Aristotle,
in his first sentence, is not simply stating a common
opinion, but stating it with approval and on the as-

sumption that it is an opinion which his hearers will accept and so which can be used as a basis for his subsequent argument. And, so regarded, it is very sweeping.

Even if he had said that in every deliberate action we have an aim or are aiming at something, we should have regarded the statement, put forward as expressing a fact obvious to everyone, and so as needing neither elucidation nor discussion, as sufficiently sweeping. But what he does say is more sweeping. In effect, taking for granted that there is always something at which we are aiming, he commits himself to a general statement about its nature, stating that it is always ἀγαθόν τι, or, as we may translate the phrase, a good.

But besides being sweeping it is obscure. Even if Aristotle had said that in all action we are aiming at something, we should have felt that the statement needed elucidation. But saying as he does that we are aiming at something good, we have an additional puzzle. If, instead, he had said that we are always aiming at a pleasure, or at an honour, or at doing some good action, then we should have at least suspected we knew what he meant, whether or not we agreed. But the meaning of ἀγαθόν is not clear.

Consequently to discover his meaning we have to find out not only what he means when he speaks of us in a deliberate action as aiming at something (ἐφίεσθαί τινος) or as having a τέλος or end, but also what he means by ἀγαθόν. And of these tasks, plainly the former has to be accomplished first.

The idea, which of course underlies the *Ethics*, that in all deliberate action we have an end or aim, is one the truth of which we are all likely to maintain when we first consider action, 'action' being a term which, for shortness' sake, I propose to use for deliberate action. The idea goes back to Plato; and Mill expresses it when he says that all action is for the sake of an end. We take for granted that in doing some action there must be some desire leading or moving us to do the action, i.e. forming what we call our motive, since, as we should say, otherwise we should not be doing the action; or, for this is only to express the same idea in other words, we take for granted that in doing the action we have a purpose, i.e. something the desire of which moves us to do the action. And, taking this for granted, we are apt to maintain that our purpose in doing the action always consists in something, other than the action, which we think the action likely to cause, directly or indirectly, such as an improvement in our health which we expect from taking a dose of medicine.

Further, taking this view of the motive of action, we are apt to express it metaphorically by saying that in any action we have an aim or that there is something at which we are aiming. For when we consider, e.g., taking a drug from the desire to become healthy, we are apt to think of the thing desired, viz. our health, as that by reference to which we have devised the action as what is likely to cause it, and so as similar to the target by reference to the position of which a shooter arranges his weapon before shooting. We are also apt to speak of our purpose metaphorically as our end, as being something which we think will come into existence at the end of the action. In either case, however, it is to be noticed that the terms 'end' and 'aim' are merely metaphorical expressions for our purpose, i.e. for that the desire of which is moving us to act. No doubt further consideration may afterwards lead us to abandon this view. For certain actions and notably acts of gratitude or revenge seem prompted by the desire to do the action we at least hope we are doing, such as the desire to inflict an injury on another equal to that to which he has done us. Yet we may not reflect sufficiently to notice this, or even if we do we may fail to notice that such actions require us to modify the view, or may even think, as Aristotle did, that the doctrine may be made to apply to them.

Plato, it may be noticed, expressly formulates this view in the *Gorgias*. In trying to show that orators and tyrants have the least power in States, he lays down generally[1] that a man in doing what he does wishes not for the action but for that for the sake of which he does it, this being implied to be some result of the action. And in support he urges that a man who takes a drug wishes not for taking the drug but for health, and that a man who takes a voyage wishes not for the sailing and the incurring of dangers but for the wealth for the sake of which he takes the voyage. He is, however, here obviously going too far in asserting that the man does not want to do the action itself, for if the man did not want to do the action, he would not be doing it. What Plato should have said and what would express the view accurately is this:

A man undoubtedly wants to do what he does, and this desire is moving him. But the desire is always derivative or dependent. His having it depends on his having another desire, viz. the desire of something to which he thinks the action will lead, and that is why this latter desire should be represented as what is moving him, since it is in consequence of having this latter desire that he has the desire to do the action.

The view, therefore, implies the idea that the desire to do some action is always a dependent desire, depending on the desire of something to which we think the action will lead. But, as we soon notice, this latter desire must either be itself an independent desire, i.e. a desire which does not depend on any other, or else imply such a desire, since otherwise, as Aristotle put it, desire would be empty and vain. We are therefore

[1]*Gorgias*, p. 467.

led to draw a distinction between an independent desire and a desire depending on a desire of something which we think the thing desired will cause. Aristotle, of course, recognized and even emphasized the distinction, but unfortunately he formulated it with a certain inaccuracy. He implies that it should be expressed as that between τὸ βούλεσθαί τι δι' αὐτό, or καθ' αὐτό, and τὸ βούλεσθαί τι δι' ἕτερον. But the latter phrase must be short for τὸ βούλεσθαί τι διὰ τὸ βούλεσθαι ἕτερόν τι, and, this being so, the former phrase must be short for τὸ βούλεσθαί τι διὰ τὸ βούλεσθαι αὐτό, which, meaning wishing for something in consequence of wishing for itself, is not sense. The distinction should have been expressed as that between τὸ βούλεσθαί τι μὴ διὰ τὸ βούλεσθαι ἕτερόν τι and τὸ βούλεσθαί τι διὰ τὸ βούλεσθαι ἕτερόν τι or, to be more accurate, between desiring something not in consequence of desiring something else, and desiring something in consequence of desiring something else to which we think it will lead. And in this connexion it should be noticed that the English phrase for an independent desire, viz. the desire of something for its own sake, which is the equivalent of Aristotle's βούλεσθαί τι δι' αὐτό, has really only the negative meaning of a desire which is not dependent on any other desire.

Further, having reached this distinction, we are soon led, as of course Aristotle was, to hold that in every action we must have some ultimate or final aim, consisting of the object of some independent desire, and to distinguish from this aims which we have but which are not ultimate.

Having drawn this distinction we do not ask: 'Of what sort or sorts are our non-ultimate aims?' since obviously anything may be such an aim. But we do raise the question: 'Of what sort or sorts is our ultimate aim in various actions?'

To this question Aristotle's answer is ἀγαθόν τι, since his opening statement covers ultimate as well as non-ultimate aims. And the most obvious way to ascertain what Aristotle considers our ultimate aim is, of course, simply to find out what he means by ἀγαθόν. But, as should now be obvious, there is also another way. Like ourselves, he must really mean by our ultimate or final aim that the independent desire of which, or, as he would put it, that the desire of which καθ' αὐτό, is moving us to act. Consequently, if he says of certain things that we desire and pursue, i.e. aim at, them καθ' αὐτά, we are entitled to conclude that he considers that in certain instances they are our ultimate aim. Now in chapter 6 of Book I he maintains that there are certain kinds of things, viz. τιμή, φρόνησις, and ἡδονή, which are διωκόμενα καὶ ἀγαπώμενα καθ' αὐτά;* and to these he adds in chapter 7, § 5, νοῦς and πᾶσα ἀρετή,† of which, together with τιμή and ἡδονή, he says that though we choose them for the sake of happiness, we also choose them δι' αὐτά, i.e. as being what they severally are, since we should choose them even if nothing resulted from them. And to say this is only to say in other words that in some instances our ultimate end is an honour, in others it is a pleasure, in others our being φρόνιμος, and so on. Consequently, if we hold him to this, the only possible conclusion for us to draw is that he considers (1) that in such cases our ultimate end is not ἀγαθόν τι, whatever he means by ἀγαθόν, and also (2) that our ultimate end is not always of the same sort, so that no single term could describe it. We thus reach the astonishing conclusion that Aristotle, in insisting as he does that we pursue these things for their own sake, is really ruling out the possibility of maintaining that

---

*"Honour, wisdom, and pleasure, which are pursued and loved for themselves"—Ed.
†"Reason and every virtue"—Ed.

our end is always ἀγαθόν τι, or indeed anything else, so that we are in a position to maintain that he has no right to assert that our ultimate end is always an ἀγαθόν, even before we have attempted to elucidate what he means by ἀγαθόν.

Further, if we next endeavour, as we obviously should, to do this, we get another surprise. Aristotle's nearest approach to an elucidation is to be found in chapter 6, §§ 7–11, and chapter 7, §§ 1–5. There he speaks of τὰ καθ' αὑτὰ διωκόμενα καὶ ἀγαπώμενα as called ἀγαθά in one sense, and gives as illustrations τιμή, φρόνησις, and ἡδονή; and he speaks of · τὰ ποιητικὰ τούτων ἢ φυλακτικά πως* as called ἀγαθά in another sense, and he implies that these latter are διωκτὰ καὶ αἱρετὰ δι' ἕτερον[2] and that πλοῦτος is an illustration.[3] Further, he appears to consider that the difference of meaning is elucidated by referring to the former as ἀγαθὰ καθ' αὑτά and to the latter as ἀγαθὰ διὰ ταῦτα, i.e. ἀγαθὰ διὰ ἀγαθὰ καθ' αὑτά. But this unfortunately is no elucidation, since to state a difference of reason for calling two things ἀγαθόν is not to state a difference of meaning of ἀγαθόν, and indeed is to imply that the meaning in both cases is the same. Nevertheless, these statements seem intended as an elucidation of the meaning of ἀγαθόν. And the cause for surprise lies in this, that if they are taken seriously as an elucidation, the conclusion can only be that ἀγαθόν includes 'being desired' in its meaning, and indeed simply means τέλος or end. For if they are so understood, Aristotle must be intending to say (1) that when we say of something that it is ἀγαθόν καθ' αὑτό what we mean is that it is διωκόμενον καὶ ἀγαπώμενον καθ' αὑτό, i.e. simply that it is an ulti-

---

*"Those which tend to produce or to preserve them somehow."
[2]*Ethics*, I 7, 4. ["Pursued and desirable for the sake of something else."—Ed.]
[3]Ibid. I 5, 8. ["Wealth"—Ed.]

mate end, and (2) that when we say of something that it is ἀγαθὸν δι' ἕτερον, what we mean is that it is διωκόμενον καὶ ἀγαπώμενον δι' ἕτερον, i.e. simply that it is a non-ultimate end. In other words, if here he is interpreted strictly, he is explaining that ἀγαθόν means τέλος, and by the distinction between an ἀγαθὸν καθ' αὑτό and an ἀγαθὸν δι' ἕτερον he means merely the distinction between an ultimate and a non-ultimate end. Yet if anything is certain, it is that when Aristotle says of something, e.g. πλοῦτος, that it is an ἀγαθόν he does not mean that it is a τέλος, i.e. that it is something at which someone is aiming, and that when he says of something, e.g. τιμή or φρόνησις, that it is an ἀγαθὸν καθ' αὑτό, he does not mean that it is someone's ultimate end, i.e. what he speaks of in VI 9, 7 as τὸ τέλος τὸ ἁπλῶς. Apart from other considerations, if he did, then for him to say, as he in effect does, that we always aim at ἀγαθόν τι would be to say nothing, and for him to speak, as he does, of the object of βούλησις as τἀγαθόν would be absurd.

But this being so, what does Aristotle mean by ἀγαθόν? Here there is at least one statement which can be made with certainty. Aristotle unquestionably would have said that where we are pursuing something of a certain kind, say, an honour, καθ' αὑτό, we are pursuing it ὡς ἀγαθόν, i.e. as a good. Otherwise there would not even have been verbal consistency between his statements, that we pursue, i.e. aim at, things of certain stated kinds, and that we always aim at ἀγαθόν τι. Again, unless we allow that he would have said this, we cannot make head or tail either of his puzzling statement in Book I, chapter 2 that since, as there must be, there is some end which we desire for its own sake, this end must be τἀγαθόν, or, again, of its sequel in chapter 7, where he proceeds to consider what that is to which the term τἀγαθόν is applicable by con-

sidering which of our various ends is a final end. For
we are entitled to ask: 'Why does Aristotle think that
if we discover something to be desired and pursued
for its own sake, we shall be entitled to say that it is
τἀγαθόν?' And no answer is possible unless we allow
that he thought that in desiring and pursuing something for its own sake we are desiring and pursuing it
ὡς ἀγαθόν.

But Aristotle in saying, as he would have said, that
in pursuing, e.g., an honour, we are pursuing it
ὡς ἀγαθόν could only have meant that we are pursuing it in virtue of thinking that it would possess a
certain character to which he refers by the term
ἀγαθόν, so that by ἀγαθόν he must mean to indicate some character which certain things would have.
Further, this being so, in implying as he does that in
pursuing things of certain different kinds καθ᾽ αὑτά
we are pursuing them ὡς ἀγαθά, he must be implying
that these things of different kinds have, nevertheless,
a common character, viz. that indicated by the term
ἀγαθόν. It will, of course, be objected that he expressly
denies that they have a common character. For he says:
τιμῆς δὲ καὶ φρονήσεως καὶ ἡδονῆς ἕτεροι καὶ διαφέ-
ροντες οἱ λόγοι ταύτῃ ᾗ ἀγαθά.[4] But the answer is
simple; viz. that this is merely an inconsistency into
which he is driven by his inability to find in these
things the common character which his theory requires
him to find, and that if he is to succeed in maintaining that we pursue these things of various kinds
ὡς ἀγαθά, he *has* to maintain that in spite of appearances to the contrary they have a common character.

Nevertheless, though we have to insist that Aristotle
in fact holds that in pursuing any of these things

[4]*Ethics* I 6, 11. "But of honour, wisdom, and pleasure, just in
respect of their goodness, the accounts are distinct and diverse."
—Ed.]

καθ' αὐτό, i.e., as we should say, for its own sake, we are pursuing it ὡς ἀγαθόν, we cannot escape the admission that in doing so he is being inconsistent. For to maintain that in pursuing, e.g., an honour, we are pursuing it καθ' αὐτό, or, as we should say, for its own sake, is really to maintain that the desire of an honour moving us is an independent desire, i.e. a desire depending on no other. And, on the other hand, to maintain that in pursuing an honour, we are pursuing it ὡς ἀγαθόν, or as a good, is really to maintain that the desire of an honour moving us is a dependent desire, viz. a desire depending on the desire of something which will possess the character indicated by the word ἀγαθόν, i.e. that we desire an honour only in consequence of desiring something which will possess that character and of thinking that an honour will possess it. It is, in fact, really to maintain that in pursuing an honour, our ultimate aim, i.e. that the independent desire of which is moving us, or what Aristotle would call that which we are pursuing καθ' αὐτό, is not an honour but a good, i.e. something having the character, whatever it may be, which is indicated by the word ἀγαθόν, i.e. that we desire an honour only in consequence of desiring a good. The principle involved will become clearer, if we take a different illustration. In chapter 6 Aristotle speaks of ὁρᾶν as one of the things which are pursued for their own sake; and if he had said that we pursue ὁρᾶν ὡς αἰσθάνεσθαι he would in consistency have had to maintain that what we are pursuing καθ' αὐτό is not ὁρᾶν but αἰσθάνεσθαι,* and that the desire of ὁρᾶν moving us is only a dependent desire depending on our desiring something else which we think ὁρᾶν will be.

It will be objected that there is really no inconsistency, since Aristotle conceives the characteristic referred

---

*"Sight . . . perception."

to by ἀγαθόν as a characteristic of an honour and of
anything else which he would say we pursue καθ' αὐτό,
and that to speak of us as desiring something in respect
of some character which it would have is not to represent our desire of it as dependent. In illustration
it may be urged that to speak of us as, in desiring to
do a courageous action, desiring it as a worthy or virtuous action is not to represent our desire to do a
courageous action as dependent. But the objection cannot be sustained. For if we desire to do a courageous
action, as something which would be a virtuous action,
i.e., really, a something which we think would be a
virtuous action, although our desire does not depend
on a desire of something which we think a courageous
action would *cause*, it does depend on the desire of
something which we think it would *be*. And as a proof
of this dependence we can point to the fact that if,
while having this desire, we were to do a good action
of another sort, e.g. a generous action, the desire would
disappear.

What is in the end plain is that Aristotle cannot
succeed in maintaining that our ultimate end is always
ἀγαθόν τι without abandoning his view that we pursue such things as τιμή and ἀρετή καθ' αὐτά, or, as
we should say, for their own sake, and maintaining
instead that we pursue them as things which we think
will have the character to which the term ἀγαθόν
refers. Nevertheless, in spite of having to allow that
we are thereby attributing inconsistency to Aristotle,
we have to admit that he, in fact, holds that in desiring
and pursuing certain things for their own sakes we are
desiring and pursuing them in respect of their having
a certain character, viz. whatever it be to which he
refers by the term ἀγαθόν.

So far the only clue reached to the meaning of
ἀγαθόν is the idea that Aristotle used it to refer to
a certain character possessed by certain things, the

thought of the possession of which arouses desire for them, and indeed is the only thing which arouses desire for anything, except where our desire depends on another desire.

We have now to try to get to closer quarters with the question of its meaning. The question is really: 'What is the character which Aristotle considered we must think would be possessed by something if we are to desire it, independently of desiring something else to which we think it will lead, that character being what Aristotle used the word ἀγαθόν to refer to?'

Here it seems hardly necessary to point out that the answer cannot be 'goodness'. To rule out this answer it is only necessary to point out two things. First, if Aristotle had meant by ἀγαθόν good, he would have had to represent us as desiring for its own sake any good activity, whether ours or another's, whereas he always implies that a good activity which we desire is an activity of our own, and in addition he would have had to drop, as he never does, the idea of a connexion between a good activity and our own happiness. And second, Aristotle's term ἀγαθόν is always ἀγαθὸν τινί, as appears most obviously in the phrase ἀνθρώπινον ἀγαθόν and in the statement in IX 8, 8–9, where he says that reason always chooses what is best for itself—πᾶς γὰρ νοῦς αἱρεῖται τὸ βέλτιστον ἑαυτῷ—and goes on to add that the man who gives wealth to a friend assigns the greater good, the having done what is noble (τὸ κάλον), to himself. Once, however, we regard this answer as having to be excluded once for all, there seems to be no alternative to attributing to Aristotle a familiar turn of thought to which we are all very prone and which is exemplified in Mill and T. H. Green.

When we consider what we desire we soon come to the conclusion, as of course Aristotle did, that there are things of certain kinds which we desire, not in

consequence of thinking that they will have an effect
which we desire, but for themselves, such as seeing a
beautiful landscape, being in a position of power, help-
ing another, and doing a good action. We then are
apt to ask, 'What is the condition of our desiring such
things?' and if we do, we are apt to answer—and the
tendency is almost irresistible—'It is impossible for us
to desire any such thing unless we think of it as something which we should like, since, if we do not think
of it thus, we remain simply indifferent to its realization.' Then, if asked what we mean by its being something we should like, we reply: 'Something which
would give us enjoyment, or, alternatively, gratification,
or, to use a term which will cover either, pleasure.'
The tendency is one to which Mill gives expression
when he says that desiring a thing and finding it pleasant are two parts of the same phenomenon; and Green
exhibits it when he maintains, as in effect he does,
that we can desire something only if we think of it
as something which will give us satisfaction, i.e. gratification. In maintaining this we are really maintaining
that the thing which we at first thought we desired
for its own sake, such as seeing a beautiful landscape,
or doing a good action, is really only being desired for
the sake of a feeling of enjoyment or gratification, or,
to put it generally, pleasure, which we think it will
cause in us. And correspondingly, where we think of
the desire as moving us to act, we are really maintaining that what we at first thought our ultimate end is
really only our penultimate end or the proximate
means, and that our ultimate end is really a pleasure
which we think this will cause. We are, however, apt
to think of a thing's giving us enjoyment, or alternatively gratification, as if it were a quality of the thing,
just as we think of the loudness of a noise as a quality
of the noise. And our tendency to do this is strength-
ened by the fact that the ordinary way of stating the

fact that something X excites a feeling of pleasure, or of gratification, is to say that X is pleasant or gratifying, a way of speaking which suggests that what is in fact a property possessed by X of causing a certain feeling is a quality of X. The tendency is mistaken, since, as anyone must allow in the end, something's giving us enjoyment is *not* a quality of it, and when we say that something *is* pleasant, we are not attributing to it a certain quality but stating that it has a certain effect. Nevertheless, the tendency exists. And when it is operative in us, we state our original contention by saying that in desiring to see a beautiful landscape for its own sake, we desire it as something which will be pleasant, and that when we are acting on the desire, our ultimate end is the seeing a beautiful landscape as something which will be pleasant, thereby representing what on our view is really the proximate means to our end as our end.

This being the line of thought to which I referred, it remains for me to try to show that it was taken by Aristotle. Before we consider details we can find two general considerations which are in favour of thinking that he took it. In the first place, if we assume it to be indisputable that he thought that there are things of a certain sort which we desire for their own sake, but that in desiring them we desire them in respect of having a certain character to which he refers by the term ἀγαθόν, and then ask 'What can be the character of which he is thinking?' the only possible answer seems to be: 'That of exciting either enjoyment or gratification.' And in particular two things are in favour of this answer. First, it is easy, from lack of consideration, to think of exciting pleasure as a quality of the thing desired—as indeed Aristotle appears to do when he speaks of virtuous actions (αἱ κατ᾽ ἀρετὴν πράξεις) as φύσει ἡδέα and as ἡδεῖαι καθ᾽ αὐτάς,[5]

[5]*Ethics* I 8, 11.

i.e. as pleasant in virtue of their own nature; and second. the perplexity in which he finds himself in chapter 6 when trying to elucidate the meaning of ἀγαθόν
would be accounted for if what he was referring to was
something which is not in fact a character common
to the various things said to be ἀγαθά, although he
tended to think of it as if it was. In the second place
he applies the term ἀγαθόν not only to the things
which we desire for themselves, but also to the things
which produce or preserve them, and it is difficult to
see how he can apply the term to the latter unless
ἀγαθόν means productive of pleasure, whether directly
or not. In fact, only given this meaning is it possible
to understand how Aristotle can speak not merely of
τιμή but also of πλοῦτος as an ἀγαθόν.

To pass, however, to special considerations, we seem
to find evidence, and decisive evidence, in a quarter
in which we at first should least expect it. At the beginning of chapter 4 he directs his hearers' attention
to the question: τί (ἐστι) τὸ πάντων ἀκρότατον
τῶν πρακτῶν ἀγαθῶν, i.e. 'What is it that is the
greatest of all achievable goods?' and he proceeds to
say that while there is general agreement about the
name for it, since both the many and the educated
say that it is happiness, yet they differ about what
happiness is, the many considering it something the
nature of which is clear and obvious, such as pleasure,
wealth, or honour, whereas, he implies, the educated
consider it something else of which the nature is not
obvious. Then in the next chapter he proceeds to state
what, to judge from the three most prominent types
of life, that of enjoyment, the political life, and that
of contemplation, various men consider that the good
or happiness is, viz. enjoyment, honour, and contemplation. And later he gives his own view, contending,
with the help of an argument based on the idea that

man has a function, that happiness is ψυχῆς ἐνέργειά τις κατ' ἀρετὴν τελείαν.[6]

Here it has to be admitted that Aristotle is expressing himself in a misleading way. His question 'What is the greatest of goods?' can be treated as if it had been the question 'What is a man's ultimate end?' i.e. τὸ τέλος τὸ ἁπλῶς. For as I 2, 1 and I 7 show, he considers that to find what is the greatest good, or the good, we must find a man's final end, i.e. that which he desires and aims at for its own sake, and in I 5 he judges what men consider the good from what their lives show to be their ultimate aim. And his answer to this question, if taken as it stands, is undeniably absurd. For, so understood, it is to the effect that, though all men, when asked 'What is the ultimate end?', answer by using the same word, viz. εὐδαιμονία, yet, as they differ about what εὐδαιμονία is, i.e., really, about the thing for which they are using the word εὐδαιμονία to stand, some using it to designate pleasure, others wealth, and so on, they are in substance giving different answers, some meaning by the word εὐδαιμονία pleasure, others wealth, and so on. But of course this is not what Aristotle meant. He certainly did not think that anyone ever meant by εὐδαιμονία either τιμή or πλοῦτος; and he certainly did not himself mean by it ψυχῆς ἐνέργειά τις κατ' ἀρετὴν τελείαν. What he undoubtedly meant and thought others meant by the word εὐδαιμονία is happiness. Plainly, too, what he thought men differed about was not the nature of happiness but the conditions of its realization, and when he says that εὐδαιμονία *is* ψυχῆς ἐνέργειά τις κατ' ἀρετὴν τελείαν, what he really means is that the latter is what is required for the realization of happiness. Consideration of the *Ethics* by itself should be enough to convince us of this, but

[6]*Ethics* I 13, 1 ["an activity of the soul in accordance with perfect virtue."—Ed.]

if it is not, we need only take into account his elucidation of the meaning of the question 'τί ἐστιν;' to be
sure that when he asks 'τί ἐστι ἡ εὐδαιμονία';
his meaning is similar to that of the man who, when
he asks 'What is colour?' or 'What is sound?' really
means 'What are the conditions necessary for its realization?' We must therefore understand Aristotle in
chapter 4 to be in effect contending that while it is
universally admitted that our ultimate aim is happiness, there is great divergence of view about the conditions, or, more precisely, the proximate conditions,
of its realization.

But, this conclusion reached, we can plainly take
one step farther and conclude that Aristotle himself
is in agreement with the view that our ultimate end
is happiness, and that, taking its truth for granted, his
Ethics is concerned first to prove that it is by virtuous
action that it will be realized, and then to work out
in detail the character of virtuous action, so that we
shall be better able to obtain our aim. In other words,
we can conclude that his real answer to the question,
'What is τὸ τέλος τὸ ἁπλῶς, i.e. our ultimate aim?'
is not, as we may at first think, ψυχῆς ἐνέργειά τις
κατ' ἀρετὴν τελείαν but εὐδαιμονία, i.e. happiness.
Putting this otherwise, we can say that the accurate
statement of his own view is to be found in I 12,
where he gives as a reason why εὐδαιμονία is τίμιον,
whereas ἀρετή is merely ἐπαινετόν, that it is for the
sake of εὐδαιμονία that we all do everything.[7]

Now, if by thus going behind Aristotle's terminology
we are driven to conclude that Aristotle really considered our ultimate end to be always our happiness,
or alternatively some particular state of happiness on
our part—for sometimes he seems to imply the one
view and sometimes the other—we are also driven to

[7][ταύτης (i.e. εὐδαιμονίας) γὰρ χάριν τὰ λοιπὰ πάντα πάντε
πράττομεν, Ethics, I 12, 8.]

conclude that, though he at times makes statements to the contrary, he also holds that where we are said to have as our ultimate end τιμή or ἐνέργειά τις κατ' ἀρετήν or anything else of a kind which we consider a condition of happiness, the thing in question is really according to him only our penultimate end, and the desire of it is only a derivative desire depending on our desire of happiness. And then it becomes obvious that when he implies, as he always does, that in desiring one of these things we desire it as an ἀγαθόν, what he means by ἀγαθόν is 'productive of a state, or rather a feeling, of happiness', i.e., as I think we may say in this context, a feeling of pleasure. Further, this being so, we have to allow that he fundamentally misrepresents his own problem. Assuming that we all always have either a single ultimate aim, or at least, alternatively, an aim of one sort, what he ostensibly maintains is that we are uncertain about its nature, and that therefore he has to discover its nature in order to help us to achieve it. But, as we must now conclude, what he is really maintaining is that though the nature of our ultimate aim, happiness, is known to us, for we all know the nature of that for which the word 'happiness' stands, we are doubtful about the proximate means to it, and that consequently he has to discover the proximate means. In other words, in maintaining ψυχῆς ἐνέργειά τις κατ' ἀρετὴν τελείαν to be our ultimate end of the nature of which we are uncertain, he is putting what on his view is really the proximate means to our end in the place of what on his view is really our end. And if we ask 'How can he have come to misrepresent his own view so fundamentally?', then, if the contentions already advanced are true, we have at hand a satisfactory answer. We can reply that the misrepresentation is due to his making two mistakes to which we are all prone: first, that of thinking of the property of causing happiness as a quality of what causes it, and secondly, that of thinking that where we are aiming at something of a certain kind for its own sake, and so having it as our ultimate end, we are nevertheless aiming at it in respect of its having a certain character.

By way of conclusion it may be well to refer to an objection which will inevitably be raised, viz. that I have been, in effect, representing Aristotle as a psychological hedonist, and that to do this is absurd. I admit the charge, but do not consider the representation absurd. It seems not only possible, but common, to hold that there are a number of things other than pleasure which we desire for their own sake, and then when the question is raised, 'How is it that we desire these things?', to reply: 'Only because we think they will give us pleasure.' In my opinion, the reply is mistaken, and is made only because we are apt to think of the gratification necessarily consequent on the thought that something which we have desired is realized as that the thought of which excites the desire. But the mistake is a very insidious one, as, if I am right, is shown by the fact that Green, in spite of all the trouble he takes to point out that Mill falls into it, falls into it himself.

'ΑΓΑΘΟΝ AND ΕΥΔΑΙΜΟΝΙΑ IN THE ETHICS OF ARISTOTLE*

J. L. AUSTIN

This article takes its start from an article by Professor H. A. Prichard (*Philosophy*, X [1935], 27–39 [241–60 above]) on "The Meaning of ἀγαθόν in the *Ethics* of Aristotle." It will be seen that I disagree with him, but I think his article has the great merit of raising serious questions.

Statement of Prof. Prichard's conclusions. Prof. Prichard begins by stating his "heretical" conclusions, as follows:

(1) Aristotle really meant by ἀγαθόν "conducive to our happiness."

(2) Aristotle maintained that when a man does an action deliberately, as distinct from impulsively, he does it simply in order to, i.e. from the desire to, become happy, this being so even when he does what is virtuous or speculates.[1]

---

*This paper was composed by the late Professor John L. Austin before World War II, while Professor Prichard was still alive. Some changes and additions were made after World War II. Its publication was made possible by the kind consent of Mrs. J. L. Austin. The author's footnotes are numbered. For the convenience of the reader some translations have been supplied by the editor of this volume. The translation employed is that of W. D. Ross, since his was the version current at the time this paper was written.

[1]This distinction between "speculating" and "doing what is virtuous" is not strictly Aristotelian: θεωρία *is* ἐνέργεια κατὰ τὴν τελειοτάτην ἀρετήν.

(2.1) A corollary: Aristotle, being anxious to persuade men first and foremost to practice speculation and secondarily to do what is virtuous,[1] conceived that, to succeed, what he had to prove was that this was the action necessary to make a man happy.

(The corollary Prof. Prichard ignores, and, at least for the present, I shall do the same.)

His reason for excluding certain passages from consideration invalid. We must first direct our attention to a curious and important reservation, which Prof. Prichard makes in stating his view. Aristotle, he says, means by ἀγαθόν conducive to our happiness "in the *Nicomachean Ethics* [abbreviated *NE* hereafter—Ed.] except in the two discussions of pleasure—where ἀγαθόν is opposed to φαῦλον and μοχθηρόν." We are not here concerned with the restriction to the *NE*, but it is necessary to examine the further restriction, by which we are precluded from using *NE* VII xi–xiv and X i–v.

The argument implied in Prof. Prichard's words seems to be as follows:

(a) In these passages ἀγαθόν means something different from what it means in the rest of the *NE*.

(b) This is shown by the fact that it is, in these two passages opposed to φαῦλον and μοχθηρόν.

With regard to (a), it is most unfortunate that Prof. Prichard does not tell us what ἀγαθόν *does* mean in these two passages.

As to (b), we clearly need further explanation. I hope that the following is a correct expansion of Prof. Prichard's argument.

(1) Throughout the *NE*, with the exception of these two passages, ἀγαθόν is never opposed to φαῦλον or μοχθηρόν, but to something else, presumably κακόν.

(2) In these two passages alone, ἀγαθόν is opposed, not to κακόν, but to φαῦλον and μοχθηρόν.

(3) Since we know on independent grounds that κακόν has a different meaning from φαῦλον or μοχθηρόν, it follows that ἀγαθόν, in these two passages, must have a meaning different from that which it has throughout the rest of the *NE*.

(To take a parallel case. Suppose that I do not know the meaning of the adjective "green": and that throughout a certain work I find it opposed to the adjective "experienced," except in two passages where it is opposed to "red" and "yellow." Then if I know on other grounds that "experienced" means something sufficiently different from "red" or "yellow," I can infer that "green" must, in these two passages, have a meaning different from that which it has throughout the rest of the work.)

If this is actually the sort of argument on which Prof. Prichard is relying, I think there are considerations which will lead him to abandon it.

(1) ἀγαθόν is opposed to μοχθηρόν elsewhere in the *NE*—e.g. in IX viii 7—where pleasure is not under discussion. (Not to mention passages in other works, e.g. *Met.* 1020b21). I have not found a case of ἀγαθόν being explicitly opposed to φαῦλον elsewhere, but cp. (3) *infra*.

(2) ἀγαθόν is constantly opposed to κακόν in the two discussions of pleasure: VII i 1–2, xiii 1 and 7, xiv 2 and 9, X ii 5. In VII in particular, the discussion is introduced and terminated by an opposition between ἀγαθόν and κακόν, and in xiv 2 we read: κακῷ γὰρ ἀγαθόν ἐναντίον.

(3) I do not know of any clear distinction between the meaning of κακόν and the meanings of φαῦλον and μοχθηρόν (or πονηρόν) any more than I can clearly distinguish between ἀγαθόν, ἐπιεικές, and σπουδαῖον. The words seem to be used almost indifferently, or at least for "species" of one another which would be equivalent in certain contexts.

Very many passages in the NE, such as III v 3, are evidence of this. But the point seems clear even from the two discussions of pleasure. σπουδαῖον seems equivalent to ἀγαθόν in VII xiv 4, ἐπιεικές to ἀγαθόν in X ii 1, μοχθηρόν seems equivalent to or a species of κακόν in VII xiv 2, φαῦλον to κακόν in X i 2. Pleasures are called ἀγαθαί, σπουδαῖαι, ἐπιεικεῖς (also καλαί, etc.) in apparently the same sense or senses not sufficiently distinguished: and similarly οὐκ ἀγαθαί, μοχθηραί, φαῦλαι (also αἰσχραί, etc.) in apparently the same sense. And these adjectives seem opposed to one another indifferently, cp. e.g. X v 6. (It must be admitted that Aristotle does not use the expression κακαί ἡδοναί: if this requires some explanation, I think one could easily be found.)

It is, of course possible that some distinction can be drawn between κακόν on the one hand and φαῦλον and μοχθηρόν on the other. But (a) It is clearly incumbent on Prof. Prichard to draw it—which he does not do. (b) Even so he would by no means be out of the wood, for (i) it does not seem to be true that ἀγαθόν is, in these passages on pleasures more commonly opposed to φαῦλον and μοχθηρόν than to κακόν. μοχθηρόν only occurs once in each book, and is only used as opposite of ἀγαθόν in VII xiv 2: and there it is only so opposed because it is equated with κακόν. φαῦλον is opposed to ἀγαθόν only once in X i 2, a rather popular passage: and there, as section 5 of the same chapter shows, it is equivalent to κακόν. (ii) Actually ἀγαθόν is in these same passages much more commonly opposed to κακόν, and so presumably has its 'normal' sense. (But we shall see that it is vital for Prof. Prichard that, when Aristotle says "ἡδονή is an ἀγαθόν," ἀγαθόν should never have its 'normal' sense of "conducive to our happiness.") (iii) In a most important passage, X ii 1, exactly the same remarks are made about ἀγαθόν as in I i 1, a passage on which Prof. Prichard relies in arriving at his interpretation of it as "conducive to our happiness." Here then ἀγαθόν must presumably have that meaning: but this is one of the places where ἡδονή is said to be an ἀγαθόν, which, on Prof. Prichard's interpretation of ἀγαθόν, does not make sense. *v.i.*

It would seem then that Prof. Prichard's ostensible argument for excluding these two discussions of pleasure from consideration will not bear examination. And it is in any case so very recondite that we may be tempted to think he would never have chanced upon it, unless he had been *searching* for some reason to justify the exclusion of these passages.

Why does he wish to exclude these passages? His interpretation of εὐδαιμονία. Why then, we must ask, should it be important for Prof. Prichard to secure the exclusion from consideration of the two discussions of pleasure? In order to understand this, we must first understand that the whole argument of Prof. Prichard's paper is based upon a premise which is never expressed, no doubt because it seems to him obvious; namely, that "happiness" (his translation of εὐδαιμονία) *means a state of feeling pleased*. This may be shown as follows:

(1) On p. 39, line 16 [p. 259, l. 37 above] "causing happiness" is substituted without remark for "causing pleasure," which was the expression used in the parallel argumentation on e.g. pp. 35–36.

(2) On p. 38, [p. 259)] at the bottom we read "what he means by ἀγαθόν is productive of a state, or rather a feeling, of happiness, i.e. as I think we may say in this context, a feeling of pleasure." This remark is interesting, since it seems to imply that "in other contexts" being happy does *not* mean feeling pleased. However, we need not worry, I think, about these other contexts, for it is quite essential to Prof. Prichard's argument at a crucial point that the word

εὐδαιμονία, or in English "happiness," should be and should be known by all to be, at least for purposes of Ethics, entirely clear and unambiguous in meaning: so that, if being happy means feeling pleased in some contexts in the *NE*, it clearly must do so in all thought that concerns the moral philosopher.[2] (The crucial point referred to is found on p. 37 [p. 257] at the bottom, and repeated on p. 39 [p. 259] at the top. Prof. Prichard there maintains that Aristotle cannot be really asking the question he "ostensibly" asks, viz. "What is the nature of happiness?" for there is no uncertainty about that—"the nature of ... happiness is known to us, for we all know the nature of that for which the word 'happiness' stands.")

(3) On p. 39 [p. 260], in summing up his own contentions, Prof. Prichard says that he has in effect represented Aristotle as a psychological *hedonist*; i.e., I understand, he claims that, according to Aristotle, all deliberate action is done from a desire to produce in ourselves feelings of *pleasure*. Now on p. 27 [p. 241], quoted above, Prof. Prichard said that, according to Aristotle, all deliberate action is done from a desire to become *happy*. Hence being happy and feeling pleased are evidently, for Prof. Prichard, equivalent expressions. (And this enables us to see why he considers his view, as he says on p. 27 [p. 241], "heretical," although, at first sight and as here stated, it does not appear very extraordinary: if we realize that "become happy" means "feel pleased" the view certainly is very strange.)

It is, therefore, clear that Prof. Prichard does not distinguish what we call "being happy" from what we

[2]Prichard's reservation, "in this context" whatever it means, is not important here; nor is the contrast between state ("disposition") and feeling. Similarly, on p. 38 [p. 258], a distinction is drawn between "happiness" and "some particular state of happiness": but I do not think that concerns us here.

call "feeling pleased": and he has in fact been good enough to tell me that that is so.

It now becomes evident why the two discussions of pleasure in the *NE* should have a peculiar interest for him.

For if ἀγαθόν means "conducive to our happiness," and if "happiness" is equivalent to "pleasure"—then how can we ask, as Aristotle does in these passages, whether ἡδονή is an ἀγαθόν? For ἡδονή must presumably be translated "pleasure": so that the question we are asking becomes "Is (our) pleasure conducive to our pleasure?" which is absurd, or at least absurdly limited. Further similar difficulties arise, if we ask, for instance, what could be meant by saying that some ἡδοναί are ἀγαθαί, and, odder still, that some are *not* ἀγαθαί.

Hence it is essential for Prof. Prichard to maintain that ἀγαθόν has in these passages a meaning different from "conducive to our happiness": but, as we have seen, his reason for saying ἀγαθόν has a new meaning in these two passages is invalid (nor does he explain what ἀγαθόν *does* mean in them).

But Prof. Prichard has another and quite radical difficulty to face in connection with Aristotle's discussions of pleasure, which in his paper he appears not to appreciate. For Aristotle there discusses the relation of ἡδονή to εὐδαιμονία in such a manner as to make it quite plain that these two Greek words do *not* mean the same.[3] Whereas Prof. Prichard's whole argument depends on translating εὐδαιμονία "happiness," and taking "happiness" to be equivalent to "pleasure" which *must* (we assume) be the translation of ἡδονή : so that ἡδονή and εὐδαιμονία ought to mean the same. Hence Prof. Prichard must hold that, in these discussions, not merely ἀγαθόν, but *also* either

[3] εὐδαιμονία *is* τὸ ἄριστον, ἡδονή is *not* τὸ ἄριστον: and so on.

εὐδαιμονία or ἡδονή changes its meaning from the
normal. Otherwise his view is untenable. As to which
alternative he would choose, I do not know: but both
are very difficult. He can scarcely hold that εὐδαιμονία
changes its meaning, for, as we shall see, much of his
argumentation depends on his view that the meaning
of εὐδαιμονία was clear and unambiguous. As to
ἡδονή, he does hold, as we shall see, that the word
is sometimes used in a special restricted sense to include only the σωματικαὶ ἡδοναί: but it is obviously
quite impossible to hold that it has only this restricted
sense throughout the two fulldress discussions of pleasure. Unfortunately, Prof. Prichard does not notice
this additional difficulty.

Even the exclusion of these passages would not suffice to save Prof. Prichard's view from refutation. It
would still be open to Prof. Prichard to maintain (and
in view of his low opinion of Aristotle's Ethics, I think
it possible he might do so) that, even apart from
other arguments such as that about φαῦλον and
μοχθηρόν, these very facts which I have just mentioned are themselves sufficient to show that the two
discussions of pleasure are inconsistent with the rest
of the NE and may therefore be neglected. It need
scarcely be pointed out how dangerous this would be:
for we are trying to discover the meanings of ἀγαθόν
(and εὐδαιμονία) and it is scarcely permissible to elim-
inate a large part of the evidence, not otherwise
known to be incompatible with the rest, on the ground
that it will not square with our interpretation of those
meanings. At least it would be necessary to prove that
εὐδαιμονία must elsewhere mean "pleasure": but, it
seems to me, Prof. Prichard does not prove this, he
assumes it.

However, it would in any case be of no use to exclude from consideration the "two discussions of pleasure." For pleasure is mentioned in many other parts

of the *NE*, and precisely the same difficulties for Prof. Prichard's view are to be found in them also.

Let us confine ourselves to Book I, since it is upon that book that Prof. Prichard principally relies, including chapters v and xii, which he cites.

In I v we are told that οἱ πολλοὶ καὶ φορτικώτατοι maintain that εὐδαιμονία is ἡδονή and that Aristotle himself *rejects* this view. According to Prof. Prichard's interpretation, it would seem that he ought to accept it, as tautological. Prof. Prichard did reply, when faced with this, that ἡδονή here, being the end of the ἀπολαυστικὸς βίος, has a special restricted meaning which includes only the σωματικαὶ ἡδοναί (cp. VII xiii 6).[4] This is scarcely obvious, and we should have expected Aristotle's rejection to take a rather different form, if he himself held that our end *is* ἡδονή, although not merely the σωματικαὶ ἡδοναί. However, we need not insist on this passage; others are plainer.

In I xii 5, what Eudoxus said about ἡδονή is compared with what Aristotle himself says about εὐδαιμονία: clearly, then, ἡδονή and εὐδαιμονία are distinct. And, whatever may be true of Sardanapallus, there is no reason whatever to suppose that *Eudoxus* meant by ἡδονή merely the σωματικαὶ ἡδοναί.

Finally, in I viii the relation of ἡδονή to εὐδαιμονία is discussed very much as in books VII and X: εὐδαιμονία is μεθ' ἡδονῆς ἢ οὐκ ἄνευ ἡδονῆς,* but quite clearly it is distinct from it. (Even if they are necessarily connected, we must not confuse one with the other: cp. *EE* I ii 5.)

We do not, naturally enough, find in Book I, a discussion as to whether ἡδονή is an ἀγαθόν. But the

---

[4]Just as, when Aristotle says ἡδονή is ἀγαθόν, Prof. Prichard says ἀγαθόν has a meaning different from the ordinary, so, when Aristotle distinguishes ἡδονή from εὐδαιμονία, Prof. Prichard says ἡδονή has a meaning different from the ordinary.

*"Accompanied by pleasure or not without pleasure."—Ed.

views that it is τὸ ἀγαθόν or τὸ ἄριστον are mentioned, and, though rejected, not rejected as absurdities
(I v and xii). Moreover, as was pointed out above,
Eudoxus' views are mentioned in I i and xii in pretty
much the same words as in X ii, so that it would seem
that the meaning of ἀγαθόν ought to be the same in
each case.

We see then, that Prof. Prichard cannot exclude
VII xi–xiv and X i–v from consideration, and that they
are fatal to his view. But even if we do exclude them,
other passages, equally fatal, can be produced even
from Book I, on which he relies. So that, if he still
maintains the view, it would seem that he must be
prepared to attribute to Aristotle even more and graver
inconsistencies and oversights than those, already so
numerous, which he attributes to him in his article.
Myself, I am not yet prepared to do this: though I am
only too well aware how imperfect the *Ethics* is in
these respects.

Present state of the problem. So far our results are
negative. εὐδαιμονία does not mean a state or feeling
of pleasure and ἀγαθόν does not mean conducive to
our pleasure. (It is, however, still possible that ἀγαθόν
may mean conducive to our *happiness*, if "happiness"
is not equivalent to "pleasure.") It certainly is important to discover, therefore, what these two words
do mean. Of the two, εὐδαιμονία is, for reasons which
will appear, considerably the easier to elucidate, and
accordingly I shall consider it first.

Τί ἐστιν εὐδαιμονία; *the meaning of the question.*
Once again I shall take my start from Prof. Prichard's
article. In a passage extending from p. 36 at the bottom
to p. 38 [pp. 256–58 above], he argues that evidence
for his view is to be found in *NE* I iv. I must quote,
I am afraid, at some length.

At the beginning of Chapter IV he [Aristotle]
directs his hearers' attention to the question...

"What is it that is the greatest of all achievable goods?" and he proceeds to say that while there is general agreement about the name for it, since both the many and the educated say that it is happiness, yet they differ about what happiness is, the many considering it something the nature of which is clear and obvious, such as pleasure, wealth, or honour, whereas, he implies, the educated consider it something else, of which the nature is not obvious. Then in the next chapter he proceeds to state what, to judge from the most prominent types of life, that of enjoyment, the political life, and that of contemplation, various men consider that the good or happiness is, viz. enjoyment, honour, and contemplation. And later he gives his own view ... that happiness is ψυχῆς ἐνέργειά τις κατ' ἀρετὴν τελείαν.

Here it has to be admitted that Aristotle is expressing himself in a misleading way. His question, "What is the greatest of goods?" can be treated as if it had been the question, "What is man's ultimate end?" ... And his answer to this question, if taken as it stands, is undeniably absurd. For, so understood, it is to the effect that, though all men, when asked "What is the ultimate end?" answer by using the same word, viz. εὐδαιμονία, yet, as they differ about what εὐδαιμονία is, i.e. really, about the thing for which they are using the word εὐδαιμονία to stand, some using it to designate pleasure, others wealth, and so on, they are in substance giving different answers, some meaning by the word εὐδαιμονία pleasure, others wealth, and so on. But of course this is not what Aristotle meant. He certainly did not think that anyone ever meant by εὐδαιμονία either τιμή or πλοῦτος; and he certainly did not himself mean by it ψυχῆς ἐνέργειά τις κατ' ἀρετὴν τελείαν. What he undoubtedly meant and thought others meant by the word εὐδαιμονία is happiness. Plainly too, what he thought men differed about was not the nature of happiness but the conditions of its realization, and when he says that εὐδαιμονία is ψυχῆς ἐνέργειά τις κατ' ἀρετὴν τελείαν, what he really means is that the latter is what is required for the realization of happiness ... this meaning is similar to that of the man who, when he asks "What is colour?" or "What is sound?" really means "What are the conditions necessary for its realization?"

Here is the passage, I iv 1–3: Λέγωμεν . . . τὶ τὸ πάντων ἀκρότατον τῶν πρακτῶν ἀγαθῶν, ὀνόματι μὲν οὖν σχεδὸν ὑπὸ τῶν πλείστων ὁμολογεῖται· τὴν γὰρ εὐδαιμονίαν καὶ οἱ πολλοὶ καὶ οἱ χαρίεντες λέγουσιν, τὸ δ' εὖ ζῆν καὶ τὸ τῦ πράττειν ταὐτὸν ὑπολαμβάνουσι τῷ εὐδαιμονεῖν. περὶ δὲ τῆς εὐδαιμονίας, τί ἐστιν, ἀμφισβητοῦσι καὶ οὐχ ὁμοίως οἱ πολλοὶ τοῖς σοφοῖς ἀποδιδόασιν. οἵ μὲν γὰρ τῶν ἐναργῶν τι καὶ φανερῶν, οἷον ἡδονὴν ἢ πλοῦτον τιμήν κτλ.*

Whence does Prof. Prichard derive his confidence that Aristotle is misrepresenting his own problem? If he is, it must be admitted that the misrepresentation is pretty consistent. Right through to Book X Aristotle always purports to be telling us "what εὐδαιμονία is." (He summarizes the present passage in almost the same words again in I vii 9.)[5] Moreover, Aristotle is, of course, aware of the very kind of misrepresentation of which Prof. Prichard accuses him: compare what he says about

---

*"Let us state . . . what is the highest of all goods achievable by action. Verbally there is very general agreement; for both the general run of men and people of superior refinement say that it is happiness, and identify living well and doing well with being happy; but with regard to what happiness is they differ, and the many do not give the same account as the wise. For the former think it is some plain and obvious thing, like pleasure, wealth, or honour; etc."—Ed.

[5]The only reasonable alternative is to hold that in both passages it is really τὸ ἄριστον ἀνθρώπῳ which is being elucidated.

pleasure in VII xii 3 and X iii 6, rebuking those who maintained that pleasure *is* a γένεσις, when they really meant that a certain γένεσις is the condition of the realization of pleasure.

The real reason for Prof. Prichard's confidence is to be found in his unquestioned assumption that εὐδαιμονία means pleasure. This assumption is stated in the passage above: "What Aristotle undoubtedly meant and thought others meant by εὐδαιμονία is happiness." (This is, of course, rather odd as it stands, since Aristotle did not know English: it would lose its plausibility if we substituted ἡδονή for "happiness.") For if εὐδαιμονία were the Greek word for 'pleasure', it might well be contended that to ask τί ἐστιν εὐδαιμονία; must be misleading: for it might very well be held[6] that 'pleasure' stands for something unanalyzable and *sui generis*, which we either know, and know with entire adequacy, from experiencing it, or do not know at all. Pleasure might, on these lines, very well be considered to be in the same case as colour and sound, to which, accordingly, Prof. Prichard without hesitation compares εὐδαιμονία. In such cases, one who asks "what is so-and-so?" will very probably be found to be asking "what are the conditions for its realization?" And whether or not 'pleasure' could in any sense be analyzed, at least e.g. the person who said pleasure is honour or wealth would obviously be suspect of only really intending to give conditions of realization.

However, εὐδαιμονία does not mean pleasure, as we have seen. And this very passage proves as well as another that it does not. This is not merely because the theory that εὐδαιμονία means or "is" ἡδονή is rejected, but also because in a most important clause omitted in Prof. Prichard's paraphrase, εὐδαιμονία is said to be equivalent to τὸ εὖ ζῆν καὶ εὖ πράττειν which can-

[6]I do not enquire whether this would be correct.

not mean "feeling pleased." To this we shall return shortly.

Prof. Prichard seems to make out that, apart from the fact that the Greeks did not disagree about what εὐδαιμονία stands for, Aristotle's actual presentation of his question makes it in general an absurd one. Certainly, Prof. Prichard's ostensible argument for maintaining that Aristotle here misrepresents his own problem is not very explicit. According to him, Aristotle says that men agree only on the *name* for the τέλος, viz. εὐδαιμονία, but disagree about what it is used to stand for, or to designate. This, he says, is undeniably absurd. Now why? Has Prof. Prichard any other reason for saying so, except his belief that there could, in fact (owing to the unanalyzable nature of what εὐδαιμονία does stand for), be no disagreement about what εὐδαιμονία stands for?

He seems to suppose that, according to Aristotle, (1) men agree *only* on the name; (2) that is a substantial measure of agreement; (3) what is being (mistakenly) asked for is some *synonym* for εὐδαιμονία, in the simplest sense—some other word or phrase which stands for precisely the same as εὐδαιμονία stands for. (Somewhat as though, when asked for the answer to a mathematical problem, all should agree that the name for the answer was 'k' while disagreeing as to the number which 'k' stands for.) I do not know whether even this would be undeniably absurd (always assuming that in fact all did *not* know εὐδαιμονία to stand for 'pleasure'): but in any case, Aristotle does none of these things.

(1) According to Aristotle, men agree, not merely on the name εὐδαιμονία, but also that εὐδαιμονία is equivalent to τὸ εὖ ζῆν καὶ εὖ πράττειν. (This statement Prof. Prichard omits in his paraphrase.) Moreover, it transpires later that they also agree on a number of other propositions about the characteristics

of εὐδαιμονία, which are listed in chapters viii and ix–xii.

(2) As is shown by I vii 9, Aristotle does not think that the agreement on the name alone is very substantial. And indeed it is clear even from chapter iv that this agreement could cover most radical disagreements.

(3) Aristotle is not, I believe, searching for some simple synonym for εὐδαιμονία, but rather for an 'analysis' of its meaning. While satisfactory as a preliminary statement, this does not make it sufficiently clear what exactly Aristotle is doing.* All men know more or less vaguely what is meant by εὐδαιμονία or τὸ εὖ ζῆν καὶ εὖ πράττειν, and agree on many propositions about it: but when they attempt to clarify that meaning, they disagree. Cp. I vii 9: ἀλλ' ἴσως τὴν μὲν εὐδαιμονίαν τὸ ἄριστον λέγειν ὁμολογούμενόν τι φαίνεται, ποθεῖται δ' ἐναργέστερον τὶ ἐστιν ἔτι λεχθῆναι.†

To search thus for an analysis of the meaning of εὐδαιμονία does not seem to me absurd, except on the false assumption that its meaning was, and was known to be, simple and unanalyzable. We might, to take a similar case, agree that the aim of the statesman is "liberty" or "justice," and yet, in a perfectly intelligible sense, disagree about "what liberty is" or "what justice is."

**There is no doubt, however, that this account of what Aristotle is asking when he asks τί ἐστιν εὐδαιμονία; is far from entirely satisfying. For we need to distinguish from the analysis of the meaning of εὐδαιμονία another procedure altogether, namely the

---

*At this point, in view of the state of the manuscript, some editing by Mr. Urmson was required.—Ed.

†"Presumably, however, to say that happiness is the chief good seems a platitude, and a clearer account of what it is is still desired."—Ed.

**See below under the same sign.

"discovery" of those things, or that life, as he would rather ordinarily say, which satisfy the definition of εὐδαιμονία when that has been discovered. As Moore has insisted, in the case of 'good' (which will occupy us later), it is important to distinguish the discovery of what a word means from the discovery of those things in which the characters meant by the word in fact reside. (Of course this latter procedure is still not what Prichard means when he speaks of discovering 'the conditions for the realization' of something.) This is too simple a view for modern times, since few will accept that goodness is a character in this simple sense. But we still would distinguish the meaning of εὐδαιμονία—the best life for man, etc.—from what we may call the specification of the good life: what the good life allegedly consists in concretely. The whole problem arises over the connection between these two.

There is justice in Prichard's remark that Aristotle "certainly does not think that anyone ever meant by εὐδαιμονία either τιμή or πλοῦτος." They were capable of having said that they meant this, but would have more plausibly claimed that τιμή or πλοῦτος was what satisfied the specification of εὐδαιμονία. But it is not so clear that "he certainly did not himself mean by it ψυχῆς ἐνέργεια τις κατ' ἀρετὴν τελείαν," at least ἐν βίῳ τελείῳ. It is hard to discover, especially in I vii, where the analysis ends and the other process begins. It is perhaps impossible to judge how much is meant to be analysis. Certainly εὐδαιμονία is analyzed (ταὐτὸν ὑπολαμβάνουσι) as τὸ εὖ ζῆν καὶ εὖ πράττειν. Then ἐν βίῳ τελείῳ (ambiguous phrase!) also seems clearly part of the meaning of εὐδαιμονία. I believe that the whole of I vii 9–16 is intended to be an analysis of that meaning. And it results, as it should, in a clear and full definition, referred to as ὁ λόγος of εὐδαιμονία or of τὸ ἄριστον. Moreover EE II i 10 says that ψυχῆς ἐνέργεια κατ' ἀρετήν is τὸ γένος καὶ τὸν ὅρον εὐδαιμονίας. If it had been said that Aristotle did not mean by εὐδαιμονία θεωρία, that would, I think, be certainly true: and it is θεωρία which, in Aristotle's theory, occupies the place of ἡδονή and πλοῦτος in rival theories, as chapter v plainly shows.

But when Aristotle discusses what are in fact the special virtues, and which is the most perfect, he cannot be said any longer to be analyzing the meaning of εὐδαιμονία. He is asking τί ἐστιν εὐδαιμονία; in a different sense: what are the virtues that fill the bill. Even in X viii 8, where the conclusion is reached: ὥστ' εἴη ἂν ἡ εὐδαιμονία θεωρία τις, it is evident that εὐδαιμονία does not mean θεωρία—ἐφ' ὅσον δὴ διατείνει ἡ θεωρία καὶ ἡ εὐδαιμονία, καὶ οἷς μάλιστα ὑπάρχει τὸ θεωρεῖν καὶ τὸ εὐδαιμονεῖν οὐ κατὰ συμβεβηκὸς ἀλλὰ κατὰ τὴν θεωρίαν.**

So Aristotle's distinction between analysis and specification is most unclear. But there is some excuse for Aristotle perhaps, in that εὐδαιμονία does not stand for some character, such as goodness might be, but for a certain kind of life, or ἐνέργεια (Aristotle is unclear as to which): in such a case it is not so easy clearly to observe Prof. Moore's distinction, or even one such as Hare's or Urmson's between meaning and criteria. Suppose we were to ask, for instance, "What is golfing?" But there is this finally to be said. If Aristotle had thought that εὐδαιμονία, like golfing, resided in fact in only one activity of one kind of creature, there would have been more excuse for him than is

**The material included between the double stars required extensive editing by Mr. Urmson because the manuscript on these pages was complicated by notes, corrections, and revisions. Ross's translation of this Greek passage reads: "Happiness extends, then, just so far as contemplation does, and those to whom contemplation more fully belongs are more truly happy, not as mere concomitant but in virtue of the contemplation; . . . Happiness, therefore, must be some form of contemplation."—Ed.

actually the case. For actually he does think that εὐδαιμονία is achieved, in different ways, by gods and by men: hence εὐδαιμονία cannot mean those activities in which human εὐδαιμονία is found. (Unfortunately, of course, his statements on divine εὐδαιμονία are rudimentary, and it is very doubtful, e.g. how ἐν βίῳ τελείῳ can be a part of the meaning of εὐδαιμονία if the gods are also εὐδαίμονες!)

Some distinctions, however, though not this requisite one, Aristotle does draw: in a way he was perhaps on his way to it. In Rhet. I v ad init. he says we must ask: τί ἐστιν εὐδαιμονία καὶ τὰ μόρια αὐτῆς; and this distinction is common, though not in the NE. In EE I v 13–14, he calls the particular virtues μόρια τῆς ἀγαθῆς ζωῆς, which συντείνουσι πρὸς εὐδαιμονίαν. (This does not, of course, mean that they are "the conditions for the realization" of εὐδαιμονία: in NE 1129b18, where the μόρια εὐδαιμονίας are mentioned, they are distinguished from τὰ ποιητικὰ καὶ φυλακτικὰ εὐδαιμονίας [cp. VI xii 5], a distinction insisted on in e.g. EE I ii 5. There is a similar distinction in EE I i of ἐν τίσι τὸ εὖ ζῆν from πῶς κτητόν; compare also MM I ii 9–11: οὐ γάρ ἐστιν ἄλλο τι χώρις τούτων ἡ εὐδαιμονία ἀλλὰ ταῦτα.)[7] Now in effect, the discovery of the μόρια εὐδαιμονίας is the discovery of the activities which together make up the life which, for man, satisfies the definition of εὐδαιμονία; and we can in a sense say, as Aristotle does, that this life is εὐδαιμονία. Nevertheless, εὐδαιμονία does not mean that life, and its discovery is posterior to the analysis of the meaning of εὐδαιμονία. Two erroneous presuppositions were, however, encouraged by Aristotle's failure to be clear what question he is asking when he writes τί ἐστιν

[7] It is important to remember this when interpreting such a passage as I vii 5. Compare EE II i 12, a better statement. [Austin's MM is a reference to Magna Moralia—Ed.]

εὐδαιμονία; first, the presupposition that εὐδαιμονία—the ideal life—is not a will-o'-the-wisp, and that there is only one possible ideal life; second, that the question of what fills the bill is throughout purely factual.

Summing up then, the question τί ἐστιν εὐδαιμονία; is sensible but ambiguous. Aristotle means to ask firstly: what is the analysis or definition of εὐδαιμονία? and secondly: what life, in particular for man, satisfies that definition or specification? (A subsidiary and distinct question is: What are the conditions ὧν οὐκ ἄνευ, and the methods necessary for the realization of such a life?)

What does εὐδαιμονία *mean? Some general considerations.* We must now concern ourselves with the first of these questions: What does εὐδαιμονία mean in Greek and incidentally what is its translation in English? But I cannot enter into details of Aristotle's own analysis: I shall only attempt to show what, according to him, was the vague and common notion of εὐδαιμονία from which his analysis starts.

According to I iv 2, τὸ εὐδαιμονεῖν was admittedly equivalent to τὸ εὖ ζῆν καὶ εὖ πράττειν. (In I vii 4 there is a weaker statement: it is admitted "that the εὐδαίμων lives and acts well"—but, as Aristotle remarks, on his own account εὐδαιμονία is living and acting well: and in both the other *Ethics* the statement is given as in I iv 2; cp. *MM* I iii 3; *EE* i 10 and I i 7.) εὐδαιμονία, then, means living a life of a certain kind—of *what* kind can of course only be discovered by analyzing the word εὖ, and hence ἀγαθόν (so that the full analysis of εὐδαιμονία includes that of ἀγαθόν). εὐδαίμων, I suppose, means literally or, what is often the same, etymologically, "prospered by a deity": and what the deities prosper is lives or careers or activities or parts of these. Aristotle insists on two further points—εὐδαιμονία means a *complete* life of activity of a certain kind. On the latter point, that the reference is to ἐνέργεια not to ἕξις, he is always firm (cp. also I xii).[8] On the former point he is not so happy: not only is βίος τέλειος hopelessly ambiguous (cp. MM I iv 5), but Aristotle often omits to remember this qualification. So much so that in the end he never explains how the βίος is made up—only the ἀρεταί which predominate it.

At any rate, what is important in all this is, that, though of course we can speak of a man as εὐδαίμων, the substantive with which εὐδαίμων naturally goes is βίος or a similar word: a man is only called εὐδαίμων because his life is so. Hence the discussion in chapter v of the various βίοι which lay claim to being εὐδαιμονία.[9] And hence the saying "call no man εὐδαίμων until he is dead" (I x i).

Similarly the forms εὐδαιμονίζειν and εὐδαιμονισμός, which seem to mean "to congratulate," "congratulation." That whereon I congratulate someone is an achievement, an activity and normally a completed one (though normally also, of course, of less extent than his whole career). With reference to this point consider I v 6 and viii 9.

These considerations show conclusively that εὐδαιμονία could not mean "pleasure": pleasure is a feeling, not a life of a certain kind nor an achievement: nor do I congratulate someone on his feeling pleased: and it

---

[8]On p. 38 [p. 258], Professor Prichard makes what seems to me serious misstatements about I xii. "In other words . . . everything else." The contrast in the first sentence I, of course, consider mistaken. As for the rest, the quotation given is actually from section viii where εὐδαιμονία is not contrasted with ἀρετή at all. The contrast with ἀρετή is in ii and vi: ἀρετή is ἐπαινετὸν qua τὸ ποῖον καὶ πρὸς τι εἶναι — viz. the ἐνέργειαι (πράξεις, ἔργα) which are εὐδαιμονία: the ἐνέργειαι are τίμια and are εὐδαιμονία. Professor Prichard talks as though in xii ἐνέργειαι κατ' ἀρετήν were ἐπαινετά: they are τίμια!

[9]And when in I iv the suggestion is made that εὐδαιμονία is ἡδονή or πλοῦτος, that is loose language (as V shows) for the life in which most pleasure or most wealth is gained.

would be silly to say "call no man pleased until he is dead."

There is, however, Aristotle's own remark in I iv that many people do maintain that εὐδαιμονία is ἡδονή, as others πλοῦτος or τιμή. This is a loose remark—as Prof. Prichard claims, though not in his way. His explanation, that Aristotle meant that some maintain that εὐδαιμονία is *produced* by ἡδονή, also πλοῦτος. etc., is incorrect. Aristotle himself shows what he meant more fully in chapter v. The view was that εὐδαιμονία is the ἀπολαυστικὸς βίος, the life in which most pleasure is felt. Likewise the identification with πλοῦτος should be taken as "the life in which most wealth is gained" (not, of course "is by definition" but "in fact resides in").

If we want a translation of εὐδαιμονία which will not mislead, as "happiness" appears to mislead Prof. Prichard, we might use as a prophylactic "success." "Success" is at least a word of the same *type*, so to say, as εὐδαιμονία. "Success" does mean living and acting well: a life or a part of it is "successful": and with some hesitations I do congratulate on "success"; it might well be said "call no man successful until he is dead." Furthermore, success demands just that fortunate supply of εὐτυχία, εὐημερία, which Aristotle admits in I viii 15–17 is also a necessary condition for εὐδαιμονία.

It is true, however, that "success" is not a moral notion for us. Perhaps this is no great disadvantage, for it is doubtful how far a pagan ethic, such as the Greek (or the Chinese) gains by a translation which imports our own moral notions: εὐδαιμονία is certainly quite an unchristian ideal. Still, we do require a word to import some form of *commendation*, as εὐδαίμων did, and to certain non-personal standards.

**That εὐδαιμονία did mean life of *activity* of a certain kind is almost certainly the correct analysis;

and that it did further mean life of ἀρεταί seems equally correct. So we may say that the analysis in I vii 8–16 is correct and is supported by I viii. However we must also say: (a) That roundabout way of bringing into the discussion ψυχή and ἔργον is a piece of unnecessary Aristotelian metaphysics. It is not really made use of until the very end, in the argument for the supremacy of θεωρία; the argument proceeds straight on to the ἀρεταί. (b) The whole discussion here is not purely factual; its nature is disguised by the transference of commendation to the ἀρεταί. (c) Of the three lives suggested none accords with the popular view which was that of Tellus the Athenian.* His ideal is omitted altogether except when allowed in by the back door suddenly in Book X. (d) It might be argued that he omits to give sufficient consideration to μεθ᾽ ἡδονῆς ἢ οὐκ ἄνευ ἡδονῆς and it might be argued further that not enough deference is shown to ψυχικόν—people may have meant by this something genuinely internal, as did later the Stoics. Quite possibly εὐδαιμονία did have this "meaning" too.**

Nevertheless, "happiness" is probably after all to be preferred as a translation, partly because it is traditional, and still more because it is fairly colourless.[10] It seems to me very rash to assume that in common English "happiness" obviously means feeling pleased: probably it has several more or less vague meanings. Take the lines:

---

*Tellus the Athenian is mentioned by Plutarch in his *Life of Solon*, where Solon is said to describe him as a happy man on account of his honesty, his having good children, his having a competent estate, and his having died bravely in battle for his country. Tellus appears to have been a plain man whose happiness, nevertheless, Solon holds up to Croesus.—Ed.

** ... ** This passage appears to be a later addition by Austin, which we inserted here in a somewhat expanded form.—Ed.

[10]Success also does not always or usually refer to life *as a whole*: and it has perhaps a nuance of *competitiveness*.

"This is the happy warrior, this is He
That every Man at arms should wish to be."

I do not think Wordsworth meant by that: "This
is the warrior who feels *pleased*." Indeed, he is

"Doomed to go in company with Pain
And fear and bloodshed, miserable train."

(Though no doubt his life is μεθ' ἡδονῆς ἢ οὐκ ἄνευ
ἡδονῆς as Aristotle likes to assume or feebly to argue
his own chosen one must be.) What every man at
arms is being incited to wish, is not so much to get
for himself *feelings* comparable to those of the paragon,
as to imitate his *life*. I think, then, that if we are on
our guard against misleading nuances, "happiness" is
still the best translation for εὐδαιμονία.

The question of the relation of εὐδαιμονία to
ἡδονή has not, it should be noticed, yet been cleared
up. It to a great extent coincides with the equally
difficult problem of the relation of τὸ ἀγαθόν to
τὸ ἡδύ. Both must be reserved for a separate discussion later.

ἀγαθόν—Does Aristotle tell us what its meaning is?
Prof. Prichard's contention is, it will be remembered,
that Aristotle really means by ἀγαθόν "conducive to
our happiness." Not concerning ourselves for the moment with the precise interpretation given, we may
notice, *firstly*, that he is purporting to give Aristotle's
answer to a question which Aristotle himself expressly
declines to answer, viz. what is the meaning of ἀγαθόν?
And *secondly*, that the answer given, implying as it does
that ἀγαθόν *does* have a *single* meaning, is of a kind
which Aristotle himself is at pains to prove impossible.

Let us take the translation of ἀγαθόν as "good"
here for granted, and let us once more, following Prof.
Moore, distinguish between two very different sorts
of question, which are commonly asked in books on
ethics. We are investigating, we may say, the Good:

but we may intend to ask: (1) What does the word
'good' mean?[11] or (2) What things are good, and in
what degrees? Of course, these two questions may be
formulated in a variety of ways. For (1) we may substitute: What is the nature of goodness? or: In saying
of anything that it is good, what am I saying about
it? even: What sort of a predicate is 'good'? and so
on. For (2) we may substitute: Of what things may
it be truly said that they are good? And which is the
best of them? and so on.

To these two different sorts of question, as Moore
claimed, we shall get two correspondingly different
sorts of answer. To (1) the answer might be: Goodness is a simple unanalyzable quality like yellow, or:
"Goodness" means "approved by me," or: To say of
anything that it is good, is to say that it is conducive
to happiness, or: 'Good' is an evaluative word. Whereas
to (2), the answer might be: Friendship is good, or:
Violence is better than justice, and so on. Note here
that it is assumed that the only sense in which ἀγαθόν
has a "meaning" is in some "factual" sense. Aristotle
assumes this too.

Now we must ask, on this distinction does Aristotle
concern himself with both these questions or with
one only? And if the latter, with which? And I think
that we must answer, that he concerns himself pro-
fessedly with the second only.[12]

For Aristotle himself is aware of and draws this distinction between the two questions, and says that, in
the *Ethics*, he is concerned only with the second. This
he does in the celebrated chapter I vi. He there con-

[11]Which is itself probably an ambiguous question, but we may
let this pass for the moment. (We also have to distinguish (a)
how to translate a word? (b) what does someone say about the
analysis of the meaning or of the definition of a word? and both
of these from (c) possibly different senses of 'mean'.)

[12]And with that only in the more special form: "What particular things are good, and in what degrees, *for man?*"

futes those who had supposed that the word ἀγαθόν always stands for a single identical predicate.¹³ But in proving this, he does not tell us what are the various meanings of ἀγαθόν—the furthest he goes in that direction is to give us a hint as to how the various meanings may be related to one another, i.e. how the variety yet forms a unity. He then dismisses the matter, 1096b30: ἀλλ' ἴσως ταῦτα μεν ἀφέτεον τὸ νῦν. ἐξακριβοῦν γὰρ ὑπὲρ αὐτῶν ἄλλης ἂν εἴη φιλοσοφίας οἰκειότερον.* He then turns to his present problem: What is that good which is πρακτὸν καὶ κτητὸν ἀνθρώπῳ, that is: What particular things are good for man, (and in what degrees)? Unfortunately, as is well known, he does not in fact discuss "the meaning of ἀγαθόν" elsewhere.

It is clear, then, that Aristotle declines in general to discuss the meanings of ἀγαθόν but argues that it has no single meaning. In both respects Prof. Prichard's view conflicts, *prima facie*, with Aristotle's statements. Nevertheless, it may be urged, both that Aristotle is unjustified in declining to explain the meaning of ἀγαθόν and that he must himself attach some meaning to it in using in throughout the *Ethics*, which we may be able to discover. And further, that meaning might be identical in all important cases (this will be explained later).

If asked to justify himself, there is no doubt how Aristotle would reply.¹⁴ The *NE* is only intended as

¹³Compare [H.W.B.] Joseph, *Some Problems in Ethics* [Oxford, 1931], p. 75.: "That goodness is not a quality is the burden of Aristotle's argument in *NE* I vi.": but this is not quite correct. Aristotle is anxious to say that ἀγαθόν *has no single meaning*—whether a quality, a relation, or anything else. As a matter of fact, he says it does sometimes stand for a quality.

*But perhaps these subjects had better be dismissed for the present; for perfect precision about them would be more appropriate to another branch of philosophy."—Ed.

¹⁴Aristotle does to some extent reply to this objection in I vi 14–16.

a guide for politicians, and they are only concerned to know what is good, not what goodness means. Probably Platonists would have said that I cannot discover what is good until I have found the definition of goodness, but Aristotle would claim that the definition, if possible at all, is only necessary if we wish to *demonstrate* scientifically that certain things are good. So much ἀκρίβεια is not called for in the *NE*, and in any case one can know what things are good without knowing the analysis of 'good'.[15] Whether this reply is satisfactory is doubtful. Certainly there is much to be said on Aristotle's side. Firstly, as Moore pointed out, we can know something to be true without knowing its analysis. Secondly, as Aristotle pointed out in I vi 4, if goodness is an isolable, definable property we should be able to study it in isolation from all subject matters, whereas in fact there is no such study. Thirdly, even those who, like Moore, find goodness "unanalyzable" still go on to discuss what is good. But in any case it must be admitted that his method has its dangers; and whether they are serious can best be judged by its results in the body of the *NE*. (In at least two cases, those of ἡδονή and φιλία and perhaps also in that of τιμή the lack of a clearer account of the meaning or meanings of ἀγαθόν is in fact most serious.)

The extent to which Aristotle does in fact attach a discoverable, and even single, meaning to ἀγαθόν will, of course, concern us largely. But before proceeding, it is worth considering an example of the extreme lengths to which Prof. Prichard is prepared to go in imputing inconsistency to Aristotle. His view, we said, implies that ἀγαθόν does have a single meaning, i.e. does always stand for an identical common character in the subjects of which it is predicated. (Note that

---

[15]I do not, however, accept Burnet's exaggerated view of the "dialectical" method of the *NE*.

we need 'character' here, not 'quality'; for, of course, one of Prof. Prichard's main contention is that Aristotle mistakes "being conducive to our happiness" for a *quality* of that which is so conducive, whereas it is not.) And this, we said, conflicts with Aristotle's own statement that ἀγαθόν does not do this.

Now it may be thought that I have been wasting unnecessary words over this, since Prof. Prichard himself notices this objection and answers it on pp. 32–33 [p. 250.]

> But Aristotle in saying, as he would have said, that in pursuing, e.g. an honour, we are pursuing it ὡς ἀγαθόν, could only have meant that we are pursuing it in virtue of thinking that it would possess a certain character to which he refers by the term ἀγαθόν, so that by ἀγαθόν he must mean to indicate some character which certain things would have. Further, this being so, in implying as he does that in pursuing things of certain different kinds καθ' αὑτά we are pursuing them ὡς ἀγαθά, he must be implying that these things of different kinds have, nevertheless, a common character, viz. that indicated by the term ἀγαθόν. It will, of course, be objected that he expressly denies that they have a common character. For he says: τιμῆς δὲ καὶ φρονήσεως καὶ ἡδονῆς ἕτεροι καὶ διαφέροντες οἱ λόγοι ταύτῃ ᾗ ἀγαθά (*Ethics* I vi 11).* But the answer is simple; viz. that this is merely an inconsistency into which he is driven by his inability to find in these things the common character which his theory requires him to find, and that if he is to succeed in maintaining that we pursue these things of various kinds ὡς ἀγαθά, he *has* to maintain that in spite of appearances to the contrary they have a common character.

* "But of honour, wisdom, and pleasure, just in respect of their goodness, the accounts are distinct and diverse."—Ed.

We are not concerned for the moment with this doctrine about "pursuing things ὡς ἀγαθά."[16] But what we must notice is that Prof. Prichard quotes the sentence about τιμή, φρόνησις, and ἡδονή, as though it were an *unwilling admission*, into which Aristotle's honesty drives him: as though Aristotle is admitting that in certain cases he *cannot* find the common character, which he *must* find. Yet a glance at the context will show that, on the contrary, the whole passage is designed to *prove* that there is no such common character: and the sentence quoted clinches the argument.[17] It is not too much to say that, if τιμή and the rest are possessed of a common character denoted by ἀγαθόν, the whole argument against the Platonists is undermined: and Prof. Prichard must accuse Aristotle not so much of inconsistency as of bad faith.

In any case, this passage cannot be thus lightly dismissed. The objection retains, it seems to me, very considerable weight.

ἀγαθόν—*Does it mean "that which is desired"?* We may now turn to the main problem, the meaning of ἀγαθόν. It must, I think, be agreed, that there is some chance of our being able to discover what Aristotle does in fact believe about the meaning of the word: but, since Aristotle appears to decline to assist us, that chance is small.

It is on p. 31 [p. 248] that Prof. Prichard begins his attempt to elucidate the meaning of ἀγαθόν: and he says that "Aristotle's nearest approach to an elucida-

---

[16]ὡς ἀγαθά does not in Greek mean "in virtue of their possessing a certain characteristic, 'goodness.'" It means rather "pursuing them *in the way in which we pursue things we say are good*." Thus the phrase is noncommittal as to whether there is a common quality or not. Cp. in English 'stating as a fact,' 'stating as a matter of opinion.'

[17]Aristotle does not say he "cannot find" a common character denoted by ἀγαθόν in these instances: he says that he knows ἀγαθόν stands for *different* characters.

tion" is to be found in I vi 7–11[18] and vii 1–5. Certain statements there made, he says, "seem intended as an elucidation of the meaning of ἀγαθόν"; nevertheless they fail, even formally, to constitute such an elucidation: and moreover, if they are "taken seriously as an elucidation," the result is to render absurd other well-known doctrines in the *NE*.

I suppose it cannot be denied that Aristotle is capable of getting himself into pretty tortuous confusions; but this time, at least, I think he can be exonerated.

In the first place, it seems to me that the statements in question are not intended at all as an "elucidation of the meaning of ἀγαθόν" in Prof. Prichard's sense.[19] It is, consequently, not surprising that they fail formally to constitute such an elucidation: what is surprising, I think, is Prof. Prichard's reason for saying that they so fail. In the second place, if they are "taken seriously as an elucidation," they do not so much render absurd the doctrines mentioned by Prof. Prichard as others which it is easy to find.

In these passages, says Prof. Prichard, Aristotle speaks of τὰ καθ' αὑτὰ διωκόμενα καὶ ἀγαπώμενα as called ἀγαθά in one sense . . . and he speaks of τὰ ποιητικὰ τούτων ἢ φυλακτικά πως as called ἀγαθά in another sense, and he implies that these latter are διωκτὰ καὶ αἱρετὰ δι' ἕτερον (*Ethics* I vii 4) . . . Further he appears to consider that the difference of meaning is elucidated (sic) by referring to the former as ἀγαθὰ καθ' αὑτά and to the latter as ἀγαθὰ διὰ ταῦτα, i.e. ἀγαθὰ διὰ ἀγαθὰ καθ' αὑτά. But this unfortunately is no elucidation, since to state a difference of reason for calling two things ἀγαθόν is not to state a difference of mean-

18For "7–11" we should read "8–11."
19If any passage deserves the description "Aristotle's nearest approach to an elucidation," it is probably I vii 10 (not mentioned by Professor Prichard); on this *v.i.*

ing of ἀγαθόν, and indeed is to imply that the meaning in both cases is the same. Nevertheless, these statements seem intended as an elucidation of the meaning of ἀγαθόν. And the cause for surprise lies in this, that if they are taken seriously as an elucidation, the conclusion can only be that ἀγαθόν includes 'being desired' in its meaning, and indeed simply means τέλος or end.

It will, I am afraid, necessarily take some considerable space to clear this matter up.

Let us, as a preliminary, remark that the passage vii 1–5 is not concerned with at all the same matter as vi 8–11. In vii 1 he asserts that τὸ ἀγαθόν of any activity whatsoever is τὸ τέλος (incidentally this passage implies that τὸ ἀγαθόν and τὸ τέλος do not mean the same): he then proceeds to ask, what is the τέλος τῶν πρακτῶν ἀπάντων? And the word ἀγαθόν is not so much as mentioned again. Moreover, though he does proceed to distinguish a τέλος καθ' αὑτὸ διωκτόν (αἱρετόν) from a τέλος δι' ἕτερον διωκτόν (αἱρετόν) he does not assert that the word τέλος has (in any sense) two meanings, only that there are some τέλη which are τέλεια (complete or final), others which are not. Still less, of course, does he assert that ἀγαθόν has two meanings, or endeavour to elucidate its meaning: he says nothing about it at all; just as, in vi 8–11, no mention is made of τέλος at all.

We may confine ourselves, therefore, to vi 8–11. Upon what is Aristotle there engaged? In the earlier part of the chapter he has been arguing that ἀγαθόν cannot have always an identical meaning. But now he produces an attempted answer to his own objections, which is to be understood by referring to his own logic (*Categories* I a1). A word (ὄνομα) may be used either συνωνύμως, ὁμωνύμως, or παρωνύμως. If, on each occasion of its use, its connotation (ὁ κατὰ τοὔνομα λόγος τῆς οὐσίας) is identical, then the word is used συνωνύμως. If, on different occasions of its use, its connotations are different, then the word is used ὁμωνύμως: e.g. κλείς may be used to mean "key" or "collarbone," ζῷον "animal" or "picture." But there is a third possibility: on different occasions of its use, the word may possess connotations which are *partly* identical and *partly* different, in which case the word is said to be used παρωνύμως.[20] There are evidently many ways in which a word can be used paronymously: Aristotle names some of them, and gives examples (τὸ ὑγιεινόν in *Met.* 1003a33 τὸ ἰατρικόν and τὸ ὑγιεινόν in *Met.* 1060b37. Also notoriously τὸ ὄν with which ἀγαθόν here is again compared, and τὸ ἕν. For more details, the reader may refer to those passages, or to Burnet's notes on p. 29 of his edition of the *Ethics*).[21]

One such type of paronymity is known as the "πρὸς ἕν." When we speak of a "healthy exercise" the word 'healthy' has a connotation which is only partly the same as that which it has in the phrase "a healthy body": a healthy exercise is an exercise which produces or preserves healthiness in bodies. Hence healthiness[a], when predicated of an exercise, means "productive or preservative of healthiness[b]" i.e. of healthiness in the sense in which it is predicated of bodies. Thus "healthiness[b]" and "healthiness[a]" have connotations which are partly identical and partly different.

Now, in our present passage, vi 8–11, Aristotle is producing as an objection against himself the fact (admitted elsewhere, cp. *Rhet.* 1362a27) that ἀγαθόν is paronymous in this way. His opponents are supposed

[20]Compare the traditional classification of terms as *univocal, equivocal,* and *analogous.*—Joseph, *An Introduction to Logic* (Oxford, 1916), p. 46: "analogous" is unsatisfactory, since κατ' ἀναλογίαν is only one form of paronymity.

[21]This supplements and amends *Cat.* I. a bit; homonymy and paronymy are defined by very limited examples there. Consider also Rhet. 1362a21 ff. with regard to this point.

to claim that, although ἀγαθόν does not always have
an identical meaning, that is merely because it is paronymous in the above manner. Sometimes it means "x,"
sometimes "productive, etc. of x," etc.; and clearly it
is only the "*nuclear*" meaning of "x" which is common
to both, with which they are concerned. And it *is* always identical. To which Aristotle replies as follows.
First, let us distinguish ἀγαθόν as used in the one
sense, from ἀγαθόν as used in the other, by substituting
for it, in the one case ἀγαθὸν καθ' αὐτό, and in the
other ἀγαθὸν διὰ ἀγαθόν τι καθ' αὐτό.[22] Then let
us disregard all cases where ἀγαθόν is used in the latter
sense. And finally observe that, even in cases where it
is used in the former sense only, it *still* has not always
an identical meaning.

Now let us ask, with reference to Prof. Prichard's
argument quoted above, does Aristotle intend here to
"elucidate the meaning" of ἀγαθόν? It is clear that
there is no simple answer, Yes or No, to this question.
He does intend to point out that it has at least two
meanings, at least in a reasonably strict sense, and to
explain how those two meanings are related, and to
show how they are in part identical. But he does not
intend to elucidate that identical part. Moreover, he
proceeds to assert that in fact ἀγαθόν, used in the
nuclear way, has at least three different meanings (so
that there may be at least six meanings of ἀγαθόν in
general): but he does not mean to elucidate any one
of the three, nor even to explain how they are related
to each other. It is not, then, surprising that Prof.
Prichard should feel dissatisfied; if we ask his over-
simplified question, the passage must "seem intended
as an elucidation" of the meaning of ἀγαθόν, and yet
fail to be one—for plainly, Prof. Prichard would only
count as a *real* elucidation, an elucidation of the mean-

[22]πρὸς might have been expected rather than διά: but διὰ is
more general.

ing of ἀγαθόν in the nuclear sense of senses, which Aristotle is not concerned to give him.

Prof. Prichard's remark, that "to state a difference of reason for calling two things ἀγαθόν is not to state a difference of meaning of ἀγαθόν, and indeed is to imply that the meaning in both cases is the same," remains to me obscure. But it seems clear that he has not appreciated the doctrine of παρώνυμα, since he uses the rigid dichotomy "same meaning—different meaning" whereas παρώνυμα are words which have meanings *partly* the same and *partly* different. His "difference of reason" might be the point about, say, healthy. Then Aristotle would accept the claim, and say that what he offers is *not* an elucidation and is not intended to be one. We have seen, however, that Prof. Prichard is prepared to believe that the passage may be seriously intended as an elucidation of ἀγαθόν in the "nuclear" sense. Seeing that he has already dismissed the distinction between ἀγαθὰ καθ᾽ αὑτά and ἀγαθὰ διὰ ταῦτα as "no elucidation," and seeing that Aristotle makes no attempt to elucidate the meaning of ἀγαθόν in the nuclear sense, and further states that it has at least three nuclear senses, it is clearly bound to be difficult for Prof. Prichard to find anything in the passage which could be described as "an elucidation of *the* meaning of ἀγαθόν." He fastens upon the words διωκόμενα καὶ ἀγαπώμενα, διώκεται, διώκομεν and concludes that, according to Aristotle here, ἀγαθόν "simply means τέλος or end."[23]

Let us proceed to consider first Prof. Prichard's arguments to prove that ἀγαθόν does *not* have that meaning. After asserting that it quite certainly is not used by Aristotle with that meaning [which in a way is true: but surely then, it is unlikely that he intends

---

[23]It seems to me doubtful whether τέλος means simply "something desired": but for present purposes it will do no harm to suppose it does so.

to ascribe that meaning to it in this passage?] he proceeds as follows: "Apart from other considerations, if he did [mean by ἀγαθόν simply τέλος], then for him to say, as he in effect does, that we always aim at ἀγαθόν τι would be to say nothing, and for him to speak, as he does, of the object of βούλησις as τἀγαθόν would be absurd."

The first of these arguments is perhaps too concise to be clear. "We always aim at ἀγαθόν τι" may perhaps mean

(1) whenever we *act*, we aim at ἀγαθόν τι, or
(2) whenever we *aim*, we aim at ἀγαθόν τι

If (1) is meant, I very much doubt whether Aristotle would maintain it; for we sometimes act from ἐπιθυμία or θυμός, and then we aim at ἡδύ τι or at ἀντιλύπησις. But he might say[24] that in all *deliberate* action we aim at ἀγαθόν τι, as he implies in the first sentence of the *Ethics*.[25] However, this qualification need not concern us here (though, since he *would* certainly have said that every action aims at some τέλος, it is clear enough that ἀγαθόν does not mean τέλος). If, then, (1) is meant, and if ἀγαθόν τι *means* τέλος τι, Aristotle will be saying "Whenever we act, we aim at some end." But to say that is not to say *nothing*: indeed, it is to say something which Prof. Prichard declares, on p. 29 [p. 243], to be false.[26] At most the sentence is *pleonastic*: for we could write τινός for τέλους τινός (or ἀγαθοῦ τινός) without loss of meaning. But that is a very minor matter. And this would serve, e.g., to define ἀγαθόν.

If (2) is meant, the sentence is certainly emptier: "whenever we aim, we aim at some end." It might be said to be a matter of definition. But it might well be

[24]Wrongly.

[25]The importance of which should not be exaggerated.

[26]Because he understands by τέλος *only* what Aristotle calls a τέλος παρὰ τὴν πρᾶξιν, I confess that his criticism at this point seems to me perverse.

said, for emphasis, in explaining the notion of "aiming," or in otherwise explaining the use of words. However, for reasons similar to those given in the preceding paragraph, I do not consider that Aristotle would ever have made such a remark about ἀγαθόν, though he might well have made it about τέλος. If we change it to "whenever we aim *deliberately*, and only then, we aim at ἀγαθόν τι," Aristotle might agree: but *then*, if we substitute τέλος τι for ἀγαθόν τι, the statement would simply be *false*. Thus proving, though not by Prof. Prichard's argument, that ἀγαθόν does not mean τέλος.

Now take Prichard's second argument. Here, no such objection applies as in the case of the first argument, for Aristotle certainly *would* say that the object of βούλησις is τἀγαθόν. If ἀγαθόν means τέλος, the statement becomes: "the object of βούλησις is τὸ τέλος." Now this is not, as a matter of fact, as it stands, absurd—it is in fact a remark which Aristotle often makes, with good sense (cp. e.g. 1111b26, or 1113a15, ἡ βούλησις τοῦ τέλους ἐστίν). However, τὸ τέλος is there being contrasted with τὰ πρὸς τὸ τέλος, and βούλησις with προαίρεσις: whereas it is clear that Prof. Prichard means, and fairly enough, to refer to a context where βούλησις is being contrasted with ἐπιθυμία and θημός, and τἀγαθόν with τὸ ἡδύ and ἀντιλύπησις. In such a context, it is clear enough that we cannot substitute τέλος for ἀγαθόν. For in the case of the other two types of ὀρέξεις we are also aiming at a τέλος, and we need ἀγαθόν not τέλος to provide the contrast. Prof. Prichard's arguments, then, reduce to one, which I think is sound: ἀγαθόν cannot mean "that which is desired," because Aristotle holds that there are *other* objects of desire besides τὸ ἀγαθόν.

Apart from this argument, it is absolutely clear from I vi itself that ἀγαθόν does not, for Aristotle, mean (or at any rate. merely mean?) "that which is desired."

It is not merely that he says that ἀγαθόν has no single meaning, and hence a *fortiori*, not that suggested. But further, he says of τιμή φρόνησις and ἡδονή that they are all διωκόμενα καθ' αὐτά, so that, presumably, their λόγοι ᾗ διωκόμενα καθ' αὐτά* are *identical*: whereas their λόγοι ταύτῃ ᾗ ἀγαθά are *different*. So that being ἀγαθόν cannot mean being desired.

I expect the reader has found the proof of this tedious. But it is important to establish the point, since the relation between "being ἀγαθόν" and "being desired" is one of the most baffling puzzles in Aristotle's, or for that matter Plato's, ethical theory. This puzzle, like that of the relation between ἀγαθόν and ἡδύ, must be reserved for a separate discussion.

*Their accounts as things pursued for their own sake." (Ed. transl.).

THE FINAL GOOD IN
ARISTOTLE'S *ETHICS*

W. F. R. HARDIE

Aristotle maintains that every man has, or should have, a single end (τέλος), a target at which he aims. The doctrine is stated in *NE* I 2. 'If, then, there is some end of the things we do which we desire for its own sake (everything else being desired for the sake of this), and if we do not choose everything for the sake of something else (for at that rate the process would go on to infinity, so that our desire would be empty and vain), clearly this must be the good and the chief good. Will not the knowledge of it, then, have a great influence on life? Shall we not, like archers who have a mark to aim at, be more likely to hit upon what is right?'[1] (1094a18–24). Aristotle does not here prove, nor need we understand him as claiming to prove, that there is only one end which is desired for itself. He points out correctly that, if there are objects which are desired but not desired for themselves, there must be some object which is desired for itself. The passage further suggests that, if there were one such object and one only, this fact would be important and helpful for the conduct of life.

From *Philosophy*, XL (1965), 277–95. Reprinted by permission of the author and the editors of *Philosophy*.

[1]Here, and in quoting other passages, I have reproduced the Oxford translation. I refer to the *Nicomachean Ethics* as *NE* and to the *Eudemian Ethics* as *EE*.

The same doctrine is stated in *EE* A 2. But, whereas in the *NE* the emphasis is on the concern of political science, statesmanship, with the human good conceived as a single end, the *EE* speaks only of the planning by the individual of his own life. 'Everyone who has the power to live according to his own choice (προαίρεσις) should dwell on these points and set up for himself some object for the good life to aim at, whether honour or reputation or wealth or culture, by reference to which he will do all that he does, since not to have one's life organised in view of some end is a sign of great folly. Now above all we must first define to ourselves without hurry or carelessness in which of our possessions the good life consists, and what for men are the conditions of its attainment' (1214b6–14). Here, then, we are told that lack of practical wisdom is shown in a man's failure to plan and organise his life for the attainment of a single end. Aristotle omits to say, but says elsewhere, that lack of practical wisdom is shown also in a man's preference for a bad or inadequate end, say pleasure or money. We learn in *NE* VI 9 that the man of practical wisdom has a true conception of the end which is best for him as well as the capacity to plan effectively for its realisation (1141b31–33).

How far do men in fact plan their lives, as Aristotle suggests they should, for the attainment of a single end? As soon as we ask this question, we see that there is a confusion in Aristotle's conception of the single end. For the question confuses two questions: first, how far do men plan their lives; and, secondly, so far as they do, how far do they, in their plans, give a central and dominating place to a single desired object, money or fame or science? To both these questions the answer that first suggests itself is that some men do and some do not. Take the second question first. It is exceptional for a life to be organised to achieve the satisfaction of one ruling passion. If asked for ex-

amples we might think of Disraeli's political ambition
or of Henry James' self-dedication to the art of the
novel. But exceptional genius is not incompatible with
a wide variety of interests. It seems plain that very few
men can be said, even roughly, to live their lives under
the domination of a single end. Consider now the
first question. How far do men plan their lives? Clearly
some do so who have no single dominant aim. It is
possible to have a plan based on priorities, or on equal
consideration, as between a number of objects. It is
even possible to plan not to plan, to resolve never to
cross bridges in advance. Hobbes remarked that there
is no 'finis ultimus, utmost aim, nor summum bonum,
greatest good, as is spoken of in the books of the old
moral philosophers. . . . Felicity is a continual progress
of the desire, from one object to another, the attaining
of the former being still but the way to the latter'
(*Leviathan*, ch. xi). But even such a progress may be
planned, although the plan may not be wise. Every
man has, and knows that he has, a number of independent desires, i.e. desires which are not dependent
on other desires in the way in which desire for a means
is dependent on desire for an end. Every man is capable,
from time to time, of telling himself that, if he pur-
sues one particular object too ardently, he may lose or
imperil other objects also dear to him. So it may be
argued that every man capable, as all men are, of
reflection is, even if only occasionally and implicitly,
a planner of his own life.

We can now distinguish the two conceptions which
are confused or conflated in Aristotle's exposition of
the doctrine of the single end. One of them is the
conception of what might be called the inclusive end.
A man, reflecting on his various desires and interests,
notes that some mean more to him than others, that
some are more, some less, difficult and costly to achieve,
that the attainment of one may, in different degrees,

promote or hinder the attainment of others. By such reflection he is moved to plan to achieve at least his most important objectives as fully as possible. The following of such a plan is roughly what is sometimes meant by the pursuit of happiness. The desire for happiness, so understood, is the desire for the orderly and harmonious gratification of desires. Aristotle sometimes, when he speaks of the final end, seems to be fumbling for the idea of an inclusive end, or comprehensive plan, in this sense. Thus in *NE* I 2 he speaks of the end of politics as 'embracing' other ends (1094b6–7). The aim of a science which is 'architectonic' (1094a26–27; cf. *NE* VI 8, 1141b24–26) is a second-order aim. Again in *NE* I 7 he says that happiness must be 'most desirable of all things, without being counted as one good thing among others since, if it were so counted, it would be made more desirable by the addition of even the least of goods . . .' (1097b16–20). Such considerations ought to lead Aristotle to define happiness as a secondary end, the full and harmonious achievement of primary ends. This is what he ought to say. It is not what he says. His explicit view, as opposed to his occasional insight, makes the supreme end not inclusive but dominant, the object of one prime desire, philosophy. This is so even when, as in *NE* I 7, he has in mind that, *prima facie*, there is not only one final end: '. . . if there are more than one, the most final of these will be what we are seeking' (1097a30). Aristotle's mistake and confusion are implicit in his formulation in *EE* A 2 of the question in *which* of our possessions does the good life consist (1214b12–13). For to put the question thus is to rule out the obvious and correct reply; that the life which is best for a man cannot lie in gaining only *one* of his objects at the cost of losing all the rest. This would be too high a price to pay even for philosophy.

The ambiguity which we have found in Aristotle's

conception of the final good shows itself also in his attempt to use the notion of a 'function' (ἔργον) which is 'peculiar' to man as a clue to the definition of happiness. The notion of function cannot be defended and should not be pressed, since a man is not designed for a purpose. The notion which Aristotle in fact uses is that of the specific nature of man, the characteristics which primarily distinguish him from other living things. This notion can be given a wider interpretation which corresponds to the inclusive end or a narrower interpretation which corresponds to the dominant end. In *NE* I 7, seeking what is peculiar to man (1097b33–34), Aristotle rejects first the life of nutrition and growth and secondly the life of perception which is common to 'the horse, the ox and every animal' (1098a2–3). What remains is 'an active life of the element that has a rational principle' (1098a3–4). This expression need not, as commentators point out, be understood as excluding theoretical activity. 'Action' can be used in a wide sense, as in the *Politics* VII 3 (1325b16–23), to include contemplative thinking. But what the phrase specifies as the proper function of man is clearly wider than theoretical activity and includes activities which manifest practical intelligence and moral virtue. But the narrower conception is suggested by a phrase used later in the same chapter. 'The good for man turns out to be the activity of soul in accordance with virtue, and if there are more than one virtue in accordance with the best and most complete' (1098a16–18). The most complete virtue must be theoretical wisdom, although this is not made clear in *NE* I.

The doctrine that only in theoretical activity is man really happy is stated and defended explicitly in X 7 and 8. Theoretical reason, the divine element in man, more than anything else is man (1177b27–28, 1178a6–7). 'It would be strange, then, if he were to choose not the life of his self but that of something else. And what we said before will apply now; that which is proper to each thing is by nature best and most pleasant for each thing' (1178a3–6). Man is truly human only when he is more than human, godlike. 'None of the other animals is happy, since they in no way share in contemplation' (1178b27–28). This statement makes obvious the mistake involved in the conception of the end as dominant rather than inclusive. It is no doubt true that man is the only theoretical animal. But the capacity of some men for theory is very small. And theory is not the only activity in respect of which man is rational as no other animal is rational. There is no logic which leads from the principle that happiness is to be found in a way of living which is common and peculiar to men to the narrow view of the final good as a dominant end. What is common and peculiar to men is rationality in a general sense, not theoretical insight which is a specialised way of being rational. A man differs from other animals not primarily in being a natural metaphysician, but rather in being able to plan his life consciously for the attainment of an inclusive end.

The confusion between an end which is final because it is inclusive and an end which is final because it is supreme or dominant accounts for much that critics have rightly found unsatisfactory in Aristotle's account of the thought which leads to practical decisions. It is connected with his failure to make explicit the fact that practical thinking is not always or only the finding of means to ends. Thought is needed also for the setting up of an inclusive end. But, as we have seen, Aristotle fails to make explicit the concept of an inclusive end. This inadequacy both confuses his statement in *NE* I 1 and 2 of the relation of politics to subordinate arts and leads to his giving an incomplete account of deliberation.

I have represented Aristotle's doctrine as primarily a doctrine about the individual's pursuit of his own good, his own welfare (εὐδαιμονία). But something should be said at this point about the relation between the end of the individual and the 'greater and more complete' end of the state. 'While it is worth while to attain the end merely for one man, it is finer and more godlike to attain it for a nation or for city-states' *NE* I 2, 1094b7–10). This does not mean more than it says: if it is good that Smith should be happy, it is even better that Brown and Robinson should be happy too.

What makes it inevitable that planning for the attainment of the good for man should be political is the simple fact that a man needs and desires social community with others. This is made clear in *NE* I 7 where Aristotle says that the final good must be sufficient by itself. 'Now by self-sufficient we do not mean that which is sufficient for a man by himself, for one who lives a solitary life, but also for parents, children, wife and in general for his friends and fellow-citizens, since man is born for citizenship' (1097b7–11). That individual end-seeking is primary, that the state exists for its citizens, is stated in Ch. 8 of *NE* VI, one of the books common to both treatises. 'The man who knows and concerns himself with his own interests is thought to have practical wisdom, while politicians are thought to be busybodies.... Yet perhaps one's own good cannot exist without household management, nor without a form of government' (1142a1–10). The family and the state, and other forms of association as well, are necessary for the full realisation of any man's capacity for living well.

The statesman aims, to speak roughly, at the greatest happiness of the greatest number. He finds his own happiness in bringing about the happiness of others (*NE* X 7, 1177b14), especially, if Aristotle is right, the happiness of those capable of theoretical activity. Speaking in terms of the end as dominant Aristotle, in *NE* VI 13, sets a limit to the authority of political wisdom. 'But again it is not supreme over philosophic wisdom, i.e. over the superior part of us, any more than the art of medicine is over health; for it does not use it but provides for its coming into being; it issues orders, then, for its sake but not to it' (1145a6–9). This suggestion that science and philosophy are insulated in principle from political interference cannot be accepted. The statesman promotes science but also uses it, and may have to restrict the resources to be made available for it. If the secondary and inclusive end is the harmonisation and integration of primary ends, no primary end can be sacrosanct. But, even if Aristotle had held consistently the extravagant view that theoretical activity is desired only for itself and is the only end desired for itself, he would not have been right to conclude that there could be no occasion for the political regulation of theoretical studies. For the unrestricted pursuit of philosophy might hinder measures needed to make an environment in which philosophy could flourish. It might be necessary to order an astronomer to leave his observatory, or a philosopher his school, in order that they should play their parts in the state. Similarly the individual who plans his life so as to give as large a place as possible to a single supremely desired activity must be ready to restrain, not only desires which conflict with his ruling passion, but the ruling passion itself when it is manifested in ways which would frustrate its own object.

In *NE* I 1 and 2 Aristotle expounds the doctrine that statesmanship has authority over the arts and sciences which fall under it, are subordinate to it. An art, A, is under another art, B, if there is a relation of means to end between A and B. If A is a productive art, like bridle-making, its product may be used by a superior art, riding. Riding is not a productive activity, but it falls under generalship in so far as generals use cavalry, and generalship in turn falls under the art of the statesman, the art which is in the highest degree architectonic (1094a27; cf. VI 8, 1141b23–25). Thus the man of practical wisdom, the statesman or legislator, is compared by Aristotle to a foreman, or clerk of the works, in charge of technicians and workmen of various kinds, all engaged in building an observatory to enable the man of theoretical wisdom to contemplate the starry heavens. In the *Magna Moralia* the function of practical wisdom is said to be like that of a steward whose business it is so to arrange things that his master has leisure for his high vocation (A 34, 1198b12–17). Perhaps the closest parallel to the function of the statesman as conceived by Aristotle is the office of the Bursar in a college at Oxford or Cambridge.

This account of statesmanship as aiming at the exercise of theoretical wisdom by those capable of it is an extreme expression of the conception of the end as dominant and not inclusive. The account, as it stands, is a gross over-simplification of the facts. When he speaks of a subordinate art as pursued 'for the sake of' a superordinate or architectonic art (1094a15–16), Aristotle should make explicit the fact that the subordinate activity, in addition to serving other objects, may be pursued for its own sake. Riding, for example, has non-military uses and can be a source of enjoyment. Again two arts, or two kinds of activity, may each be subordinate, in Aristotle's sense, to the other. Riders use bridles, and bridle-makers may ride to their work. The engineer uses techniques invented by the mathematician, but also promotes the wealth and leisure in which pure science can flourish. Aristotle does not fail to see and mention the fact that an object may be desired both independently for itself and dependently for its effects (*NE* I 6, 1097a30–34). He was aware also

that theoretical activity is not the only kind of activity
which is independently desired. But he evidently
thought that an activity which was never desired except for itself would be intrinsically desirable in a
higher degree than an activity which, in addition to
being desired for itself, was also useful. It is, so to say,
beneath the dignity of the most godlike activities that
they should be useful. Aristotle is led in this way, and
also by other routes, to give a narrow and exclusive
account of the final good, to conceive of the supreme
end as dominant and not inclusive.

Aristotle describes deliberation, the thinking of the
wise man, as a process which starts from the conception of an end and works back, in a direction which
reverses the order of causality, to the discovery of a
means. Men do not, he asserts, deliberate about ends.
'They assume the end and consider how and by what
means it is to be attained; and if it seems to be produced by several means they consider by which it is
most easily and best produced, while, if it is achieved
by one only, they consider how it will be achieved by
this and by what means *this* will be achieved, till they
come to the first cause, which in the order of discovery
is last' (*NE* III 3, 1112b15–20). Such an investigation
is compared to the method of discovering by analysis
the solution of a geometrical problem. Again in VI 2
practical wisdom is said to be shown in finding means
to a good end. 'For the syllogisms which deal with acts
to be done are things which involve a starting-point,
viz. "since the end, i.e. what is best, is of such and
such a nature" ...' (1144a31–33).

This is Aristotle's official account of deliberation.
But here again, as in his account of the relation between political science and subordinate sciences, a too
narrow and rigid doctrine is to some extent corrected
elsewhere, although not explicitly, by the recognition
of facts which do not fit into the prescribed pattern.

Joseph, in *Essays in Ancient and Modern Philosophy*, pointed out that the process of deciding between alternative means, by considering which is easiest and best, involves deliberation which is not comparable to the geometer's search (pp. 180–81). But he remarks that Aristotle does not 'appear to see' this. What the passage suggests is that the agent may have to consider the intrinsic goodness, or badness, of the proposed means as well as its effectiveness in promoting a good end. A less incidental admission that there is more in deliberation than the finding of means is involved in Aristotle's account of 'mixed actions' in *NE* III 1. Aristotle recognises that, if the means are discreditable, the end may not be important enough to justify them. 'To endure the greatest indignities for no noble end or for a trifling end is the mark of an inferior person' (1110a22–23). 'It is difficult sometimes to determine what should be chosen at what cost, and what should be endured in return for what gain' (1110a29–30). Alcmaeon's decision to kill his mother, on his father's instruction, rather than face death himself is given as an example of a patently wrong answer to a question of this kind. This kind of deliberation is clearly not the regressive or analytic discovery of means to a preconceived end. It is rather the determination of an ideal pattern of behaviour, a system of priorities, from which the agent is not prepared to depart. It is what we described earlier as the setting up of an inclusive end. It is a kind of practical thinking which Aristotle cannot have had in his mind when he asserted in *NE* III 3 that 'we deliberate not about ends but about means' (1112b11–12).

I have argued that Aristotle's doctrine of the final human good is vitiated by his representation of it as dominant rather than inclusive, and that this mistake underlies his too narrow account of practical thinking as the search for means. But to say that the final good

is inclusive is not to deny that within it there are
certain dominant ends corresponding to the major interests of developed human nature. One of these major
interests is the interest in theoretical sciences. Of these,
according to Aristotle, there are three; theology or first
philosophy, mathematics and physics (*Metaphysics* E
1, 1026a18–19, cf. *NE* VI 8, 1142a16–18). His account
of contemplation in the Ethics, based on the doctrine
of reason as the divine or godlike element in man (*NE*
X 7, 1177a13–17; 8, 1178a20–23), exalts the first and
makes only casual mention of the other two. Elsewhere,
in the *De Partibus Animalium* I 5, he admits that
physics has attractions which compensate for the relatively low status of the objects studied. 'The scanty
conceptions to which we can attain of celestial things
give us, from their excellence, more pleasure than all
our knowledge of the world in which we live; just as
a half-glimpse of persons that we love is more delight-
ful than a leisurely view of other things, whatever their
number and dimensions. On the other hand, in cer-
titude and in completeness our knowledge of terrestrial
things has the advantage. Moreover their greater near-
ness and affinity to us balances somewhat the loftier
interest of the heavenly things that are the object of
the higher philosophy' (644b31–645a4).

I cannot here discuss the theological doctrines which
led Aristotle to place 'the higher philosophy' on the
summit of human felicity. But there is an aspect of
his account of the theoretic life which has an immediate
connection with my main topic. He remarks in *NE*
VII 14 that 'there is not only an activity of movement
but an activity of immobility, and pleasure is found
more in rest than in movement' (1154b26–28). This
doctrine that there is no 'movement' in theoretical
contemplation, and the implication that its immobility
is a mark of its excellence, is determined primarily by
Aristotle's conception of the divine nature. The latest

commentators on the *NE*, Gauthier and Jolif, say, with justification, that he here excludes discovery from the contemplative life. 'On pourrait même dire que l'idéal, pour le contemplatif aristotélicien—et cet idéal le Dieu d'Aristote le réalise—ce serait de ne jamais étudier et de ne jamais découvrir...' (855–56). In *NE* X 7 we are told that 'philosophy is thought to offer pleasures marvellous for their purity and their enduringness' and that it is 'reasonable to suppose that those who know will pass their time more pleasantly than those who enquire' (1177a25–27). It is not reasonable at all. It is a startling paradox. I shall now suggest that Aristotle's apparent readiness to accept this paradox, like his confusion between the dominant and the inclusive end, is to be explained, at least in part, by his failure to give any explicit or adequate analysis of the concept of end and means.

Aristotle states in *NE* I that an end may be either an activity or the product of an activity. 'But a certain difference is to be found among ends; some are activities, others are products apart from the activities that produce them. Where there are ends apart from the actions, it is the nature of the products to be better than the activities' (1094a3–6). The suggestion here is that, when an activity leads to a desired result, as medicine produces health or shipbuilding a ship or enquiry knowledge, the end-seeking activity is not itself desired. As he says (untruly) in the *Metaphysics*, 'of the actions which have a limit none is an end' (Θ 6, 1048b18). But an activity which aims at producing a result may be an object either of aversion or of indifference or of a positive desire which may be less or greater than the desire for its product. It is necessary to distinguish between 'end' in the sense of a result intended and planned and 'end' in the sense of a result, or expected result, which, in addition to being intended and planned, is also desired for itself while

the process of reaching it is not. It is true that
travel may be unattractive, but it may also be more
attractive that arrival. A golfer plays to win. But,
if he loses, he does not feel that his day has
been wasted, that he has laboured in vain, as he
would if his only object in playing were to win a prize
or to mortify his opponent or just to win. Doing cross-
word puzzles may be a waste of time, but what makes
it a waste of time is not the fact that we rarely get one
out. It would be a greater waste of time if we never
failed to finish them. In short, the fact that an activity
is progressive towards a planned result leaves quite
open the question whether it is the process or the result
which is desired, and, if both, which primarily. If Aristotle had seen and said this, he might have found it
more difficult than he does to suggest that the pleasures
of discovery are not an essential element in science as
a major human interest. Philosophy would be less attractive than it is if only results mattered. God's perfection requires that his thinking should be unpro-
gressive. But men, who fall short of perfect simplicity,
need, to make them happy, the pleasures of solving
problems and of learning something new and of being
surprised. For them the best way of life leads, in the
words of Meredith,

'through widening chambers of surprise to where
throbs rapture near an end that aye recedes'.

We have seen that Aristotle's doctrine of the final
human good needs clarification in terms of a distinction
between an end which is inclusive, a plan of life, and
an end which is dominant as the satisfaction of theoretical curiosity may be dominant in the life of a philosopher. No man has only one interest. Hence an end
which is to function as a target, as a criterion for deciding what to do and how to live, must be inclusive. But
some men have ruling passions. Hence some inclusive

ends will include a dominant end. I shall now try to look more closely at these Aristotelian notions, and to suggest some estimate of their relevance and value in moral philosophy.

It will be best to face at once and consider a natural and common criticism of Aristotle; the criticism that his virtuous man is not moral at all but a calculating egoist whose guiding principle is not duty but prudence, Bishop Butler's 'cool self-love'. Aristotle is in good company as claiming that rationality is what makes a man ideally good. But his considered view, apart from incidental insights, admits, it is said, only the rationality of prudent self-interest and not the rationality of moral principle. Thus Professor D. J. Allan, in *The Philosophy of Aristotle*, tells us that Aristotle "takes little or no account of the motive of moral obligation" and that "self-interest, more or less enlightened, is assumed to be the motive of all conduct and choice" (p. 189). Similarly the late Professor Field, a fair and sympathetic critic of Aristotle, remarked that, whereas morality is 'essentially unselfish', Aristotle's idea of the final end or good makes morality 'ultimately selfish' (*Moral Theory*, pp. 109, 111).

When a man is described as selfish what is meant primarily is that he is moved to act, more often and more strongly than most men, by desires which are selfish. The word 'selfish' is also applied to a disposition so to plan one's life as to give a larger place than is usual or right to the gratification of selfish desires. But what is it for a desire to be selfish? Professor Broad, in his essay 'Egoism as a theory of human motives' (in *Ethics and the History of Philosophy*), makes an important distinction between two main kinds of 'self-regarding' desires. There are first desires which are 'self-confined', which a man could have even if he were alone in the world, e.g. desires for certain experiences, the desire to preserve his own life, the desire to feel respect for himself. Secondly there are self-regarding desires which nevertheless presuppose that a man is not alone in the world, e.g. desires to own property, to assert or display oneself, to inspire affection. Broad further points out that desires which are 'other-regarding' may also be 'self-referential', e.g. desires for the welfare of one's own family, friends, school, college, club, nation.

A man might perhaps be called selfish if his other-regarding motives were conspicuously and exclusively self-referential, if he showed no interest in the welfare of anyone with whom he was not personally connected. But usually 'selfish' refers to the prominence of self-regarding motives, and different kinds of selfishness correspond to different self-regarding desires. The word, being pejorative, is more readily applied to the less reputable of the self-regarding desires. Thus a man strongly addicted to the pursuit of his own pleasures might be called selfish even if his other-regarding motives were not conspicuously weak. A man whose ruling passion was science or music would not naturally be described as selfish unless to convey that there was in him a reprehensible absence or failure of other-regarding motives, as shown, say, by his neglect of his family or of his pupils.

The classification of desires which I have quoted from Broad assumes that their nature is correctly represented by what we ordinarily think and say about them. *Prima facie* some of our desires are self-regarding; and, of the other-regarding desires, some are and some are not self-referential. But there have been philosophers who have questioned or denied the reality of these apparent differences. One doctrine, psychological egoism, asserts in its most extreme form that the only possible objects of a man's first-order independent desires are experiences, occurrent states of his own consciousness. Thus my desire to be liked is really a desire to know that I am liked; and my desire that my children should be happy when I am dead is really a desire for my present expectation that they will be happy. The obvious criticism of this doctrine is that it is preposterous and self-defeating: I must first desire popularity and the happiness of my children if I am to find gratifying my thought that I am popular and that my children will be happy. To most of us it seems that introspective self-scrutiny supports the validity of this dialectic. We can, therefore, reject psychological egoism. A *fortiori* we can reject psychological hedonism which asserts that the *only* experiences which can be independently desired are pleasures, feelings of enjoyment. This further doctrine was stated as follows by the late Professor Prichard. 'For the enjoyment of something which we enjoy, e.g. the enjoyment of seeing a beautiful landscape, is related to the thing we enjoy, not as a quality but as an effect, being something excited by the thing we enjoy, so that, if it be said that we desire some enjoyment for its own sake, the correct statement must be that we desire the experience, e.g. the seeing of some beautiful landscape, for the sake of the feeling of enjoyment which we think it will cause, this feeling being really what we are desiring for its own sake' (*Moral Obligation*, p. 116). Surely most of us would be inclined to say that we *can* desire for its own sake 'the seeing of some beautiful landscape' and that we do not detect a distinct 'feeling of enjoyment'.

Was Aristotle a psychological egoist or a psychological hedonist? A crisp answer would have been possible only if Aristotle had explicitly formulated these doctrines as I have defined them. So far as I can see, he did not do so even in his long, but not always lucid, treatment of friendship and self-love in *NE* IX. This being so, he cannot be classed as a psychological egoist in respect of his account of first-order desires. When Aristotle confronts the fact of altruism, he does not refuse to accept benevolent desires at their face value (*NE* VIII 2, 1155b31; 3, 1156b9–10; 7, 1159a8–12). But he shows acuteness in detecting self-referential elements in benevolence. Thus he compares the feelings of benefactors to beneficiaries with those of parents for their children and of artists for their creations. 'For that which they have treated well is their handiwork, and therefore they love this more than the handiwork does its maker' (*NE* IX 7, 1167b31–1168a5).

The nearest approach which Aristotle makes to the formulation of psychological hedonism is, perhaps, in the following passage in *NE* II 3. 'There being three objects of choice and three of avoidance, the noble, the advantageous, the pleasant, and their contraries, the base, the injurious, the painful, about all of these the good man tends to go right and the bad man to go wrong, and especially about pleasure; for this is common to the animals, and also it accompanies all objects of choice; for even the noble and the advantageous appear pleasant' (1104b30–1105a1). But there are passages in his discussion of pleasure in *NE* X which show that, even if he had accepted psychological egoism, he would not have accepted psychological hedonism. 'And there are many things we should be keen about even if they brought no pleasure, e.g. seeing, remembering, knowing, possessing the virtues. If pleasures necessarily do accompany these, that makes no odds; we should choose them even if no pleasure resulted' (1174a4–8). This reads like a direct repudiation of the doctrine in my quotation from Prichard. In *NE* X 4 he asks, without answering, the question whether we choose activity for the sake of the attendant pleasure or vice versa (1175a18–21). The answer which his doctrine requires is surely that neither alternative can be accepted, since both the activity and the attendant pleasure are desired for their own sake. But it is open to question whether, when we speak of a state or activity, such as 'the seeing of some beautiful landscape', as pleasant, we are referring to a feeling distinct from the state or activity itself.

The charge against Aristotle that his morality is a moraliy of self-interest is directed primarily against his doctrine of the final good, the doctrine which I have interpreted as a conflation of the distinct notions of the 'inclusive end' and the 'dominant end'. But the critic may also wish to suggest that Aristotle overstates the efficacy of self-regarding desires in the determination of human conduct. To this the first answer might well be that it is not easy to overstate their efficacy. The term 'self-regarding' applies, as we have seen, to a wide variety of motives; and there is a 'self-referential' factor in the most potent of the other-regarding motives. Altruism which is pure, not in any way self-regarding or self-referential, is a rarity. The facts support the assertion that man is a selfish animal. But the criticism can be met directly. Aristotle does not ignore other-regarding motives. Thus, while he points out that the philosopher, unlike those who exercise practical virtue, does not need other men 'towards whom and with whom he shall act', he admits that the pleasures of philosophy are enhanced by interest in the work of colleagues. 'He perhaps does better if he has fellow-workers, but still he is the most self-sufficient' (*NE* X 7, 1177a27–b1). When, in the *EE*, Aristotle speaks of philosophy as the service of God, he seems to imply that the love of wisdom is not directed merely to the lover's own conscious states (1249b20). Again, in *NE* IX 8, he can attribute to the 'lover of self' conduct which is, in the highest degree, altruistic and self-sacrificing. 'For reason always chooses what is best for itself, and the good man obeys his reason. It is true of the good man too that he does many acts for the sake of his friends and his country, and, if necessary,

dies for them; for he will throw away both wealth and
honours and in general the goods that are objects of
competition, gaining for himself nobility (τὸ καλόν);
since he would prefer a short period of intense pleasure
to a long one of mild enjoyment, a twelvemonth of
noble life to many years of humdrum existence, and
one great and noble action to many trivial ones. Now
those who die for others doubtless attain this result;
it is, therefore, a great prize that they choose for themselves' (1169a17–26).

But it is not enough, if we are to do justice to the
criticism that Aristotle makes morality selfish, to quote
this passage, or the passage in *NE* I 10 where Aristotle
speaks of the shining beauty of the virtue shown in
bearing disasters which impair happiness (1100b30–33).
Such passages, it may be said, show Aristotle's moral
sensibility and moral insight. But the question can still
be asked whether their commendation of the ultimate
self-sacrifice, and of endurance in suffering, is consistent
with Aristotle's doctrine of the final human good. Perhaps he is speaking more consistently with his own
considered views when, again in *NE* IX 8, he makes
the suggestion (or is it a joke?) that a man may show
the finest self-sacrifice, the truest love, by surrendering
to his friend the opportunity of virtuous action (1169a
33–34). Perhaps Aristotle's commendation of the sur-
render, in a noble cause, of life itself needs to be
qualified, from his own point of view, as it was qualified
by Oscar Wilde:

> And yet, and yet
> Those Christs that die upon the barricades,
> God knows it I am with them, in some ways.

To this question I now turn. My answer must and can
be brief.

We have found two main elements in Aristotle's
doctrine of the final good for man. There is, first, the

suggestion that, as he says in *EE* A 2, it is a sign of 'great folly' not to 'have one's life organised in view of some end'. Perhaps it would be better to say that it is impossible not to live according to some plan, and that it is folly not to try to make the plan a good one. The inevitability of a plan arises from the fact that a man both has, and knows that he has, a number of desires and interests which can be adopted as motives either casually and indiscriminately or in accordance with priorities determined by the aim of living the kind of life which he thinks proper for a man like himself. But in an agent naturally reflective the omission to make such a plan is not completely undesigned: the minimal plan is a plan not to plan. To this side of Aristotle's doctrine I have applied the term 'inclusive end', inclusive because there is no desire or interest which should not be regarded as a candidate, however unpromising, for a place in the pattern of life. Wisdom finds a place even for folly. The second element which we have found in Aristotle's doctrine is his own answer to the question what plan will be followed by a man who is most fully a man, as high as a man can get on the scale from beast to god. Aristotle's answer is that such a man will make theoretical knowledge, his most godlike attribute, his main object. At a lower level, as a man among men, he will find a place for the happiness which comes from being a citizen, from marriage and from the society of those who share his interests. I have called this the doctrine of the dominant end. The question whether Aristotle's doctrine of the final good can be reconciled with the morality of altruism and self-sacrifice must be asked with reference both to the inclusive end and to the dominant end.

To say that a man acts, or fails to act, with a view to an inclusive end is to say nothing at all about the comparative degrees of importance which he will ascribe to his various aims. His devotion to his own good, in the sense of his inclusive end, need not require him to prefer self-regarding desires to other-regarding desires, or one kind of self-regarding desire to another. All desires have to be considered impartially as candidates for places in the inclusive plan. To aim at a long life in which pleasures, so far as possible, are enjoyed and pains avoided it is a possible plan, but not the only possible plan. That a man seeks an inclusive end leaves open the question whether he is an egoist or an altruist, selfish or unselfish in the popular sense.[2]

While a man seeking his inclusive end need not be selfish, he can be described as self-centred in at least three different ways. First and trivially his desire to follow his inclusive plan is his own desire; it is self-owned. Secondly, a man can think of a plan as being for his own good only if he thinks about himself, thinks of himself as the one owner of many desires. His second-order desire for his own good is self-reflective. Thirdly, this second-order desire, being a desire about desires, an interest in interests, can be gratified only through the gratification of his first-order desires. Even the martyr plans to do what he wants to do. We can express this by saying that the pursuit of the final good is self-indulging as well as self-reflective. But 'self-indulgence' as applied to a way of life in which pleasures may be despised and safety put last carries no pejorative sense. That action in pursuit of an inclusive end is self-centred in these ways does not mean

[2] I owe this point, and less directly much else in my discussion of the criticism of Aristotle's ethical system as egoistic, to Professor C. A. Campbell's British Academy Lecture (1948), "Moral Intuition and the Principle of Self-Realisation" (especially pp. 17–25). Professor Campbell's lecture discusses the ethical theory of T. H. Green and F. H. Bradley, and I do not know whether he would think of his arguments as being relevant to the interpretation of Aristotle. But I have found his defence of 'self-realisation' as a moral principle helpful in my attempt to separate the strands of thought in Aristotle's doctrine of the final good.

that the agent is self-regarding or self-seeking in any sense inconsistent with the most heroic or saintly self-sacrifice.

To the question whether the pursuit of the human good, understood in terms of Aristotle's conception of the dominant end, can be reconciled with the morality of altruism, and in particular the extreme altruism of the man who gives his life for his friends or his country, a different answer must be given. Here reconciliation is not possible. In order to see this it is necessary only to reflect on Aristotle's definition in *NE* I 7 of the dominant end, which he calls happiness, and to compare this definition with what is said about the self-love of the man who nobly gives up his own life. 'Human good turns out to be activity of soul in accordance with virtue, and if there are more than one virtue, in accordance with the best and most complete. But we must add "in a complete life." For one swallow does not make a summer nor does one day; and so too one day or a short time does not make a man blessed and happy' (1098a16–20). How then can the man who, to gain nobility (τὸ καλόν) for himself, gives his life for his friends or his country be said to achieve happiness? Aristotle's answer, as we have seen, is that such a man prefers 'a short period of intense pleasure to a long one of mild enjoyment, a twelvemonth of noble life to many years of humdrum existence, and one great and noble action to many trivial ones' (1169a22–25). But the scales are being loaded. For why should it be supposed that the man who declines to live the final, if crowded, hour of glorious life will survive to gain only 'mild' enjoyments and a 'humdrum' or 'trivial' existence? If such existence is, or seems, humdrum *because* the 'intense pleasure' of self-sacrifice has been missed, then Aristotle's thought here is circular and self-stultifying. The intensity of the brief encounter, it is suggested, is such that by contrast the remainder of life would be humdrum. But, unless the alternative would be humdrum in its own right, the encounter would not be intense enough to compensate for the curtailment of life and happiness. A 'complete life' either is, or is not, a necessary condition of happiness. Aristotle as a theorist cannot justify the admiration which, as a man, he no doubt feels for the 'one great and noble action'. Confronted with the facts he would have to admit that the man who, whether by good fortune or design, survives a revolution or a war may live to experience intense enjoyments and to perform activities in accordance with the best and most complete virtue. He may become a professor of philosophy or at least a prime minister. We must conclude, therefore, that Professor Field was right: the doctrine of the good for man, as developed by Aristotle in his account of the dominant end, does make morality 'ultimately selfish' (*Moral Theory*, pp. 109, 111).

Aristotle offers us in his *Ethics* a handbook on how to be happy though human. To some it may seem that a treatise on conduct with an aim so practical and so prudential can do little to clarify the concepts with which moral philosophy is mainly concerned, the concepts of duty and of moral worth. 'He takes little or no account', Professor Allan tells us, 'of the motive of moral obligation' (*The Philosophy of Aristotle*, p. 189). Perhaps not. The topic is too large for a concluding paragraph. Certainly most men feel moral obligations which cannot be subsumed under the obligation, if there is one, to pursue their own happiness by planning for the orderly satisfaction of their self-regarding desires. But 'obligation' and 'duty' are words with many meanings, meanings variously related to the concept of moral worth. Perhaps Aristotle is not wrong, as he is not alone, in connecting the concept of moral worth with the fact that man is not just the plaything of circumstance and his own irrational nature but also the responsible planner of his own life. This aspect of Aristotle's teaching is what I have called his doctrine of the 'inclusive end', and I have argued that there is no necessity for the doctrine to be specified and developed as a recommendation of calculated egoism. Aristotle himself, as we have seen, does not adhere consistently to his own exaltation of self-regarding aims. He is, indeed, always ready to notice facts which are awkward for his own theories. Thus in *NE* I 10 he recognises that the actual achievement of happiness, virtuous activity, is largely outside a man's control. 'A multitude of great events if they turn out well will make life happier ... while if they turn out ill they crush and maim happiness; for they both bring pain with them and hinder many activities' (1100b25–30). He adds that, even when disaster strikes, 'nobility shines through, when a man bears with resignation many great misfortunes, not through insensibility to pain but through nobility and greatness of soul' (1100b30–33). 'The man who is truly good and wise', he goes on to say, 'bears all the chances of life becomingly and always makes the best of circumstances as a good shoemaker makes the best shoes out of the hides that are given to him' (1100b35–1101a5). The suggestion of this passage is that a man's worth lies not in his actual achievement, which may be frustrated by factors outside his own control, but in his striving towards achievement. In an earlier chapter (5) of *NE* I he speaks of the good as something which 'we divine to be proper to a man and not easily taken from him' (1095b25–26). Aristotle's doctrine of the final good is a doctrine about what is 'proper' to a man, the power to reflect on his own abilities and desires and to conceive and choose for himself a satisfactory way of life. What 'cannot be taken from him' is his power to keep on trying to live up to such a conception. Self-respect, thus interpreted, is a principle of duty. If moral philosophy must seek one comprehensive principle of duty, what other principle has a stronger claim to be regarded as the principle of duty?

ARISTOTLE ON PLEASURE

J. O. URMSON

Aristotle's most mature and careful account of pleasure or enjoyment—he uses the noun ἡδονή and its cognates and the verb χαίρειν without any apparent discrimination—is to be found in Book X of the *Nicomachean Ethics* (1174a13 ff.). I propose to summarize this very acute account and then to discuss some of the problems arising out of it.

Like sight, Aristotle holds, pleasure is not a process (κίνησις) but an activity. As such, it is complete at any time. When you build a temple, you begin, continue, and perhaps finish it, and until you have finished it, you have not built a temple; but if at any moment you see or are enjoying something, then you have seen or enjoyed it. Sight and enjoyment cannot be left half-finished.

Perception, of which sight is an example, thought, and contemplation have objects. When the perception or thought is high-grade and its object is worthwhile, then the perception or thought or contemplation is enjoyable (pleasant). The higher grade the perception and the more valuable its object, the more pleasant and more perfect the activity. But the excellence of the perception or thought and its object make the activity perfect in a different way from that in which enjoyment perfects it; the former are constitutive of its perfection while the enjoyment is a manifestation of it as the grace of youth is a manifestation of physical prime. We might say that it adds zest to the activity. When, through tiredness or illness, the activity is impaired, so is the enjoyment of it. Again, novelty commands effortless attention and therefore enjoyment, but when novelty wears off, the attention wanders and enjoyment wanes. So activity and life itself are bound up with enjoyment (pleasure); there is no enjoyment without activity enjoyed and enjoyment is the mark of activity at peak performance.

Different activities (1175a21) are differently enjoyable. Just as perception and thought are different species of activity, so the pleasures of perception are different in species from the pleasures of thought. Every activity has its own 'proper' (οἰκεῖα) pleasure; one could not chance to get the pleasure of, say, reading poetry from stamp collecting. The enjoyment proper to an activity promotes that activity, whereas the enjoyment of something else impedes it. If we are doing two things at once, perhaps arguing and listening to music, the more enjoyable gets in the way of the other. So when we enjoy something very much, we do not do anything else at the same time; we only eat sweets at the theater when we are not enjoying the plot very much. So, if two enjoyments can conflict, they must be distinguishable. Just as the enjoyment of something else maims the enjoyment of an activity, so does the 'proper pain', that is, the dislike of that activity. We are disinclined to draw or reason if we find it disagreeable.

As activities differ in worth (1175b23) so do their enjoyments (proper pleasures). Even desires for the worthwhile or the base are praised and blamed, although the appetite is not so intimately bound up with the activity of pursuing them; how much more so are the enjoyments of these activities which are scarcely distinguishable from the activities themselves.

This very acute analysis of the enjoyment of activities can be supplemented from elsewhere in the NE. As a prologue to his discussion of temperance in Book III, Aristotle says that the pleasure of the soul need be distinguished from the bodily pleasures, instancing the love of honour and love of learning. He adds that the lover of each of these "enjoys what he loves, his body being in no way affected, but rather his intelligence." This remark puzzled the commentator Aspasius to the point of exasperation: "What does he mean," he protests, "when he says that the enjoyment of lovers of learning or honour involves a condition of the intelligence? For enjoyment and the pleasures are not in the intelligence but in the affective (παθητικῷ) part of the soul." Aspasius never understands Aristotle's view that enjoyment of learning is exhibited in the effortless concentration of the intelligence on its problems rather than in getting some feeling as a result or concomitant of one's study.

It has, indeed, been commonplace in the history of philosophy to regard doing something for the pleasure of it as doing something for the sake of gaining some sensation or feeling named 'pleasure'. Psychological hedonists have typically assumed this analysis and concluded therefrom that mankind has only one goal of action which they call pleasure. Sometimes their opponents have seemed to think that to reject psychological hedonism, they must say that we do not do things for pleasure but for their own sake, thus consenting to the analysis; they take the pleasure of an activity to be a feeling resulting from it but claim that the pleasure is a mere bonus resulting from gaining what one wanted rather than the end for the sake of which the activity was performed. It is not surprising, perhaps, that the fascination of this analysis should have made Aspasius and many of his successors among the commentators on Aristotle's ethics unable to see that Aristotle has no inclination to accept it. The enjoyment of an activity is for him not a result of it but something barely distinguishable from the activity; it is more like the effortless zest with which the activity is performed than a result or concomitant of it. His account is, indeed, very similar to the account of enjoyment given by G. Ryle in his *Concept of Mind* (London, 1949), a fact which should surprise nobody. Ironically enough, we shall find that Aristotle is at his weakest in discussing just those aspects of pleasure to which the 'traditional' analysis is most plausibly applicable. He is in the end most interested in the enjoyment of intellectual activities, and it is here that his view is most obviously attractive.

But what of the bodily pleasures? It is clear that in Book X Aristotle wishes to give the same general account of them as of intellectual enjoyment. Thus, bodily pleasures (σωματικαί ἡδοναί) are construed as the enjoyment of activities of sense-perception. Aristotle gives the same account of them in general in Book III. He makes it clear that he is thinking of the enjoyment of colors and shapes and pictures (sight), of music (hearing), and smells. But the objects of taste and touch have a special position among the objects of bodily pleasure, so that usually when Aristotle speaks of bodily pleasures (e.g. at 1104b5, 1153b33, 1154a8, 1154a10, 1154a26, 1177a7) he seems to have them alone in mind. They also are the only objects of bodily pleasure which fall within the sphere of temperance.

Aristotle, we have said, allots a special position to the objects of taste and touch; at times he was little inclined to distinguish between them, as when he treats χυμός as a ἁπτόν in *De Anima* 414b6–11. But in a remarkable passage (*NE* 1118a26–33) he makes it clear that touch is the true sphere of temperance: "They [the intemperate] seem to make little use of taste. For to taste belongs the judgment of flavors, as is done by wine-tasters and cooks. But it is not these that people enjoy, intemperate ones at any rate, but the experience which is all a matter of touch, whether in the field of food or drink or sex." Here, it seems to me that Aristotle is on the brink of making a distinction far more important than his distinction of the enjoyment of perceptual and intellectual activities. To this further distinction, that he never quite makes clear even, I think, to himself, we must now turn.

The account of the enjoyment of activity, whether it involves the exercise of thought or the senses, given in Book X seems to me to be remarkably acute; it is surely, at least in general, correct. But Aristotle appears to offer it as an account of pleasure in general and as such it raises problems, of which we shall immediately raise the most acute.

One is inclined to say that it is a correct account of the enjoyment of an activity in contrast to those accounts of it which make such enjoyment the obtaining of pleasant experiences which accrue from the activity, accounts such as, apparently, Aspasius and Prichard in his essay in this volume [pp. 241–60] would be inclined to give. But surely there is such a thing as gaining pleasant experiences as a result of activity, even if this is not what it is to enjoy that activity? Let us suppose that I am engaged in geometrical thinking and on the verge of completing an important proof. Certainly such a situation as this could result in a glow of excitement and elation welling up within me, though this is not the enjoyment of the activity, which Aristotle held to be scarcely distinguishable from the activity itself. Moreover, this excitement might well intercept and impede my geometrical thought in the way that 'foreign pleasures' are said by Aristotle to do; I might have to light a pipe and pace about until the pleasurable excitement died down and I could again become absorbed in my geometry. Yet in his account of pleasure Aristotle seems to leave no room for this sort of pleasurable feeling. Even the bodily pleasures are regarded as the enjoyment of activities of sense perception; they are less clear or pure than the pleasures of intellectual activity and arise from painful conditions such as thirst, but Aristotle seems to think that they can be subsumed under the same general analysis.

But it is pretty clear that the pain of thirst, which is alleged to be the opposite of the pleasure of drinking, is not like the disagreeableness of doing geometry, which is also in some way the opposite of finding geometry enjoyable. When we find geometry disagreeable, Aristotle tells us, we tend to avoid geometry and can attend to it only with difficulty. But Aristotle cannot wish to claim that the pain of thirst is such that we find it hard to pay attention to our thirst, nor does he speak of the 'proper pleasure' of thirst or the 'proper pain' of drinking. And the reason for these facts is clear; thirst is not an activity, and the pangs of thirst are an unpleasant sensation unconnected with activity; similarly when Aristotle refers to the pleasure of drinking he is not referring to the enjoyment of the activity of drinking but the pleasant feeling engendered by drinking when thirsty.

Certainly Aristotle's account of enjoyment can be applied to activities essentially involving sense perception. One can, as he points out, be interested in tastes (enjoy tasting things) in the way that an expert cook or connoisseur of wines is likely to be; one might be interested in tastes as one is interested in geometry and enjoy tasting things as one enjoys doing geometry. Or, again, watching plays and looking at colors, shapes, and pictures are activities which essentially involve sense perception, as also does listening to music. If these are to be called bodily pleasures, as involving

the senses, we do not have to exclude them from the
field happily covered by Aristotle's account.

But we should notice that the activities are looking
at (or watching), listening to, tasting (as understood
in wine tasting), and smelling (understood as sniffing
at things), not merely seeing, hearing, having a taste
in one's mouth or an odor in one's nostrils. There
could be a comparable pleasant activity of active touch-
ing, a quasi-aesthetic enjoyment of textures; touch is
not essentially different here from the other senses.

Now surely if we look attentively at Aristotle's discussion of temperance and intemperance in Book III,
especially the passage from it quoted earlier, it is clear
that when the intemperate man eats, drinks, and in-
dulges in sexual activity, he is characterized not as
enjoying these activities, but as performing them for
the sake of the pleasant feelings they produce. It is
the feelings that are enjoyed by the intemperate, not
the activities that engender them. But Aristotle fails
to make explicitly clear to himself the central point;
he persuades himself that the intemperate pleasures
are to be distinguished from the pleasure of looking
at pictures because they involve the sense of touch
and thus fails to see that he has really made a distinction between enjoying activities essentially involving
use of the senses and doing things which produce a
pleasant feeling. Pleasant bodily feelings such as those
engendered by food, drink, and sex are merely conspicuous examples of the latter. We must surely recognize that one might smell roses not because one enjoyed smelling roses but because one enjoyed the smell
—a passive experience to which the activity of smelling
is but a means. Similarly, one might, though the possibility is remote, do geometry not because of an interest in geometry and enjoyment of geometrical work,
but in order to produce the feeling of exhilaration

which successful work can sometimes give rise to, the feeling being what was enjoyed.

In the *Topics* (106a36 ff.) Aristotle remarks that "the pain from thirst is opposite to the pleasure from drinking, but there is none opposite to the pleasure from contemplating the incommensurability of the side and the diagonal. So the term 'pleasure' is used ambiguously." But in the *NE*, he has rightly noticed that there can be a 'proper pain' of thinking; I might find the contemplation of this incommensurability infinitely tedious. In the same way, I might find the activity of drinking tedious. Moreover, abstinence from geometrizing, like abstinence from drinking, might produce pangs of deprivation akin in principle to the pangs of thirst. What again we need is what Aristotle only half sees, a distinction between the pleasantness (welcomeness) and unpleasantness (unwelcomeness) of things, in particular feelings, which may be produced by or be otherwise concomitants of an activity and the pleasantness or unpleasantness of the activity itself. No doubt the pleasantness of the feelings produced by drinking is causally dependent on their being preceded by unpleasant feelings of thirst, whereas the pleasure of geometrizing is not so closely bound to the unpleasantness of anything. But these are contingent facts, for we might conceivably have pleasant sensations from drinking until we burst and enjoyed doing geometry only after a toothache.

So it would seem that Aristotle, having adumbrated a distinction between the enjoyment of perceptual activity (bodily pleasure in the wider sense), and the enjoyment of feelings produced by the bodily, but scarcely perceptual, activities of eating, drinking, and sex; fails to recognize its proper significance, making it, wrongly, a question of what sense is employed. It is remarkable that while most philosophers have wrongly assimilated the enjoyment of activity to the enjoyment of feelings, a mistake for which Aristotle duly castigates them, he himself makes the uncommon error of assimilating the enjoyment of feelings to the enjoyment of activity.

Yet at times, it seems that Aristotle effectively has the distinction clear, particularly in Book VII of the *NE*. There he is attacking the views of those who denigrate pleasure and it seems that he has two main contentions to make. First, he sees in such views a mere excess of asceticism; the activities from which pleasant feelings arise are essential features of human life and thus have their place if not cultivated in excess. Further, if one wishes to engage in theoretical work a neutral state is no doubt preferable to either pleasant or unpleasant bodily feeling; but no one would wish to regard this as a reason for a general attack on pleasure who did not think of pleasant bodily feeling as the whole of pleasure so that (1153b33) "the bodily pleasures have gained a proprietory right to the name." As he duly points out (1153a22), the enjoyment of speculative thought can hardly be claimed to impede speculative thought. Throughout these discussions in Book VII, one has to take the term 'bodily pleasure' as meaning 'pleasant feelings' rather than 'enjoyment of activities involving use of the senses'. And yet even in Book VII, he gives a summary definition of pleasure as 'unimpeded activity', which I take to be essentially similar to that of Book X; that is, I take him to mean that an activity is enjoyable when it is unimpeded (by, for example, "foreign pleasures").

To sum up, then, I should contend that Aristotle gives us a clear and valuable account of the enjoyableness of an activity. What leads to the obscurity and insufficiency in his position is an ambiguity in his use of the term 'bodily pleasure' of which he himself is unaware. At times, he uses it to refer to the enjoyment of any activity essentially involving the use

of any of the senses, including listening to music and
watching plays. At other times, he uses it to refer,
sometimes quite clearly, to the pleasant sensations
which can be gained by activity. But, since he draws
his examples from localized bodily feelings resulting
from contact, and since there are no familiar examples
of enjoying active employment of the sense of touch,
he gives a mistaken formal account of the matter as
if there were no ambiguity but the generic case of
enjoyable use of the senses and the specific case of
enjoyable use of the sense of touch. Thus, in Book X
of the *NE*, he gives a final account of pleasure which
is appropriate as an account of enjoyable activity in
general, including those involving the senses, but, fail-
ing to see the ambiguity of 'bodily pleasure', he falsely
believes that he has given a general account of pleasure
in giving an account of the enjoyment of activity.

I would like to add a few remarks about the terminology employed by Aristotle and its translation. It
is plain that at times, particularly outside his official
discussions of 'pleasure', Aristotle is referring to pains
and other very unpleasant bodily feelings when he uses
the word λύπη; obvious examples can be found in Book
VII, chapter 7. But the verb λυπῖσθαι frequently cannot be idiomatically translated 'be pained', but means
rather 'find distasteful' as when Aristotle says that the
musician λυπεῖται by bad songs—he is repelled by
them, finds them distasteful. It is abundantly clear that
to speak of the 'proper pain' of an activity is highly
suggestive of just that analysis of enjoyment and its
opposite which Aristotle rejects; to perform an activity
λυπούμενος is not to perform it with pain but finding
it disagreeable, irksome, boring, or repulsive. Moreover,
while λύπη is used by Aristotle as the opposite of
ἡδονή, pain is not the opposite of pleasure. It is not
even the opposite of pleasant feeling, a position occupied by unpleasant feeling (there are many un-

pleasant feelings which are not pains). It is hard to translate λύπη because there is no obvious opposite in English to 'enjoyment' or 'pleasure'; 'displeasure' will only do in certain rather special contexts; but we ought to abandon the word 'pain' as a translation. Pains have no opposite; in this respect they resemble tickles. It is also notable that while the word ἡδονή is common, and sometimes refers to a pleasant feeling, the verb ἥδεσθαι is far less common in the *NE* than χαίρειν, which is the usual opposite of λυπεῖσθαι; I have noticed no case where ἥδεσθαι could mean 'have a pleasant feeling', and I suppose nobody would suggest that χαίρειν has such a meaning, though one can χαίρειν σωματικῇ ἀπολαύσει. It would seem that for Aristotle χαίρειν is the verb most commonly corresponding to the noun ἡδονή rather than ἥδεσθαι and if this is so, it is surely suggestive for our understanding of the word ἡδονή in Aristotle.

NOTES ON CONTRIBUTORS

John L. Ackrill is Professor of Ancient Philosophy at Oxford University and Fellow of Brasenose College, Oxford.

Miss G. E. M. Anscombe is Lecturer in Philosophy and sometime Research Fellow in Somerville College, Oxford.

John L. Austin was White's Professor of Moral Philosophy at Oxford University and Fellow of Corpus Christi College from 1952 until his death in 1960.

John Cook Wilson was Wykeham Professor of Logic at Oxford University and Fellow of New College, Oxford. He died in 1915.

Irving M. Copi is Professor of Philosophy at the University of Michigan.

W. F. R. Hardie is President of Corpus Christi College, Oxford.

K. J. Hintikka is Professor of Philosophy at the University of Helsinki and at Stanford University.

G. E. L. Owen is Professor of Philosophy at Harvard University.

Father Joseph Owens teaches at the Pontifical Institute of Medieval Studies at Toronto.

H. A. Prichard was White's Professor of Moral Philosophy at Oxford University. He died in 1947.

Manley Thompson is Professor of Philosophy at the University of Chicago.

J. O. Urmson is Fellow of Corpus Christi College, Oxford.

M. J. Woods is Fellow of Brasenose College, Oxford.

SELECTED BIBLIOGRAPHY

This is a bibliography relevant to the topics discussed in this anthology. The selections are designed primarily for the student of philosophy.

(A) TRANSLATIONS

Oxford Translation under the editorship of J. A. Smith and W. D. Ross. 12 vols. Oxford: Oxford University, 1908–52.

Clarendon Aristotle Series, ed. by J. L. Ackrill. Oxford: Clarendon, 1963– (translations and commentaries of selected portions of the *Organon, Metaphysics,* and *Physics,* with most volumes still under preparation).

(B) GENERAL

Allan, D. J., *The Philosophy of Aristotle.* Oxford: Oxford University, 1952.

Anscombe, G. E. M., and Geach, P. T., *Three Philosophers.* Oxford: Blackwell, 1961.

Bambrough, R. (ed.), *New Essays on Plato and Aristotle.* London: Routledge & Kegan Paul, 1965.

Bonitz, H., *Aristotelische Studien,* I–V. Vienna, republished 1962–67.

Cherniss, H. F., *Aristotle's Criticism of Plato and the Academy.* Baltimore: Johns Hopkins, 1944.

Düring, I., and Owen, G. E. L. (eds.), *Aristotle and Plato in the Mid-fourth Century*. Göteborg: Almquist & Wiksell, 1957.

Jaeger, W., *Aristotle*. 2d ed.; Oxford: Clarendon, 1950.

Mansion, A., (ed.), *Aristote et les problèmes de méthode*. Louvain: Publications Universitaires de Louvain, 1961.

Mure, G. R., *Aristotle*. London: E. Benn, 1932.

Ross, W. D., *Aristotle*. 5th ed.; London: Methuen, 1949.

(C) LOGIC

Bochensky, I. M., *Ancient Formal Logic*. Amsterdam: North Holland Publishing Company, 1951.

Hintikka, K. J., "An Aristotelian Dilemma," *Ajatus*, XXII (1959), 87–92.

——, "Aristotle and the Ambiguity of Ambiguity," *Inquiry*, II (1959), 139–51.

——, "Necessity, Universality, and Time in Aristotle," *Ajatus*, XX (1957), 65–90.

Joseph, H. W. B., *An Introduction to Logic*. 2d ed.; Oxford: Clarendon, 1916.

Kneale, W. C. and M., *The Development of Logic*. Oxford: Clarendon, 1962.

Lukasiewicz, J., *Aristotle's Syllogistic*, 2d ed.; Oxford: Oxford University, 1957.

review of Lukasiewicz (1st ed.) by J. L. Austin, *Mind*, LXI (1952), 395–404.

McCall, S., *Aristotle's Modal Syllogisms*. Amsterdam: North Holland Publishing Company, 1963.

Patzig G., *Aristotelische Syllogistik*. 2te Aufl.; Göttingen: Vandenhoeck & Ruprecht, 1963.

review of Patzig (1st ed.) by J. L. Ackrill, *Mind*, LXXI (1962), 107–17.

(D) "CATEGORIES" AND "DE INTERPRETATIONE"

Albritton, R., "Present Truth and Future Contingency," *The Philosophical Review*, LXVI (1957), 29–46.

Bonitz, H., *Über die Kategorien des Aristoteles*. Vienna: Staatsdruck, 1853.

Butler, R. J., "Aristotle's Sea Fight and Three-Valued Logic." *The Philosophical Review*, LXIV (1955), 264–74.

De Pater, W. A., *Les Topiques d'Aristote et la dialectique platonicienne*. *Etudes Thomistes*, X. Fribourg, 1965.

Hintikka, K. J., "The Once and Future Sea Fight," *The Philosophical Review*, LXXIII (1964), 461–92.

Husik, J., "The Categories of Aristotle," in *Philosophical Essays*. Oxford: Blackwell, 1952.

Owen, G. E. L., "Inherence," *Phronesis*, X (1965), 97–105.

Owens, J., "Aristotle on Categories," *Review of Metaphysics*, XIV (1960–61), 73–90.

Saunders, J. T., "A Sea Fight Tomorrow," *The Philosophical Review*, LXVII (1958), 367–78.

Steinthal, H., *Geschichte der Sprachwissenschaft*. 2d ed.; Hildesheim: Olms, 1890 (1961).

Strang, C., "Aristotle and the Sea Battle," *Mind*, LXIX (1960), 447–65.

Taylor, R., "The Problem of Future Contingencies," *The Philosophical Review*, LXVI (1957), 1–28.

Trendelenburg, A., *Geschichte der Kategorienlehre*. Hildesheim: Olms, 1846 (1963).

(E) METAPHYSICS

Albritton, R., "Forms of Particular Substances in Aristotle's Metaphysics," *Journal of Philosophy*, LIV (1957), 699–708.

Cook Wilson, J., "Aristotle *Metaphysics* 1048a30 sqq.," *Journal of Philology*, XXXII (1913), 300–1.

Cousin, D. R., "Aristotle's Doctrine of Substance," *Mind*, XLII (1933), 319–37; XLIV (1935), 168–85.

Eslick, L., "What Is the Starting Point of Metaphysics?" *Modern Schoolman*, XXXIV (1957), 247–63.

338

Guthrie, W. K. C., "The Development of Aristotle's Theology," *Classical Quarterly*, XXVII (1933), 162–71; XXVIII (1934), 90–98.

Harring, E. S., "Substantial Form in Aristotle's *Metaphysics* Z 1," *Review of Metaphysics*, X (1956), 308–32; XI (1957), 482–501, 698–713.

Heidel, W. A., *The Necessary and the Contingent in the Aristotelian System*. Chicago: Chicago University, 1896.

Lacey, A. R., "OUSIA and Form in Aristotle," *Phronesis*, X (1965), 54–69.

Mansion, S., "La doctrine aristotélicienne de la substance et le traité des Catégories," Library of the Tenth International Congress of Philosophy. Amsterdam: North Holland Publishing Company, 1949.

McMullin, E. (ed.), *The Concept of Matter in Greek and Medieval Philosophy*. Notre Dame: University of Notre Dame, 1963.

Mure, G. R., "Aristotle's Doctrine of Secondary Substances," *Mind*, LVIII (1949), 82–83.

Owen, G. E. L., "A Proof in the PERI IDEOON," *Journal of Hellenic Studies*, LXXVII (1957), Pt. I, 103–11.

———, "Aristotle on the Snares of Ontology," in R. Bambrough (ed.), op. cit.

———, "Logic and Metaphysics in Some Earlier Works of Aristotle," in I. Düring and G. E. L. Owen (eds.), op. cit.

Owens, J., *The Doctrine of Being in the Aristotelian Metaphysics*. 2d ed.; Toronto: Pontifical Institute of Medieval Studies, 1963.

Sachs, D., "Does Aristotle Have a Doctrine of Secondary Substances?" *Mind*, LVIII (1948), 221–25.

Sellars, W., "Substance and Form in Aristotle," *Journal of Philosophy*, LIV (1957), 688–99.

Solmsen, F., *Aristotle's System of the Physical World*. Ithaca: Cornell University, 1960.

Sorabji, R., "Function," *Philosophical Quarterly*, XIV (1964), 289–302.

Tugendhat, E., *TI KATA TINOS*. Freiburg: K. Alber, 1958.

(F) ETHICS

Adkins, A. W. H., *Merit and Responsibility*. Oxford: Clarendon, 1960.

Allan, D. J., "The Practical Syllogism," *Autour d'Aristote*. Louvain: Publications Universitaires, 1955.

Anscombe, G. E. M., *Intention*. Oxford: Blackwell, 1958.

Burnet, J., *The Ethics of Aristotle*. London: Methuen, 1900.

Cook Wilson, J., *On the Structure of the Seventh Book of the Nicomachean Ethics*. Oxford: Clarendon, 1912.

Frankena, W. K., *Three Historical Philosophies of Education*. Chicago: Scott, Foresman & Co., 1965.

Gauthier, R., *La morale d'Aristote*. Paris: Presses Universitaires de France, 1958.

Grant, C. K., "AKRASIA and the Criteria of Assent to Practical Principles," *Mind*, LXV (1956), 400–7.

Horsburgh, H., "The Criteria of Assent to a Moral Rule," *Mind*, LXIII (1954), 345–58.

Jackson, R., "Rationalism and Intellectualism in the Ethics of Aristotle," *Mind*, LI (1942), 343–60.

Joachim, H. H., *The Nicomachean Ethics*. Oxford: Clarendon, 1951.

Mothersill, M., "Anscombe's Account of the Practical Syllogism," *The Philosophical Review*, LXXI (1962), 448–61.

Owens, J., "The Ethical Universal in Aristotle," *Studia Moralia* III (Rome: Desclée, 1965), 27–47

Ritchie, O. G., "Aristotle's Explanation of AKRASIA," *Mind*, VI (1897), 536–41.

Robinson, R., "L'acrasie selon Aristote," *Revue Philosophique*, CXLV (1955), 261–80.

Walsh, J., *Aristotle's Conception of Moral Weakness*. New York: Columbia University, 1963.

Williams, B. A. O., "Aristotle on the Good; A Formal Sketch," *Philosophical Quarterly*, XII (1962), 289–96.

340

(G) CONTEMPORARY PHILOSOPHY
RELATED TO ARISTOTLE

Austin, J. L., "A Plea For Excuses," *Proceedings of the Aristotelian Society*, LVII (1956), 1–30.

Bennett, J., "Substance, Reality, and Primary Qualities," *American Philosophical Quarterly*, II (1965), 1–17.

Copi, I., and Gould, J. (eds.), *Readings on Logic*. New York: Macmillan, 1964.

Frankena, W. K., *Ethics*. Englewood Cliffs: Prentice-Hall, 1963.

Gauthier, D., *Practical Reasoning*. Oxford: Clarendon, 1963.

Geach, P. T., *Reference and Generality*. Ithaca: Cornell University, 1962.

———, "Subject and Predicate," *Mind*, LIX (1950), 62–83.

Grice, H. P., "Some Remarks about the Senses," *Analytical Philosophy*, ed. by R. Butler. Oxford: Blackwell, 1962.

Hamlyn, D. W., "Categories, Formal Concepts, and Metaphysics," *Philosophy*, XXXIV (1959), 111–24.

Hampshire, S., *Thought and Action*. London: Chatto and Windus, 1959.

Harrison, B., "Category Mistakes and Rules of Language," *Mind*, LXXIV (1965), 309–25.

Hart, H. L. A., "A Logician's Fairy Tale," *The Philosophical Review*, LX (1951) 198–212.

Jarvis, J., "Practical Reasoning," *Philosophical Quarterly*, XII (1962), 316–28.

Ryle, G., "Categories," *Logic and Language* (2d ser.), ed. by Flew. Oxford: Blackwell, 1955.

———, "Pleasure," *Dilemmas*. Cambridge: Cambridge University, 1954.

Strawson, P. F., *Individuals*. London: Methuen, 1959.

———, *Introduction to Logical Theory*. London: Methuen, 1952.

von Wright, G. H., "Practical Inference," *The Philosophical Review*, LXXII (1963), 159–79.

———, *The Varieties of Goodness*. London: Routledge & Kegan Paul, 1963.

Williams, D. C., "The Sea Fight Tomorrow," *Structure, Method, and Meaning*, ed. by P. Henle. New York: Liberal Arts, 1951.